A Collector's Guide to
FANS OVER THE AGES

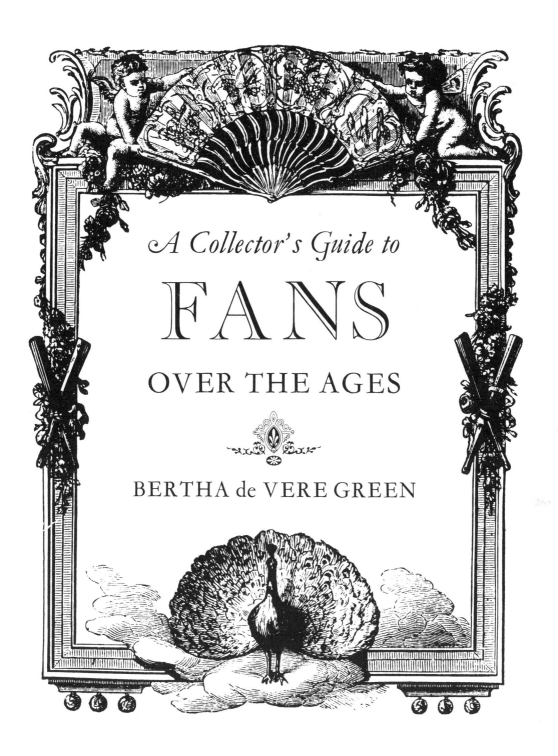

A Collector's Guide to

FANS

OVER THE AGES

BERTHA de VERE GREEN

FREDERICK MULLER · LONDON

First published in Great Britain in 1975 by
Frederick Muller Limited, Edgware Road, London NW2 6LE

Copyright © Bertha de Vere Green 1975

ISBN 0 584 10101 5

Printed in Great Britain
by W & J Mackay Limited, Chatham
by Photo-litho

CONTENTS

5

LIST OF COLOUR ILLUSTRATIONS

(Colour plates are referred to in italics.)

7

LIST OF BLACK AND WHITE ILLUSTRATIONS

LIST OF LINE ILLUSTRATIONS

ACKNOWLEDGEMENTS

In preparing this book, I freely acknowledge the enthusiastic help and assistance which I have received from many sources. First let me state that I would have been unable to extend my researches into the history of the fan were it not for the work of those who saw fit to record their findings on the fan in times past. I have drawn freely from the writings of George Woolliscroft Rhead and MacIver Percival, published, respectively, in 1910 (limited to 450 copies) and 1920. The Fan Guild of Boston published its 100-only edition of *Fan Leaves* in 1961, and I acknowledge the permission granted to me by Esther Oldham, on behalf of the Guild, for the use of material published by them.

Many museums and galleries have contributed to my work, among these being The British Museum (which houses, in the Print Room, the Schreiber Collection), The Victoria & Albert Museum, The London Museum, The Guildhall Library and The Horniman Museum. Many thanks go also to The Ashmolean Museum, Oxford. Overseas museums which have provided help to me include the Conservatoire des Arts et Metiers in Paris, the Peter Cooper Museum, New York, and the Metropolitan Museum of Art, also in New York.

I wish to express my thanks to the Worshipful Company of Fan Makers for allowing me to reproduce material from its records and also to the Rector of St Botolph Without, Bishopsgate; the Rev. Stanley Moore, for showing me over the hall used by the Company. The Rev. Moore is also Chaplain and a Member of the Livery.

Great help has been provided by many collectors, specialists and historians. I must mention the late Helen I. Doble of the Fan Guild whose excellent collection is now preserved in Tufts University, Medford, Massachusetts, in the United States of America. Others who have been of assistance to me include Mrs Jane Heuston of

13

Boca Ratón, Florida; Felix Tal in Amsterdam; and the redoubtable Esther Oldham who, through her many writings on fanology in various American periodicals, has done much to publicise fan collecting. Mrs Helen Fitch of Summit, New Jersey, has been a stoic friend for many years and has searched for, and copied for me, many items of fan history which she has found in her readings. Mr B. E. Lynch of the Directors Office at The British Museum has provided help and encouragement. Mr Arthur W. J. G. Ord-Hume, author of books on mechanical musical instruments, has provided valued information on materials and technical processes for fan making and has also provided free access to references to fans in his own extensive reference library. Mr Richard Baines of the London College of Fashion has also kept a helpful and practised eye on references to fans in the history of costume.

The work of the photographer in a book such as this is easily overlooked, yet without pictures its value would be considerably less. Many of these, both black and white and colour, are the work of Mr Jack MacLean of Harvey Johns Studios, Camden Town, whose care and patience I much appreciate. Mr C. R. Day has been responsible for most of the remainder and my thanks also go to him.

There does, though, have to be a starting place for an interest in a subject which leads to the acquisition of knowledge and, finally, the presumption which leads one to write a book. In my case, my experience and awareness is largely due to the encouragement and help provided to me by Mr J. Duvelleroy, descendent of the famous Parisian company of fan makers, who remained in business selling and repairing fans in London's Bond Street until 1965. He is now living in retirement in the South of France. It was he who allowed me to share as much of his great knowledge and experience as I could assimilate during the occasions when he kindly tolerated an incessant barrage of questions from a lady who loved fans.

Mr A. W. Fowles, 1972/3 Master of The Worshipful Company of Fan Makers, has very kindly contributed a special foreword to this book. I am deeply grateful both to Mr Fowles and the Company for their support and encouragement.

In conclusion, I must express the very real debt of gratitude which I owe to my dear husband, Cyril, for without his encouragement and constant interest in the progress of compiling this work, *Fans over the*

Ages could not have been written. Through his devotion to me and very real appreciation of the fan, my collection of fans and fan motifs is by far the richer.

BERTHA DE VERE GREEN

London, January 1973

FOREWORD

It is a great privilege to be associated with and to be permitted to write in appreciation of such an eminently complete and delightful work, as Mrs de Vere Green's study of the Fan.

The title describes this book as a Collector's Guide, but it provides so much more and is of immense interest to those, be it expert or beginner, anxious to advance in knowledge of and to learn about, this fascinating subject. It is many years since any such authoritative publication has been presented and the Worshipful Company of Fan Makers is greatly indebted to the author for this detailed and comprehensive work.

Our Charter as a Trade Guild was granted by Queen Anne in 1709 and the Company was then truly representative of the skilled craftsmen and the dealers of that time. There are now no makers of the ladies' fan left in this country, but the modern industrial counterpart will find real joy in reading so much about the work of his ancient predecessors.

There could have been nothing more charming than "My Lady" with her fan and Mrs de Vere Green's book, so beautifully illustrated, reminds us of the grace, and perhaps helps us to recover some of the elegance, of a bygone age.

A. W. FOWLES

Master 1972/3
The Worshipful Company of Fan Makers

The Fan shall flutter in all female hands
And various fashions learn from various lands.
For this shall elephants their ivory shed;
And polished sticks the waving engine spread;
His clouded mail the tortoise shall resign,
And round the rivet pearly circles shine.
On this shall Indians all their art employ,
And with bright colours stain the gaudy toy,
Their paint shall here in wildest fancies flow,
Their dress, their customs, their religions show:
So shall the British Fair their minds improve,
And on the Fan to distant climates rove.

JOHN GAY, London, 1759

PREFACE

To the average person, the shape and texture of a beautiful fan instantly conjures up thoughts of times past; tall girls with classic features and taffeta crinolines, stately music, the decorous and decorum. The very fact that the fan should be so inseparably associated with what we might term the classical lady is itself an indication of the important part which the fan played in society. As an inseparable part of the accoutrements of the lady and, indeed, of costume as a whole, the importance of the fan is only matched by the singular lack of authoritative literature available on the fan today.

At this point in time, the fan has to be considered from two standpoints—that of the historical and sociological on the one hand, and from the aspect of the collector on the other. Of the former, the history of the fan is closely bound with the ceremonials, both religious and secular, of Man through the ages. For the latter, collectors of fans are numerous and, like collectors of all things, those who aspire to collect fans fulfil a function in the survival of these frail artifacts. The more knowledge available to collectors, the greater the interest and involvement which they may have in their hobby, and the more certain we may be that fans will be preserved for posterity outside the relatively few which are in our museums today.

The first question invariably asked by the novice who takes an interest in fans is usually "Who first used the fan?", meaning, no doubt, who invented the fan. And, more often than not, a second question comes tumbling out—"Where does the word 'Fan' come from?"

The short answer is that the first fan known to us was used in Egypt around 3200 BC, and the word "fan" is derived from the Latin word *vannus*. To the casual enquirer, then, there is the answer. What is not so easy to explain, though, is the true history of the fan. Nor is it a simple matter to describe and evaluate the enormous variety of fans which have been used throughout the world for so many purposes since those far-off days in Egypt and China from whence the fan probably came. Nor is it a simple matter to equate this salutory information with the present-day thirst for knowledge on fans, a demand which has in some measure arisen from the expansion of artistic and intellectual education during the present century, and partly from the current encouragement of the latent acquisitive urge in many people.

When the novice collector today (or indeed, the established collector or expert) wishes to refer to the pages of an authoritative guide to the subject of fans, he or she will find no English book currently available. Indeed, the most recent of those reference works which have appeared in the past is more than fifty years old.

And so emerges the objective of this work which is to produce an up-to-date reference on the wide range of fans which have been made, thereby serving as a guide or handbook of the fan for museums, historians, collectors and dealers. The basis of this book is the knowledge and experience which I have amassed throughout the years I have collected and worked with fans. The purpose, then, is to place this knowledge at the beck and call of all who are interested in the fan. I have found in my years of collecting that to know just the fan and no more is impossible, for a knowledge of fans and a study of them uncovers a surprisingly broad educational spectrum. It taught me, for instance, some revealing, lost aspects of history. It taught me the changing trends of etiquette, sociology and decorum. It opened to me the minds of men and taught me the arts and the wiles of a woman's mind in a past age. I learned the intricacies of a language by which the intimacies of relationship might be transmitted without the need for recourse to the oft ineffectual, inexpressive spoken word. I saw also the artfulness behind the art, and the way, no matter in which country or circumstance she lived, the lady might have a man falling at her feet or even at her mercy—just by the propitious use of the simple fan.

Is this, then, just a romantic story? Or is there yet more behind the fan? The answer is again a simple one. The fan has been known to us for nearly 5,500 years. It has served in the chaste annals of many religions. It has inspired love to the point of being almost a symbol of love (and certainly a weapon of love!), and from its rudimentary yet curvacious shape has inspired a form of decoration and embellishment which is still with us today. The fan as a shape is at once beautiful. As a form in engineering, for example, it is light, efficient and robust—aspects which did not escape the attention of the ancient architects of the cloisters at Gloucester, or King's College Chapel, Cambridge, who used fan-vaulting in structural stonework. But, I hasten to assure you, this is no textbook on structural design, architecture or decoration, although we will examine all these briefly in Chapter 11. The body of this book is concerned with the development of the fan in its form as a costume accessory.

In preparing what is intended as a standard book of reference on the fan which might be sufficiently comprehensive to serve equally well the needs of the serious student, the museum, the collector and the antique dealer; it is necessary to research into the history and customs of many countries and different ethnic groups, in order to pursue the diverse purposes for which the fan has been employed through the ages. For the casual collector, the thought of a history of this type may be anathema. Well, to each and every reader his own opinion, but I can assure you that perhaps no history is more fascinating than that of the frail fan whose gentle flutter or violent agitation has in times past changed the lives and probably fortunes of so many.

Bertha de Vere Green

London
January 1973

INTRODUCTION

English Dictionary, N. Bailey, London 1764

A Fan (*vannus*, Lat. *evantail*, Fr. *ventaglio*, It. abanillo, Sp. ғan, Sax.)
1. An instrument to winnow corn, whereby the chaff is blown away.
For the cleaning of corn is used a wicker-fan, or a fan with tails.
Mortimer. 2. (*Van*, Fr.) A utensil used by ladies for raising wind, and
for cooling themselves. 3. Any thing spread out like a woman's fan
into a triangle. The peacock spreads his tail, and challenges the
other to show him such a *van* of feathers. *L'Effrange*. 4. Any thing by
which the air is moved, wings. Then stretch'd his feather'd *fans*
with all his might. *Dryden*. 5. An instrument to raise the fire. Nature
worketh in us all a love to our own counsels: the contradiction of
others is a *fan* to inflame that love. *Hooker*.

To Fan (*vanner*, Fr. *vanno*, Lat.) 1. To winnow corn. 2. To cool
with a fan, as women &c. do. 3. To ventilate, to affect by air put in
motion. Calm as the breath which fans our eastern groves. Dryden.

The Imperial Dictionary, John Ogilvie, London 1854

FAN, *n*. (Sax. *fann*; G. *Wanne*; L. *vannus*; Fr. *van*. The word, in
German, signifies a *fan* and a tub, as if from opening or spreading;
if so, it seems to be allied to pane, pannel.) 1. An instrument used
by ladies to agitate the air and cool the face in warm weather. It
is made of feathers, or of thin skin, paper, or taffeta mounted on
sticks, &c. 2. Something in the form of a woman's fan when spread,
as a peacock's tail, a window, &c. 3. An instrument for winnowing
grain, by moving which the grain is thrown up and agitated, and the
chaff is separated and blown away. The modern *fan*, or *fanners*,
however, is a machine for separating the chaff, husks, dust or other
light matters from grain seeds which are to be preserved for sowing,
or for some other purpose in general, or domestic economy . . . 4.
Something by which the air is moved; a wing. 5. An instrument to
raise the fire or flame; as a *fan* to inflame love.

FAN, *v.t*. To cool and refresh, by moving the air with a fan;

to blow the air on the face with a fan. 2. To ventilate; to blow on; to affect by air put in motion. 3. To move as with a fan. 4. To winnow; to ventilate; to separate chaff from grain, and drive it away by a current of air; as to *fan* wheat.

The Concise Oxford Dictionary, 1938

fan[1], n. Winnowing-machine; instrument, usu. folding & sector-shaped when spread out, on radiating ribs, for agitating air to cool face; anything so spread out, as bird's tail, wing, leaf, kind of ornamental vaulting (f. tracery); rotating apparatus giving current of air for ventilation &c.

The above references, quoted from three sources selected as being contemporary with the peak of the fan in the French courts (Bailey), the Victorian period in London (Ogilvie) and the present age (Oxford), provide derivation and insight to the fan. It will be seen that there are two apparent Saxon derivatives, the first being ꜰan (the character ꜰ being the same as the modern F) as quoted by Bailey, and the second being *fann* as shown in contemporary characters by Ogilvie. The Gothic *wanne* may well have engendered the Saxon ꜰan (or *fann*). Certainly the Romans waged battle (albeit largely without success) for many years in Germania before their final expulsion during the 3rd century AD. Their occupation of parts of that territory would have been accompanied by the introduction of a degree of Roman culture and customs. And the Romans had fans. On the other hand, both derivations, i.e. *wanne* and ꜰan, may have been pure descendants from the *vannus*, since, of course, the Roman occupation of Britain was both more successful and of greater duration. It must remain conjectural just how much culture rather than just custom was introduced by soldiers such as Divitiacus, Plautius and Vespasian into a land where the order was often battle. Nevertheless, the existence of such luxurious palaces and extensive homesteads as have been unearthed in southern England reveals a degree of permanency of occupation by wealthy and respected Romans of title and trade. It is at these places as well as the temples and shrines of worship where the fan would have been found. Now *vannus*, as we have seen, was not to the Romans the fan which we know. The *vannus* was a fan-shaped implement used for winnowing corn and, as we know, the Romans farmed southern England with a high degree of success, serious agriculture being then largely unknown to the Ancient Britons.

Did then the Romans introduce into Europe the fan as we know it? If this was so, then like many other Roman introductions into Britain (viz. central heating, heated baths and civil engineering) it was lost again until much later, in this instance not until the reign of Richard II (1377–99).

What is more surprising, though, is that the word *vannus* from which has come the present word fan was not the Latin word for what we mean by fan at all. The two words used to describe a fan were *ventilabrum* and *flabellum*. Strangely enough, it was *ventilabrum* which also could mean a winnowing fan, and yet the Roman poet Vergillius Maro wrote *vannus mystica Iacchi* (borne at the Bacchic festival), the connection with winnowing and Bacchus (the Latin name of Dionysus, God of wine) being allegorical. Our authority for understanding *ventilabrum* as a winnowing fork comes from the writings of Marcus Terentius Varro who earned for himself the apellation "Most learned of the Romans". In the connection of the fan, *ventilabrum* is the name under which ecclesiastical fans are mentioned in old inventories and it is thus uncertain whether this determination is accurate, i.e. Roman Latin, or whether it is "scholar's Latin".

The second word, *flabellum*, is much easier to understand as being a contemporary Latin word for fan. The word derives from *flabrum* which translates as a blast of wind or breezes. *Flabellum* is formed as the diminutive of *flabrum* and means not so much a small wind as the device for producing a small wind—a small *fan*. Marcus Tullius Cicero wrote *cuius lingua quasi flabello seditionis illa tum est egentium contio ventilata. Flabellum*, as *ventilabrum*, is to be found in ancient writings with ecclesiastical connections.*

So at this stage we find ourselves with a choice of derivation in our quest for the origin of the name "fan". However the etymologist

---

* George Woolliscroft Rhead in his *History of the Fan* published in London in 1910 mistakenly instances Osiris, when judge of Amenti, as holding "in his crossed hands the crook and flagellum", the mystical *vannus*—"whose fan is in his hand", and quotes Wilkinson's *Manners and Customs of the Ancient Egyptians. Flagellum* is, of course, a whip in this case and nothing to do with "the improvement of the world by tillage" as Rhead has inferred.

will tell you that it is no precedent for a word to have a confused or even an erroneous derivation and it is these very irregularities and corruptions of languages which serve to give them character and standing. The collector may now be shrugging his or her shoulders and saying "What's in a name!" and so I will hope that we can accept the basic terminology expressed by the word "fan".

I find it very interesting to see how easily unrelated things in our lives gradually develop propinquity. Take two obvious ones—salt and pepper. Could there ever be two more dissimilar things, and yet mention salt and the word pepper is instantly in the mind. By the same token, unrelated things assume a position amounting almost to symbiosis. Why, no well-dressed Edwardian gentleman would venture forth without his watch and chain. Yet what could be more dissimilar than a watch and chain? So it was with the fan. The fan underwent a subtle change of rôle from that of being a necessity (to cool the heated brow) to that of being an indispensable part of costume. A lady has always needed something to hold and no artist has ever successfully painted a woman holding her empty hand in space. Today it is the handbag; in a past era it was the fan.

Unlike the handbag, however, the fan became endowed with far greater responsibilities. It was a means of communication and, in the hand of some, a force to be reckoned with. No young lady of breeding would dream of venturing forth without her fan. Today, the young lady is told that her wardrobe cannot be considered complete unless she has in addition to the usual variety of outer garments, a brassiere for every dress. Two hundred years ago, she was instructed to have a fan for every dress. The pretty woman would use it to add to her charms; the clumsy woman would use it in order to occupy her hands; and the ill-bred and the ugly woman used it as thereby she might at least earn credit for elegance.

The fan was used and cherished by women of all types, and not necessarily always by those to whom we euphemistically benefit by the cognomen "ladies". It was not only the House of Valois and Bourbon where the ownership of expensive fans was assumed to form part of the trappings necessary to ladify. Balzac made the point succinctly in *Cousin Pons* with the passage:

> It is high time that having served vice, this fan should now be in the hands of virtue. It has taken a hundred years to bring

about such a miracle. You may be sure that no royal princess
has anything comparable to this treasure; for, unfortunately,
human nature is so constituted that it will do more for a
Madame de Pompadour than for a virtuous queen.

The other interesting point is that, as a general rule, the size of
the fans at any given period increased or decreased in proportion
to the ground area covered by the woman's skirts. When the skirts
considered fashionable by the ladies of the 1820s began to increase
in size, there was a corresponding increase in the size of their fans.

From size we come to shape. An interesting statement is contained in the definition from Bailey at the head of this Introduction.
He infers that a lady's fan might be triangular. Other writers speak,
loosely, of semi-circular. Still more refer to fan-shape as if there is a
clearly-defined shape to be followed by all fans. The truth is that the
fan comes in many shapes. If we exclude the more obvious variations
such as the circular, square and spear-shaped Asian fans and
consider for the moment only those which our loose tradition calls
"fan-shaped", we find some interesting variations. First of all, we
find that there are comparatively few fans which are truly semi-
circular. Some open up to an angle considerably less than 180
degrees—in my own collection are fans which only open half that
amount—whilst others open up to the greater part of a circle. Then
we find the elliptical fan formed from that part of an oval circum-
scribed from the minor axis, thereby having a greater radius at the
centre than at the open sides. It soon becomes apparent that there is
no fixed fan shape from the aspect of uniform proportions.

Another consideration of fan shape is the mount or leaf. In the
majority of fans, this comprises a web which has the pin or rivet
of the fan as its point of radius for both the superior and inferior
diameters. However, two other varieties exist. One is the "new-
moon" shape where the two diameters have different centres along
the bisector of the angle of the open fan. The other has what is
best described as a "spiral mount" where the mount is narrower on
one guard than on the other.

After almost 5,000 years of history, it is reassuring to find that the
fan still has a place in these closing decades of the 20th century.
The fan's long associations with Asia are still active, and the modern
Japanese fan and its Chinese counterpart retain both the purpose

and some shade of quality found in history. On a more mundane level, the invention of the electric motor in the 19th century united with the rotary fan (whose ancestry is that of the windmill, the earliest known reference to which is the so-called "windmill Psalter" of *c.* 1290 in the British Museum) up-dated the *punkah* of the Hindus as a means of creating a current of air. The electric fan, ostensibly bearing only the relationship of purpose to the hand fan, is thus deserving of at least a branch in the family tree. However, other than acknowledging its presence, this branch is one which we do not need to explore.

Before taking a meaningful look at the history of the fan, its origins and development, one important point must be made, even though this be at the expense of interrupting the chronology of the story. The folding fan, that is the fan which closes to form a narrow shape with sticks and leaf (or in the case of the brisé fan, the sticks and the ribbon) superimposed between the guards, was, on all available evidence, invented in Asia in the 7th century AD. All fans prior to this (with certain notable exceptions) although they were not necessarily unifoliate and in such cases not necessarily even uniserial, were fixed and they could not be closed up. The exceptions are some remarkable relics, one of which is reliably attributed to Theodelinda, the Lombardic queen who died in AD 628. Naturally, though, those fans comprising feathers or loose grasses or hairs (like the fly-fans or whisks) could be closed up by gathering together the extremities, but this could not be classed as folding in the proper meaning of the word. Folding fans in Europe appeared several centuries after their Asian nascence.

I have striven to shape this book in the most usable way possible. For this reason, I have chosen to put the Glossary of Terms, by unjustifiable tradition normally *ad extremum*, at the beginning since the use of some specialist terminology throughout the following chapters must be unavoidable. The balance of the book is broadly divided into two sections, separated by a Chapter devoted to the types of fans. The first part is concerned solely with the history and development of the fan and its progress from Asia into Europe and finally into England. This half terminates with a Chapter devoted to the language of the fan.

After the Chapter describing the various types of fans, the second section of the book concerns the collecting and preservation of fans. Here I have endeavoured to describe not only those hints and tips of collecting which I have learned, but also how to handle, clean and repair fans. Novices may raise eyebrows at the thought of the need for a description as to how to handle a fan, yet the fact remains that more damage can be done to a fragile example of early craftsmanship by well-intentioned but inadvised handling than may generally be appreciated. Immediately preceding this, however, is a description of the manufacture of fans and this knowledge forms the groundwork for the following advice on cleaning and repairing the fan.

The fan considered as an art form in design is the subject of a following Chapter. Here we see the important part which the fan motif played in 18th and 19th century art of all types. We take a look, for example, at the fan in furniture design and building decoration, the fan in embellishment. We will also have a look at some of the more unconventional meanings and references to fans.

The concluding Chapter of this book comprises a list of fan makers, designers and painters, and a description of some of the subjects depicted on fan leaves.

Sadly, the majority of fans to be found today can truly and accurately be described as of Victorian origin. Whilst some of these are very beautiful and a good representative selection should no doubt be included in every collection, the older and better quality fans are very scarce and the collector must search hard and long, armed with knowledge as to what to look for, in order to find good, genuinely-old specimens. He or she must learn to steer a wise track through the plethora of valueless and broken fans which are to be found in the hands of those dealers who may have a paucity of expert knowledge of the fan. I hope that this book may help to smooth that path and help both the collector and the dealer to a closer understanding and better knowledge of this, the most romantic adjunct of ladies' costume.

GLOSSARY

The following terms are used when referring to basic formats of the fan and to the component parts of the fan. Types of fans themselves are to be found in the listing forming Chapter 7, whilst the materials of fan-making and the manufacturing details of fans are to be found in Chapter 8.

BAROQUE   The baroque period extended.from 1660 to about 1735 and it is used as a broad classification for fans manufactured between these years. Whilst there is no such thing as a "baroque fan", fans of the baroque period have certain characteristics which are identifiable under this broad classification. In almost all cases, however, further classification is necessary to define a fan by manner of type, style and construction. See Chapters 4 and 5.

BATTOIR   An unusual style of fan having very few sticks, usually no more than eight. To encompass the broad width at the folded leaf, the guards are very wide at the top, being characteristically spade or racket shaped.

BRIN   The French term for the inner sticks of a fan, i.e. those between the guards.

BRISÉ   A fan which does not have a leaf but which consists of sticks of rigid material joined with a ribbon. The sticks themselves would be decorated by painting, incising or piercing. See also Chapter 7.

CABRIOLET   A fan with two, sometimes three concentric leaves. See also Chapter 7.

CAMAIEU   Decoration in the form of painting executed in different shades of the same colour, most commonly rose or blue. Extremely popular in the mid-18th century.

32

CARTOUCHE   A painting or other pictorial medium placed in the decorated part of a fan mount and isolated from the remainder of the decoration of the mount by a decorative, contrasting border. A cartouche may be found on a painted ivory brisé fan or on a paper or chicken-skin mount. See also MEDALLION and RESERVE.

CHICKEN-SKIN   A type of fine vellum used by fan makers for the leaves of better-quality fans. The skin, which provided an admirable surface for inks, water-colours and lithography, comes from very young animals and the finest was obtained by the barbarous practice of killing the mother before the birth of her offspring. It is extremely thin and combines both delicacy with suppleness. When held up to the light, it shows no grain as found in laid papers, but presents a slightly mottled appearance. See references in Chapter 8.

COCKADE   A folding fan which opens out into a circular form. The guards, each considerably longer than the sticks, are held together to form the handle. A feature of the cockade fan is often a decorative and necessarily large open-ended box to receive the closed fan. The number of folds and sticks needed to permit 360 degrees of opening often makes this type of fan relatively thick at the rivet.

ETCHING   The decoration of the fan leaf formed by printing from copper plates before the leaf is mounted. See Chapter 8.

ÉVENTAILLISTE   The French name for a maker of fans.

FEATHERS   The decoration of fans by the addition of the feathers of the peacock or ostrich is of considerable antiquity. Early fans often comprised an ornamental handle into which each feather was separately fixed to form a screen-shaped fan. Their use in folding fans was originally as an ending (i.e. an extension of each stick) but during the 19th century folding fans were made which comprised nothing but large feathers each set in a small socket and rivetted, the whole ribboned together.

FEUILLE   See LEAF.

GOLDFISH   A form of mother of pearl, richly coloured, used principally for inlay.

GORGE   That portion of the stick between the shoulder and the head. From the French for neck.

GOUACHE   A form of painting using opaque colours ground in water and thickened with gum and honey in order to preserve elasticity. Unlike water colour or Chinese white, gouache painting will not crack.

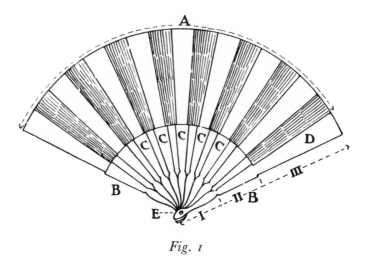

Fig. 1

The parts of a fan. There are two principal parts—the stick (B B) which is known to the French as *la monture*, and the mount (A) known in French as *le feuille*. The mount may consist of two leafs (leaves) pasted together on either side of the sticks (C C C C). The sticks, sometimes called blades and known to the French as *brins* fold between two outer, heavier sticks which are called guards (D). The French call these *panaches*. The frame of the fan, i.e. the sticks and the guards, is united at the head by a rivet or pin (E), *rivure* in French. The guard is made up of three named parts: I is the head; II is the shoulder (*gorge* in French) which reaches to the lower, inner edge of the mount; and III which is the guard proper. The sticks themselves are usually narrowed down to very thin, narrow sections of material where they extend into the mount. These parts, sometimes visible by holding the fan up to the light and looking through the mount, are called slips.

GRISAILLE   Painting without colour using only black and white, texture being determined by the intermediate shades of grey. Competently executed, this is an extremely beautiful medium. Not to be confused with CAMAIEU (q.v.) which is a single colour work.

GUARDS   The outer sticks which are always much stronger and thicker than the inner sticks and are often decorated by PIQUÉ, carving, inlay or appliqué work.

HEAD   The portion of the stick through which the pin or rivet passes so uniting it with the other sticks as a common pivot. (See GORGE.)

LEAF   French: *Feuille*. The broad band, truly a segment of an annulus, which unites the upper parts of the sticks of a folding fan. Also known as the Mount. This may be made of skin, paper, silk or other textile fabric and in all but the cheapest of fans is the major part of the fan devoted to overt decoration. See further details in Chapter 8.

LITHOGRAPHY   A printing process invented at the end of the 18th century and used either for printing the outline of a fan leaf design for subsequent hand-colouring, or for printing in several colours. See Chapter 8.

MEDALLION   A painting or other pictorial medium placed in the decorated part of a fan mount, similar to a CARTOUCHE (q.v.). However, whereas the cartouche may be of an irregular or *art nouveau* shape, the medallion is almost always circular or oval and, where there is a wide border, it is of classical proportions and decoration. See also RESERVE.

MOSAIQUE (Mosaic)   A form of decoration wherein the design is formed from very small pieces of colour or metal. The French *oeuvre mosaique* is reserved for one of the most common forms of ivory ornamentation and is totally different. Here the design consists of two differing treatments. The background is pared away to extreme thinness and is then pierced, these perforations as a rule taking the form of closely-set slits or a diaper pattern. The RESERVES, which may take the form of MEDALLIONS (q.v.) or designs such as trophies, festoons, amorini, figures, busts or groups, are left in apparent silhouette raised above the pierced ground. These were afterwards carved more or less finely so that upon completion they are sustained in low relief but nevertheless higher than the ground. Occasionally the reserves are left flat and then painted rather like a cameo. See Chapter 8.

NEO-CLASSICAL   The neo-classical period came after the rococo period (q.v.) and more or less mirrored the reign of Louis XVI. The neo-classical fan may be taken as falling between the years 1765 and 1800. See that general remark under BAROQUE and also Chapters 4 and 5.

PANACHES   The French term for the guards or outer sticks of a folding fan.

PAPER   Practically all printed fan leaves and many painted ones are executed on a paper ground. The paper was naturally enough hand-made and displayed the characteristic watermark lay when held up to the light. (For reference, see under CHICKEN-SKIN). Machine-made papers, introduced in the last century, are generally easily identified by their smoother, more even texture and, of course, by the fact that the paper fan, other than cheap fans and advertising fans, was not in wide use during the last century.

PASTE   Imitations of so-called precious stones used, in connection with the fan, for decoration and often used in the head of the pin and sometimes in the guards. More often than not, these are translucent white like imitation pearls, but red for the ruby, green for the emerald and blue for the sapphire may also be found. Very small pastes are also to be found set into the guards of some horn "Empire" fans (see Chapter 7). These, unlike those alluded to previously, have no metal settings but are set in small depressions provided in the horn.

PEN-AND-INK   DRAWINGS   Self-explanatory form of fan-leaf decoration, often mistaken for etchings. Many 18th-century fans feature finely-executed pen-and-ink drawings which are often given the additional treatment of a wash of sepia or Indian ink or, occasionally, colour. Percival* states that these fans appear to have been intended as mourning fans but suggests that this was not always the case.
* *The Fan Book*, 1920.

PIN See RIVET.

PIQUÉ A form of decoration consisting of small gold or silver points or pins set flush with the surface and used for sticks although more generally for the guards of a folding fan.

RESERVE An area which may be in the form of a MEDALLION (q.v.), oval, vignette, or a shield. This can be a feature found on both mounts and sticks. When a characteristic of the mount, it is frequently the place used for a thematic illustration, for a monogram, or for a scene making up part of the decoration of the whole. When featured as a portion of the sticks it is usually characteristic of ivory sticks and covers an area of several between shoulder and rivet. Here it is in the form of a change in the decoration, sometimes left as a plain ground which may be used to show a pierced monogram or a painted portrait. See also CARTOUCHE and MEDALLION.

RIBBON A feature of the BRISÉ (q.v.) fan is the ribbon by means of which the sticks are maintained in relation to one another when the fan is open. On many 17th- and 18th-century fans, particularly those upon which are executed very fine and delicate paintings, this positioning must be maintained with extreme accuracy otherwise the whole effect would be spoiled. The ribbon thus has a delicate task to perform and examination will show that, rather than one complete length of silk, the ribbon consists of a series of flat loops or doubled "pockets", there being as many loops as there are brins or sticks. Thus the ribbon does not simply pass through the stick but actually entraps it so ensuring positioning when open. The Vernis Martin fans,* whose decorative paintings were among the finest, always fixed the ribbon at the very top of the fan, the ribbon being painted to fit in with the rest of the decoration. The reason for this could be two-fold: it keeps the ribbon from interfering with the major decorative painting on the brins and, in having the ribbon at the furthest point from the pin, it (a) prevents the brins from separating in the plane of the fan, so making the fan stronger and more durable, and (b) allows the ribbon to exert the maximum mechanical efficiency in sustaining the brins in their correct places.
* See Chapter 8.

RIVET   The pin about which the sticks of a folding fan pivot. It passes through the head of both guards and sticks. Originally the pivot was actually rivetted over an ivory or mother of pearl washer. This made any subsequent repair work very difficult and, once unrivetted, usually meant the fitting of a new rivet. So was introduced the pin which comprises two parts—a threaded female portion and a screw. During the early 19th century, the pin was enhanced by a loop, usually of flat wire, which passed around the heads of the sticks and formed a washer under the pin head on one side and under the screw head on the other. To this loop was attached a ribbon or tassel.* Where this loop is found on an earlier fan, it is a clear indication that it is a later addition accompanied by the replacement of the rivet by a pin and screw and probably occasioned by the need of some past repair. The head of both pin and screw is often set with stones which, in the majority of cases, are PASTES (q.v.).

ROCOCO (Rocaille)   The rococo period followed the BAROQUE (q.v.) and is delineated as starting in 1735 and terminating around 1765. The remarks concerning the baroque also apply here. See also Chapters 4 and 5. The term is used to describe the extravagant style of decoration which was characteristic of the Louis XV period. It frequently included all manner of ornamental features such as birds, foliage, scrolls, flowers, figures, wreathes, rockwork, stalactites, trellis-work and like forms. The style is characterised by an overt avoidance of symmetry, irregular-shaped panels and scroll-work bounded by curves. Whilst some examples of this style, the products of craftsmen artists, are extremely good and cleverly contrived, it was often used *in extremis*.

SEQUINS   See SPANGLES

SHOULDER   The change in width of the GORGE (q.v.). That part of the stick immediately below the leaf. In early fans, this part of the stick, being wider than the part to which the leaf was affixed (the slips), was formed by a sharply-defined step whereas by the end of the 18th century the top of the shoulder was rounded on each side of the leaf portion of the stick. Brisé fans, generally speaking, do not
* *ibid.*

38

have a shoulder, although a slight indication is preserved on the guards.

SLIPS   Those portions of the sticks of a folding fan which extend through (under or between) the leaf/leaves. They are generally of wood although the visible portion of the stick may be ivory, tortoise shell or mother of pearl. See Chapter 8.

SPANGLES   This form of decoration was applied to almost every article of the lady's attire during the second half of the 18th century, the fan being no exception. On many Empire fans, they represent the sole form of decoration and appear as small circular metal plates with, usually, a small central hole through which it is sewn to the fabric of the fan leaf. The early spangles were made from small rings of wire beaten flat. This results in the consolidation and burnishing of the surface to produce a mirror-like brilliance which in so many instances is still retained today. Other forms of spangles followed: these are detailed in Chapter 8. They are not to be confused with PIQUE (q.v.).

STICK   The framework of the folding fan comprises two thick sticks (GUARDS or PANACHES) and a series of thinner, inner sticks (BRINS).

WATER COLOUR   The term used to describe a painting done in transparent colour without body colour and is distinct from GOUACHE (q.v.).

CHAPTER ONE

THE ORIGIN OF THE FAN

The chronicling of Man's slow ascendancy from the primitive being of pre-history to the civilisation of today is generally of such an imperfect and imprecise character that our historians invariably face almost insurmountable problems in presenting anything approaching definitive material. Indeed, although certain aspects of ethnology are clear and concise, these facets are exceptions to the rule and stand out in an ocean of circumstantial evidence, intelligent guesswork and barely justified assumptions.

The history of the fan is no exception. The primitive fan appeared in a distinct form 5,000 years ago, and yet its representation during the intervening millenia is in parts but scant. A reason for this could be postulated in that the fan of pre-history had more than one use and it was purely the uses of the fan in religious and ceremonial applications which were recorded. One may prudently interject here that earliest, primitive *homo sapiens* was not unaware of the cooling effect produced by the agitation of a flat-surfaced object close to his hot brow. And such a truly utilitarian device would hardly justify the efforts of the artisan chronicler in his day-to-day records.

If one can accept this last suggestion as a possible precept, it ought to follow that the fan originated in equatorial rather than temperate latitudes. It would therefore be logical to deduce this as an acceptable statement if on the one hand we can find evidence of the fan in equatorial regions and, at the same time, back this up with evidence that the fan was unknown in cooler regions.

Here, though, our otherwise clear-cut parameters become blurred for whilst we can certainly find that the fan was known in Asia more than 5,000 years ago, we cannot disprove its existence in, say, Europe prior to Roman times. We must therefore fall back on the somewhat unsatisfactory basis of supposition and generalisation, tempered by the elementary doctrines of logic.

Since many of the early references to fans emanate from China, and since the Chinese civilisation was highly developed at a time when the rest of the world was primaeval, it is difficult to avoid the assumption (made by other authors) that the fan originated in China.

An early Chinese legend suggests that the origin of the screen fan was the sudden inspiration of the daughter of a distinguished mandarin. When the maiden was attending the Feast of Lanterns, she felt faint with the heat, slipped off her mask and held it close to her face, moving it to and fro to create a cool breeze. The other beauties in the Court noticed what she was doing, and they quickly did the same.

Whether fact or fantasy, one thing is certain and that is that, contrary to the beliefs of many a writer and poet, and Mr Woolliscroft Rhead* in particular, Cupid had no hand in the invention of the fan, for it was not as an instrument of coquetry that the fan first appeared, but as a down-to-earth tool for cooling the sweated brow, keeping flies off the nobility and brightening the slow fire. The fan in this form must, in the warm parts of the world, rival the stone axe as Man's first tool and thus pre-date the wheel.

These pre-historic fans one can safely assume to have been little more than things rather than artifacts. They would have comprised the nearest available object which experiment or experience suggested might fulfil the objective. Stylised, purpose-made objects were of a later genre.

The only forms of ethnic recording available during these early times were the skills of the sculptor and the artist. The use of the fan in high ceremony accorded to it a measure of importance and thus it is to be found represented in sculpture and ancient art. Similarly, fans were in some cases preserved with the remains of their owners. However, this surviving evidence of the fan which, in the majority of cases, can be dated very accurately as we shall see further on, must be viewed in the proper context. It is, for example, unlikely that a hitherto unknown object would be depicted in these art forms and thus the discovery of evidence of the existence of the fan at a particular time proves only that the fan was extant at that time. For instance, on a tomb at Sakkarah which is said to date from *c.* 2366–2266 BC a wedge-shaped hand fan is shown being used to

* *History of the Fan*, London, 1910.

keep a fire burning. It would be illogical to assume from this that the fire-fan dates from this period when in truth it may already have been known for a millenium.

Among the first manufactured fans were the long-handled ceremonial fans used by the ancient people as a symbol of authority. Forming part of the *entourage* of the king, fan-bearers would carry the semi-circular feather fan to wave over his head. The office of fan-bearer was in no way demeaning and it was a dignified and prized position usually accorded to a person of Royal birth. A sculpture from Hierakonpolis, once a thriving city on the Nile between Luxor and Aswan, includes a mace-head of the Scorpion King* which shows ceremonial fans being borne by fan-bearers.

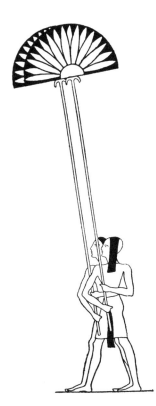

Fig. 2

Numerous representations of long-handled, semi-circular standard fans are to be found on the monuments in the Nubian Desert. Rosellini sketched these two standard bearers from Thebes (Rhamessium).

Fig. 3

The primitive fly-whisk formed of grassy reeds or similar material was used all over Egypt and Asia as a whole. This fan is similar to that type featured on Assyrian monuments.

* The ruler referred to here reigned over the so-called "Upper" Egypt and the Scorpion is the hieroglyph by which he is indicated. *Vide; The Art of the Ancient Near East* by Seton Lloyd, published by Thames & Hudson, 1961.

This dates from the end of the Predynastic period about 3200 BC and is now in the Ashmolean Museum, Oxford.

In the museum at Boulak, *flabellum* dating from 1657 BC are to be seen. The wooden palm at the top of the handle is bored with holes to enable ostrich feather plumes to be inserted. A similar specimen survives from the tomb of Tut-ankh-amen from 1350 BC and this fine specimen of an 18th-dynasty fan is beautifully preserved.* The length of the handle, with its characteristic terminal knob at the lower end, is 95 cm long and the palm stands 10.5 cm high and 18.5 cm wide.

Preserved in the British Museum is a slab of stone from the reign of Assur-Nissapal, King of Assyria 880–860 BC. This depicts attendants fanning a king.

In early China, fans were in use to keep the dust from chariot wheels, presumably to avoid dust blowing into the eyes of the occupants. It is known that this down-to-earth application, in which it became more a besom than a fan, was in use during the Chow dynasty about 1106 BC and that the fans so used were sometimes made of dyed pheasant and peacock feathers.

If the Chinese fan predates the Egyptian fan, as indeed all the evidence might suggest, we may well postulate how the fan came to Egypt from China. Normally the spread of culture and ethnology from one nation to another is achieved by the intercourse of trade and commerce, or by travellers from one place to another. But how

---

* Howard Carter (*The Tomb of Tutankhamen*, Sphere Books, 1972) makes several references to his discovery of fans during his exploration of the young King's tomb in the Valley of the Kings:

> Upon a golden fan, found between the sepulchral shrines that covered and protected his sarcophagus, a fan, such as we see pictured in Roman times, and actually used today in the Vatican, is a beautifully embossed and chased picture of Tutankhamen, hunting ostriches for the plumes for that very flabellum. On its reverse side he is seen returning home triumphant, his attendants carrying his quarry—two dead ostriches—and the coveted feathers under his arm.

Describing later in greater detail, Carter wrote:

> We found between the third and fourth (innermost) shrines ceremonial bows and arrows, and with them, a pair of gorgeous flabella—the insignia of princes, fans so prominent in scenes where kings are depicted, carried by inferior officers behind their chief. Beautiful specimens they were—

diversified was trade between Egypt and China 4,000 years ago is difficult to define accurately and it could well be that the presence of the fan in these two nations was the result of independent development. Once more there is a measure of circumstantial evidence to support this assumption. The early Chinese fan bore but passing similarity to the appearance of the Egyptian fan and, other than fulfilling a similar function, the two were sufficiently different in shape, materials and execution to suggest independent evolution. If there be truth in the adage that "necessity is the mother of invention", then the environment necessary to breed thought towards producing a cooling medium was certainly common to both territories.

The progress of the fan from Egypt to fresh territories is far more easily apparent. The Argonauts voyaged in a somewhat indeterminate manner around the northern waters (according to Orpheus), the southern waters (according to Apollonius), and deviously around the Mare Internum (according to Pindar). Whether, in their passage to Colchis they ever found China is uncertain but very unlikely. However, Oceanus Fluvius still surrounded the known world at the time of Homer who mapped out, with a high degree of accuracy, the Mediterranean area 1,000 years before the birth of Christ. Of significance on Homer's map of the world is the detail accorded to the northern part of Egypt, and the naming of Pharus and Thebae, the two centres of culture and, by corollary, ceremony. Even Herodotus, 550 years later, denied

one lying at the head, the other along the south side of the innermost shrine. The one at the head, wrought in sheet-gold, bears a charming and historical scene of the young King Tutankhamen in his chariot, followed by his favourite hound, hunting ostrich for feathers for the fan, as the inscription says in "the Eastern desert of Heliopolis"; on the reverse side of the fan, also finely embossed and chased, the young "Lord of Valour" is depicted returning triumphant, his quarry, two ostriches, borne on the shoulders of two attendants who precede him, the plumes under his arm. The second fan, larger and perhaps more resplendent, was of ebony, overlaid with sheet-gold and encrusted with turquoise, lapis lazuli, and carnelian-coloured glass, as well as translucent calcite: the palm of the fan being emblazoned with the titulary of Tutankhamen. Unfortunately, only the debris remained of the actual feathers of these two flabella. Although these had suffered from the havoc of insects, enough still remained to show us that they once had been alternate white and brown plumes—forty-two on each fan.

the existence of anything East of the River Indus.

When Eratosthenes mapped the world in 220 BC, he depicted, for the first time, Brettania (England) and pushed eastwards as far as Taprobane (Ceylon). Not until the map of Ptolemy in AD 150 were we to receive the first clear indication of lands further east, of Trans Gangem and the Sinus Magnus; although almost 500 years earlier, in 326 BC, Alexander the Great led his officers and soldiers to within a short distance of the Ganges. His travels might conceivably have brought both him and his men into contact with travellers from the Far East. Travellers were the recognised purveyors of goods and tales.

From this, two things may be suggested. First of all, if the Egyptians knew of the existence of the Chinese, they never let on to the Romans. Secondly, at the time Latin culture spread through the Mediterranean area and Europe, the Romans knew intimately

Fig. 4

Ostrich feather ceremonial fans feature in much early Egyptian art. These two were sketched by Rosellini in 1830 from the Temple of Rameses XII, 1135 BC

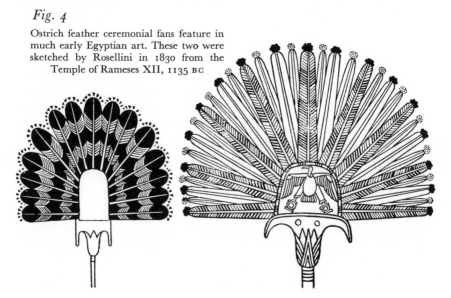

only the Egyptians (Aegyptus) to the south of the Great Sea (Mediterranean).

Now the Egyptian empire in 1450 BC extended from the south of the Nile north-east beyond the Euphrates to border on the land of the Hittites, embracing both Jerusalem and Damascus on the way. By 560 BC, the rise of the Babylonian Empire had pushed the

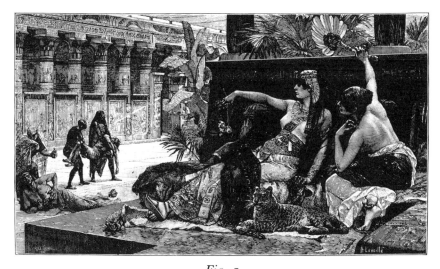

Fig. 5

This engraving shows the painting which Alex. Cabanel exhibited at the
Paris Salon in 1887. It shows Cleopatra after the battle of Actium (31 BC)
being tended by a servant with a fan.

Egyptians back to the Red Sea and extended north-east to Nineveh
and the Tigris. The fall of the Babylonians before the Persians
thirty years later marked the unification under one flag of territories
from Cyrenaica in the west, Thebae in the south right up through
Assyria and over into Thracia and Macedonia. And, of course, the
empire pushed eastwards to the Indus. The annexing of the entire
Persian empire to the Greeks at the time of Alexander the Great
now brought the Egyptians into direct cultural contact with the
Assyrians, the Phoenicians and the Greeks. The Roman empire,
at the time of Caesar now pushed west beyond the legendary Pillars
of Hercules and east into Syria.

The Greeks most likely received the fan from Egypt and Assyria
through the Phoenicians who were prolific traders between the
north, south and west. The earliest Greek fans would appear to have
been made from the leaves of the myrtle, acacia and lotus. The
Romans may likewise have received the fan from the Egyptians
although it is just possible that its birth might once again have
become self-generative. Certainly, the Romans knew of the uses of
the Egyptian fan. However, there is one significant difference and

47

that is that the major use of the Roman *vannus* was as an instrument for winnowing the grain. This shovel-shaped fan was used to scoop up a small quantity of grain which would then be thrown into the air. The chaff would then blow away, leaving the heavier seed to fall. There would seem to be little connection between this fan and the frescoes found on the palace of Medinet-Abu at Thebes which show Rameses the Great of Egypt with twenty-three sons of the Pharaoh each bearing *flabella*. These date from about 1300 BC.

The Roman equivalent was the fly-flap made of peacock's feathers. This was often provided with a long handle so that the servant could gently wave the fan over his mistress and thereby protect her from insects while she slept. There was no ceremonial connection between this and its Egyptian counterpart.

There are several references to fans of various types in The Bible. Most of these are concerned with the fan as a means of winnowing. The majority of the references appear in the Old Testament. These are Isiah XXX, 24; XLI, 16; and Jeremiah IV, 15. Two references in the New Testament are in Matthew III, 12 and Luke III, 17, both these being similar almost word for word.

The Biblical fans refer to the fan of a type which, whilst far removed from that to which we are accustomed today, was nevertheless a fan. We have seen how the fan was, in truth, a tool of many trades and might be best described as just that—a tool. Instead of "fan" as a definable noun, we discover a whole genus of *fan*.

A connection also exists between the fan and the showing of colours. Just as the Egyptians and the Japanese went to war displaying their fans as an indication of military division and allegiance, so later did soldiers in battle display their colours in related, if different manner. The Roman banner was as much a symbol of the unification under one colour as was the fan. Although the shield performed a more vital and utilitarian function, it also was used as a ground for colours and was but a much larger and more practical version of the Japanese battle fan. The shield came into its own against the penetrating powers and speed of the arrow, a medium- to long-range weapon (speaking contemporarily). The Japanese battle fan was more for close-combat use and thus had to be small enough for high-speed manoeuvre by the wrist, rather like a table-tennis bat, to parry the attacks of the adversary.

From this it may be seen that there is a definite, if somewhat tenuous connection between the fan both as a carrier of military battalion insignia and a weapon, and the colours and insignia which still play an important part today in the ceremony and formality of the armed forces. Of course, such matters also relate to lesser orders and, by the same token, touches on the bearing of heraldic arms.

The original purpose of a crest was to make a commander known to his men in battle or, if his crest represented a monster or other tremendous object, to render him warlike and terrific. But, as Joseph MacLaren says,* there is no satisfactory proof whether the crest was really meant to render a leader easily recognised by his men, to make him look more formidable in battle, or as an ornamental mark of distinction. Significantly, among the earliest forms of crests were plumes of hair or feathers. The great seal of Richard I (died AD 1199) first represents the English king with something on his helmet resembling a plume of feathers and after this reign, most of the English kings had crowns on their helmets. (See also Chapter 3.)

At this point we must turn aside from these fringe associations of the fan and concern ourselves with the burgeoning fan. It is possible to classify the fans of these early times under the following headings:

(a) Rigid Screen, featuring a long handle and a sun-burst of feathers, usually of peacock, and used for ceremonial purposes.
(b) The natural fan, usually the palm leaf, used extensively in those lands to which the palm is indigenous.
(c) Plaited rush, grass or cane fans used generally by tribal man.
(d) Hide-fans made from the skins of animals.
(e) Feather hand fans of ostrich and other feathers.
(f) The Chinese screen fan of bamboo and paper or skin.

Variations and mutations abound: the long-handled fan of plaited grass, semi-circular in shape, was used to protect the Ruler from insects and to protect the offerings during sacrifices. And fly-flaps and fire-fans could fit into any of the last five categories.

* *Royal Book of Crests of Great Britain & Ireland* by Joseph MacLaren, Edinburgh, 1882.

The instrument we are considering is, therefore, clearly established as not just being one object, but a number of related objects whose main purpose was the agitation of the air, the shielding of the sun's rays as a primitive parasol, or the separation of grain from chaff.

If it can be accepted that Man's earliest needs consisted of eating and keeping warm, then the fan fulfilled both objectives. And the Tombs of the Pharaohs, dating from 2366 BC, depict the winnowing fan (held sacred by the people of the ancient world) and the fire-fan.

A Spanish story pictures Cupid tearing a wing from Zephyrus (the west wind) to fan his wife, Psyche, as she lay asleep on her bed of roses. A far cry indeed from keeping the flies off her face and blowing up the fire on a cold night!

A useful summary of the history of the fan was contained in the Reports of the Juries to the Commission of the Great Exhibition held at the Crystal Palace, Hyde Park, London, in 1851:

Upwards of three thousand years ago, the artist of ancient Egypt painted the fan on the walls of the tombs at Thebes. There the Pharaoh sits surrounded by his fan-bearers, each in his due rank; and there is seen an investiture of a fan-bearer, which realises the description in Genesis of the honours paid by Pharaoh to Joseph. The office of fan-bearer must have been honourable, and the insignia of office were long, slender, vividly-coloured fans on variegated or twisted handles. In war the same officers acted as generals, using their fans as standards; and in peace they assisted in the temple, and waved their variegated fans, both to produce a cooling breeze, and to guard the sacred offerings from the contamination of noxious insects. The fan is mentioned by Euripides, and its origin from "barbarous countries"; its use in Greece was similar to that in Egypt, but its forms were far more beautiful. The wings of a bird joined laterally and attached to a slender handle, formed the simple yet graceful fan of the Priest of Isis, when Isis became a Grecian deity; but it had not this form alone, for the Greek vases of Sir William Hamilton show that feathers of different lengths were taken and spread out somewhat in the form of a semicircle, but pointed at the top; a thread connected the feathers at the base, and another near their summit, and the fan thus made was fixed in a handle. This fan, the precise type of the state-fan of India and China of the present day, was waved by a female slave.

The fan, according to Virgil and Apuleius, was sacred to Bacchus, and the mystica "Vannus Iacchi" was carried in procession in the feast of that deity, as well as in the Eleusinian Mysteries. Its appellations multiplied, though its office remained the same, and it was termed indifferently "Flabellum", or "Muscarium". The modern Greek church is careful to place a fan in the hands of its deacons, to guard the officiating priest and the elements from desecration. The Roman ladies certainly enjoyed the luxury of the fan, which, gorgeous with peacock's feathers, or delicate with the tinted plumes of the ostrich, could not yet be folded, and rendered the services of an attendant necessary.

Thus summarised, the fan is without any shadow of doubt no ephemeral whimsy which warrants dismissal with humour or disdain. True its sanctity, fortunes and respect vacillated with changing rituality, custom and fashion, but its very endurance through so long a period of Mankind is indicative of the reverence, in varying degree, which has been accorded to this simple artifact.

CHAPTER TWO

THE FAN IN ASIA

Western civilisation goes back little more than a thousand years and, as far as Great Britain is concerned, the Middle Ages stand as the penumbra from which all our subsequent development burgeoned. Earlier than that, we were variously dominated by other nations and their customs, notably the Romans. Amidst all these foreign influences, the early Briton emerges as a somewhat primal being.

With our sights adjusted to the evolutionary time-scale of our own development, it is understandably hard for us to appreciate that Eastern civilisations were ancient 2,000 years before the birth of Christ. Oriental Man, if we may term him that, had reached a stable state of development a thousand years earlier still, and art, craft and science prospered in a hospitable environment where curiosity and achievement enjoyed an amicable coexistence. It is a little humbling for us to realise that Chinese chronologers go back 43,000 years before Christ for the earliest tidings of their race, and doubtless their records are but dim traditions, not of China as we know it today, but of their primitive home by the Tigris and the Euphrates. So the civilisation came to blossom with art, literature and craft encouraged to flow forth freely from an instinctively creative people.*

It was into this pleasant age that the fan was born. There appears to be uncertainty amongst the Chinese as to who invented the fan and precisely when. It has been attributed to the Emperor Shun in 2255 BC and, later still, to the first ruler of the Chou dynasty in 1122 BC. Again, in a Chinese book sanguinely entitled *A Child's*

---

* Hwang-te (sometimes Huang ti), the Yellow Emperor, formulated the rules that were held to govern music with the invention of the twelve semitone scale—the 12 *lüs*—about 5,200 years ago. He is not to be confused with the Emperor Che Huang-ti who, in 246 BC, was responsible for the destruction of all books, except those on medicine, agriculture and divination, and all musical instruments. Just a few books escaped this Cromwellian act of vandalism, the oldest to survive being *The Book of Changes* published 1,150 years before Christ.

Fig. 6

The crescent-shaped hand-fan dates from a very early period and it is to be found in the painted decorations of the Buddhist cave-temples of Ajanta (which date from the 1st century BC to the 8th century AD). This one, copied from the cave paintings, was probably made of cane or pith and may have been ornamented with strips or panels of mica.

Fig. 7

Also from the Ajanta cave-paintings is this representation of a flag-fan. What is so interesting is that it is an exact forebear of the hand flag or standard which we still know and use today. Rhead comments that there can be no doubt at all that this form of fan was common to the whole of the East and to a greater portion of the West. They originated in two forms: rigid and flexible.

Guide to Knowledge, the origin of the fan is attributed to the Emperor Hsein Yüan who came to the throne in the year 2699 BC. Other writers, basing their assumptions on a fragment of poetry by Lo-ki, assign its invention to the time of the Emperor Wee-wang, the first ruler of the Chow dynasty, the date here given as 1106 BC.

The Chinese legend concerning the invention of the fan has already been given (Chapter 1, page 42). These early fans were of dyed feathers of various birds, and those of the peacock. Rhead gives an account of a present of two fans of feathers of *tsio rouge* offered to the Emperor Tchao-wang of the Chou dynasty in 1052 BC by the King of Thou-sieou, and it is affirmed in the *Tchéou-li* that one of the chariots of the empress carried a feather-fan for the purpose of keeping the wheels free from dust.*

* *History of the Fan.*

The poet Thou-fou, in the *Song of Autumn*, mentions fans of pheasants' feathers as in royal use. Rhead refers to the Emperor Kao-Tsong of the Chang dynasty, 1323–1266 BC, having heard the cry of the pheasant, decided to use only fans composed of the tail feathers of this bird as an omen of good luck.*

Feather fans of this type have continued in the service of royalty until modern times. A large lacquered screen in the Victoria &

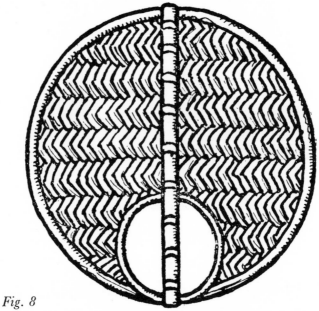

Fig. 8

A variant of the semi-circular or crescent-shaped hand-fan is this plaited grass fan which is seen in one of the sculptured roundels of the Buddhist tope or tower at Amaravati in Southern India. This dates from about the 2nd century AD

Albert Museum represents the Taoist Genii worshipping the God of Longevity. An attendant is shown holding a wing-shaped feather fan which is set laterally in a red lacquered handle. The painting, by an artist of the Ming dynasty, portrays the occupations of Court ladies. The feathers of the fan number seven, this being a sacred number corresponding to the constellation of seven stars on the left of the moon (the Great Bear) which is said to be the seat in the Taoist heavens of their supreme deity, Shang Ti, and around whom all the

* *ibid.*

other gods circulate in homage. This type of fan constantly appears in pictorial and other representations.

Similar fans having several rows of pointed feathers appear in painted and decorative work. Rhead quotes a curious example seen in a large drawing from Tonkin (Louvre) wherein the outer row of feathers are white and pale blue; the 2nd row is yellow, and the 3rd are those of the peacock. The body of the fan is coloured green, red, white and blue.*

Curiously, most surviving known Chinese art is of a later era and thus the earliest representation of fans in Chinese art are probably those of the sculptures of the Han dynasty, 206 BC–AD 25. In these, Hsi-wang Mu, wearing a coroneted hat, is attended by ladies carrying cup, mirror and fan. On the same relief, the Emperor Mu Wang of the Chou dynasty (1001 BC) is attended by a servitor with a fan and either a towel or a handkerchief. In the frieze forming the lower part of the relief, says Rhead, can be seen the "Chariot of the Sage" preceded by two men on foot, with staves and fans.†

Another of these reliefs shows servitors bearing screen fans or hand screens (*pien-mien*) which have an unusual, slightly pear shape. These small hand screens appear in a variety of shapes including circular, heart-shaped and egg-shaped, and are made of various materials. Examples recorded by Rhead include those made from the natural palm leaf, the palm leaf with a bamboo handle running up the middle (this style also being common to Japan), and of bamboo on its own. Chinese records assert that on the fifth day of the fifth month of the year corresponding to our AD 219, the Emperor presented to the members of the Imperial Academy a fan of bamboo carved and painted blue. Other examples of screen fans used turtle shell (the two portions held together with metal plates and equipped with a handle usually made of wood), or a light frame covered with stretched silk which was then painted or otherwise decorated. A form of embellishment which was greatly used by the Chinese, and one in which they excelled, was the use of feathers such as the turquoise tinted plumes of the kingfisher. Sometimes these were alternated with peacocks' feathers to produce a very beautiful effect.

A favourite decoration of the larger screen fans was provided by the representation of the fabled phoenix, the *Ho* bird of the Japanese.

* *ibid.*   † *ibid.*

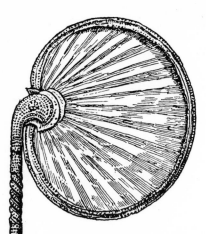

Fig. 9

The Burmese used ceremonial fans including some of an unusual shape having the leaf set sideways on the stem. These were sometimes decorated with talc inlays, painting or embroidered with silk, spangles and beetles' wings. The one illustrated here (from A. K. Coomaraswarmy's *Mediaeval Sinhalese Art*) is of gold, jewelled with rubies and the "nan-ratan" or nine stone, the handle overlaid with gold and also jewelled. It forms part of the Burmese Regalia.

A painting of the Chinese school of Japan in the British Museum (B.M. 822) shows two attendants on a Chinese emperor carrying a long oval screen bordered with peacocks' feathers and ornamented with two phoenixes.

Chinese lore decrees that there are eight sound-producing bodies corresponding to the eight symbols of *Fu Hsi*, which they believe are the expression of all the changes and permutations which take place in the universe. These eight substances are stone, metal, silk, bamboo, wood, skin, gourd and clay and they each hold symbolic relations to the eight points of the compass and the eight seasons of the year. Coincidentally, silk (a truly Chinese "invention"), bamboo, wood, metal and skin were all used individually or severally in the making of Chinese fans.

The ceremonies and the customs associated with the fan and in which the fan played a part were practically identical with the ancient peoples of the East and West. The same order of development was followed, its origin in the natural suggestion of the wings of birds and the broader leaved plants; the exact counterpart of the Han dynasty reliefs being found in Egypt and Assyria; the rigid hand-screens corresponding to those *tabellae* which the Romans derived from the Greeks (who in turn received them from the people of Asia Minor to whom they had doubtless come from the more remote East); and the employment of the fan in both religious and civil ceremony and in war.

The Chinese fan has long been associated with calligraphy and there is an early account of the supposed birth of the affinity between the fan and writing. It seems that the great scholar and calligrapher Wang-Hsi-chih (321–379 AD) once came upon an old lady selling fans in the street. Now Wang was saddened by the sight of the plain paper fans and quickly he took them from her and wrote a few words upon each before returning them. The aged vendor was justifiably angry at the defilement of her wares but her anger turned to delight when she found that she sold all her fans within minutes. Wang later became known as the "sage of calligraphy" and from that time forward, Chinese fans have excelled in the exhibition of the written word. By the 12th century, the writing of elegant inscriptions on fans had achieved the highest

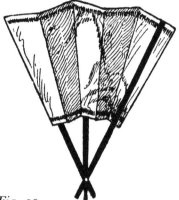

Fig. 10

The Japanese tea fan (*Rikiu ogi*) is used as a small cake tray or salver and comprises just three sticks and a simple mount. Etiquette dictates that it shall be used for no other purpose.

Fig. 11

From Madras in India comes this 19th-century ivory cockade fan. The only decoration is in the delicate carving of the guards which together form the handle when it is open as shown.

popularity and were to be found in the Royal Courts bearing the handwriting of emperors and their princesses. With handles of rare speckled bamboo gathered from the banks of the central lakes in

Fig. 12

Illustrated here from *The Penny Magazine* of July 6th, 1833, is the talipot
palm in various stages of growth. In Ceylon, where these palms grow in
profusion, the leaf is widely used as a natural folding fan. It is also sometimes
worked into the design of fixed fans (see Fig. 13.)

Hunan province, these royal fans became known as palace fans and
were of very slender wood with silk mounts.

Flory* comments that the artists of the Celestial Empire were
probably the originators of calligraphic and pictorial decorations
on fans. Certainly the Chinese have always been prolific diarists and
the *album fan* (a form of plain *ogi* fan with an undecorated, tinted
leaf) was invented to serve as a surface on which to record contemporary history. The once-famous Negroni Collection, sold in
London in 1866, included many album fans and some fetched £900
apiece. These were richly ornamented and covered with amorous
and complimentary inscriptions, and were supposed to have
belonged to the emperors and empresses of China. The first fan of
this type of which mention can be found in Chinese poetry was that

* *A Book About Fans*, p. 11.

of Princess Pan, AD 550.* The princess was for a time the favourite of the Emperor Chi'eng Si and finding herself losing this favour, she sent him a circular fan on which she had inscribed verses describing herself as an Autumn Fan—a neglected wife.†

The folding fan, however, was to come from another part of the Orient. If China gave us the ordinary fan, then Japan gave us the folding fan. Tradition claims that it was designed by an artist who lived in the reign of the Emperor Jen-ji in about AD 670, who thought up the idea using the principle of the construction of a bat's wing. This conforms to the general practice of ancient Japanese designers whose inventions were always inspired by natural constructive forms. The date when the folding fan reached China is unrecorded but there is a reference to it in a Chinese work dated AD 960 which states that the *tsin-theou-chen* (folding fan) was introduced by Tchang-ping-hai and was supposed to have been offered as a tribute by the barbarians of the south-east who came holding in their hands the pleated fan, which occasioned much laughter and ridicule.

The invention of the folding fan is attributed to a number of people. Another traditional story is that it was invented by a fan maker of the Jen-ji period (AD 668–72) whose name, unfortunately, is forgotten. He lived, legend decrees, at Tamba near Kyoto with his shrewish wife. One night a bat entered their sleeping-room and the wife reviled her husband for not getting up and throwing the animal out. Meanwhile, the unfortunate bat flew too close to the lamp, scorched its wings and fell to the floor. The fan maker picked it up and noticed how the creature's wing opened and closed. From this, he thought of a method of making a fan which might be carried in one's sleeve—the first folding fan. The Suye *hiro ogi* (wide end) fan has a similar divergence of the sticks with the addition of a slight curving of the outward sticks. This was used in the execution of dances in the Japanese *Nō* plays. The number of sticks varies between fifteen and twenty-five and this form of fan also dates from the 7th century.

It is generally believed that the rigid or screen fan remained in more or less general use in Asia until around the time of the Ming dynasty (AD 1368–1644). Thereafter, the folding fan gradually

* Woolliscroft Rhead gives a dynastical date of 32 BC.
† This story is recounted in full in Chapter 11.

Fig. 13

The Cingalese used the leaf of the talipot palm, or natural folding fan, to form the *sēsata* or rigid screen fan used for ceremonial occasions involving royalty and religion. These consisted of an embroidered cloth disc or palm leaf decorated with images of the sun, moon, etc. Mica and other materials were introduced and the whole was mounted on a decorated and lacquered wood handle anything up to seven feet long.

usurped the position formerly held by the rigid form. The fan in the Orient was held in far higher esteem than its western version in the years to come. To the Chinese and the Japanese, nations where long-standing cultures have bred gracious behaviour as second nature, the fan was a revered artifact. Each caste, every social occasion and all religious ceremony was dependent for part of its institution or liturgy on the use of a fan, and a different fan was required for each occasion.

Even what is to us so mundane an event as drinking tea is to the Chinese an event accompanied by ceremony and during the warm weather, the fan is included in the ceremony. As soon as tea is drunk, the host takes his fan and, bowing to the company, announces "Thsing-chen" which translates as "I invite you to fan yourselves". Each guest then commences to use his fan with great gravity and modesty. It is considered a breach of etiquette on such occasions either to be without a fan or to refrain from its use.

Chinese authors agree that the fan which folded was the invention of the Japanese who, together with the Tartars, possessed folding fans before they were known in China. Rondot records the fact that in the beginning, only courtesans used folding fans and "honest" women used round screens.* A curious parallel to this is to be found in Howes's 1632 edition of *Stow's Chronicle* which says:

> Women's Maskes, Buskes, Muffes, Fanns, Periwigs, and Bodkins were first devised and used in Italy by *Curtezans*, and there received of the best sort for gallant ornaments, and from thence they came to England, about the time of the massacre of Paris.

The extreme antiquity of Chinese civilisation meant that China possessed a very great lead over the rest of the world in practically every sphere. The working of materials was one aspect of craftsmanship in which China reigned supreme for several thousands of years. And of all the materials in which she excelled, perhaps in none were her talents displayed greater than in the working of ivory. Ivory fans date from a very distant period and Rhead gives a date of 990 BC as the earliest known.†

The Chinese also excelled in lacquer work; indeed lacquering is one of the earliest and most prized of all the Chinese arts (see Chapter 8). Fans finished in lacquer first appeared in China but

* *Raport sur les Objets de Paruse*, Paris, 1854.
† *History of the Fan*, London, 1910.

subsequently the art was taken up by the Japanese who brought it to a greater perfection.

Fans of China were also made of sandalwood, a timber indigenous to India from whence it is imported. Sandalwood is also, incidentally, used in the making of joss sticks, so common throughout the East. Mother of pearl and tortoise shell were also used but the finest skill of all was that displayed in the making of filigree ivory. Filigree was also used in gold and in silver gilt, often enriched by enamel or kingfisher feathers which were stuck to the surface. Enamelwork is another ancient art which has been practised in western Asia since pre-Christian times. It reached China about the 13th century AD and was used as a decoration, usually to filigree work (see Chapter 8).

Painting as a form of decoration, and the skills of the miniature painter in particular, was also highly developed at an early date in Chinese history. The Chinese fan frequently bears witness to the talents and abilities of the early craftsmen. The so-called Hundred Faces fan, depicting a large composition of figures, features perfectly detailed *appliqué* faces carved in ivory and then painted. Sometimes even the costumes worn by the characters are of silk appliquéd.

Almost every important city or district in China has its own characteristic fan displaying distinctive design, colour or ornamentation. In the Chekiang province, for example, large plates of bamboo cut from the giant bamboo which grows in that area were carved and these were known as Jade-plaque. In Kuangtung province a type of fan was made which was known as the "duck's foot". In this, a length of bamboo was split to the half-way position to form a number of thin strips which were then splayed out and covered with paper. This was also known as the Swatow fan during the last century after the town wherein was specially practised its decoration. Another type which underwent a rapid social change from Hangchou and was termed an "oiled fan". This was a folding fan covered with black, oiled paper made from persimmon-bark. Because black was originally associated with moral indelicacies, its use during the middle of the last century was confined to the lower classes it later underwent a drastic revision of social acceptance and, by the end of the 19th century, had become fashionable with the aristocracy. The folding fan was as much part of everyday life then as any comparable utilitarian device today—such as the air-

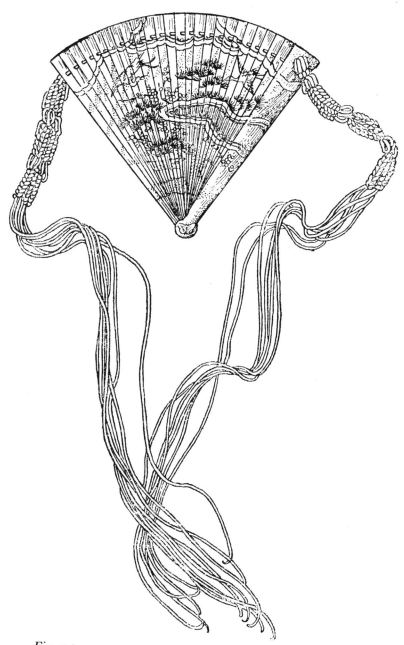

Fig. 14

Japanese lady's court fan. The long coloured streamers attached to each
guard trail gossamer fashion upon the ground.

conditioner which, after all, does just about the same job. The Chinaman would keep his folded fan in the top of his dress boot, or concealed in the ample folds of his dress.

Fig. 15a

A principle of Japanese art is the studious avoidance of exact repetition and symmetry in ornamentation. Here are two Japanese screen fans which demonstrate this. In the one there are several shapes which are so arranged that the chief objects are broken in their line. In the other, the juxtaposition of the square, the fan-form and the landscape and the birds and sun serves to produce a similar discontinuity more by implication than by overt display. The Japanese, either by natural instinct or by an aesthetic love of variety, have learned by an awareness of Nature that the greatest imaginable variety is secured automatically. This, through their treatment of art and decoration, is one of the fundamental points upon which the recognition of a Japanese fan may be founded.

In Japan, the fan is regarded as an emblem of life signified by the radiating sticks widening outwards from the rivet or starting point. From this it is understandable that the Japanese traditionally select the fan as a New Year's gift. The fan enters into almost every aspect of the life of the people ranging from Emperor down to lowliest peasant. Friends greet one another with a wave of the fan, the bride uses it as a gift which she takes with her to the house of her husband, and the youth receives a fan when he reaches his majority.

Fig. 15b

Both feather fans and hand-screens with bamboo handles appear in Japanese paintings. Fly-whips were also used.

The more important types of Japanese fan, together with their dates of invention (or earliest known *floruit*) are as follows:

Rigid fans or hand-screens introduced from China at the end
 of the 6th century AD.
Folding fans (bamboo) invented by the Japanese AD 668–71.
Gumbai Uchiwa, the flat iron battle-fans, invented during the
 11th century AD.
Gun Sen, the folding iron battle-fans, invented during the 12th
 century AD.
Hi ogi, the court fans, invented during the 11th century AD.

65

Mai ogi, the dancing fans, invented at the beginning of the 17th century AD.

Rikiu ogi, the tea fans, invented at the beginning of the 17th century AD.

Water fans, for kitchen use, invented during the 18th century AD.

The earliest form of folding fan is the *Kōmori* or bat's wing. It is formed from fifteen bamboo sticks having a slight re-divergence springing from the handle end, so that when held closed in the hand as it is by courtiers whilst fulfilling the office of fan-bearing, it still appears partially open. There is a reason for this which would appear to be well-founded. The use of the dagger fan (and its misuse) made identification of the real thing a necessity of goodwill.

The mount of the *Kōmori* is of paper which may be painted with any design and in any colour with the exception of green and light purple which are considered to be unlucky colours.

Another form of Japanese fan is the *Akomé ogi* and this, the earlier court-fan, dates from the invention of the folding fan in the 7th century. This has thirty-eight blades of wood painted white and decorated with cherry, plum, pine or chrysanthemum on a ground of gold and silver powder. The fan is characteristically ornamented at the corners with an arrangement of artificial flowers in silk with 12 long streamers of different coloured silks. The rivet is formed either in the shape of a bird or a butterfly. This form of fan was apparently used by the court ladies until as late as 1868.

Woolliscroft Rhead quotes a description of these fans left by Pierre Loti:

> They wave with constant motion, or carry shut, their court-fans, on the pleated silk (?) of which are delicately painted dreamy fancies, of inexpressible charm, picturing the reflection in the water of cloud forms, of moons wintry pale, the flight of birds, or showers of peach blossom wafted by the wind in April mists. At each angle of the mount is tied an enormous tassel with shades of chenille, the ends of which trail along the ground, brushing the fine sand at each movement of the fan.

A lengthy description of the use of the fan in Japanese ceremonials is contained in *Fans of Japan* by Mrs Salwey. Woolliscroft
Rhead quotes extensively from this.

The decoration of Japanese fans includes illustrations of a
number of the legends of Japanese history. Innumerable fans
bearing illustrations of Hotei, the Chinese God of prosperity,
appear by Japanese artists, some of which date from the 15th
century. The practice of inscribing sacred texts on fans was in-
dulged during the latter part of the 11th and the beginning of the
12th century, the period when the Buddhist religion was openly
professed by the wealthy and warmly supported by the luxurious.
Fragments of Buddhist *sûtras* written on fans and fan leaves exist
at the temples at Yamato, Osaka, the Imperial Museum at Tokyo,
and elsewhere. These fans, according to Rhead, although differing
somewhat in size, are all alike in paper, pigments and the style of
painting, and apparently had a common origin. They are overlaid
with gold-leaf and dusted with fine sand upon which has been
applied a thin wash of red or black pigment. The sacred text is
written in ink over a painting, usually a figure subject and bearing
no reference to the text. The faces are sketched in a curious convention known as Hikimé Kagihana (literally "eye with a line; nose
with a key") in which the eye is represented by a straight line and the
nose with a somewhat acute angle. This style of representation has
been traced to Kasuga Takayoshi (*c.* the beginning of the 12th
century) who painted a number of picture rolls illustrating the tales
of the Genii.

Significantly, the caligraphers who could produce skilful ideo-
graphs were rated above the artist in merit since beautiful writing
is a quality highly prized both in China and Japan.

China and Japan. For the fanologist it is to these far-off countries
that we owe our interest and our love of the fan. But it would be an
egregious oversight to assume that the art and craft which gave the
world the fan is one which is past. All the trappings of the nuclear,
supersonic age in which we live have served not to stifle the fan in
Asia. True the Japanese and Chinese businessman now wears a
western-type suit and enjoys the benefits of high-rise living, the
motor car, air-conditioning and television; but the fan is still to be
found in everyday ceremony. The peak period of the fan may have
passed, but tradition dies hard.

In concluding this outline of the fan in Asia, it is interesting to turn to Tallis's description of the Great Exhibition (1851) and quote from his words regarding the Chinese fan exhibit:

In fan-making the Chinese and French are the great rivals, and may be said to monopolise the supply of the whole world. In the lacquered fans the superiority of the natives of China is fully admitted. They are unrivalled, especially when price is taken into consideration, in the sculpturing and piercing of the wood, bone, ivory, or mother of pearl framework. Even their commonest fans are remarkable for boldness and originality of design, brilliancy of colouring, sharpness of drawing, and solidity and correctness of workmanship. The manufacture of fans is carried on almost exclusively at Canton, Soutchou, Hangtchou, and Nankin. The fans of ivory and bone and of feathers, are made exclusively for exportation to Europe or America; those used by the Chinese are of bamboo polished or japanned, and covered with paper. They are sold at from 10d to 14s 6d per dozen, according to the quality of the frame and the design of the leaf. The examples which were in the Great Exhibition did not, however, come direct from any Chinese maker, but were contributed by three English exhibitors, viz. Messrs C. T. Braine, J. Daniell, and Hewett and Co. The examples exhibited comprised fans of painted and embroidered feathers; a feather-fan painted with silver outlines, representing groups of Chinese figures, the feathers being alternately blue and white; an ivory fan elaborately carved and pierced, and, considering the amount of work, very cheap, its price being only 20s. There were also several very common paper-fans, ornamented either with rude delineations of landscapes, or besprinkled with gold-spangle.

CHAPTER THREE

FANS ENTER EUROPE

We have already seen how very different the Chinese fan was from that of Egypt and from this I have put forward the suggestion that the fan may have been self-generative in these two geographically far-removed locations.

How the fan progressed into Europe is another unanswerable question to which we can but state possible stages. First we know of the ˙ many levels of commerce between the Romans and the Egyptians. And we also know that the Phoenicians were avid traders and that the Romans and the Greeks shared much in culture and custom. If we take as a first starting point Heliopolis or Alexandria, the route to Rome was a sea voyage of more than a thousand miles. The alternative was a largely overland journey via Damascus, through Asia Minor and into Thracia via Byzantium, allowing access to Macedonia and Hellas, and thence to the Roman Empire.

Were we now to assume the starting point to be the Far East, the only practical passage into Europe lay by sea and from what we know of commerce with the Far East, the direct influence of Chinese culture on Europe is much less than 2,000 years old.

In Chapter 2, I traced the development of the fan in Asia. There may be a link here in that it was the Chinese who first employed the intriguing products of the mulberry silk-moth, *bombyx mori*. Silk has been known to the Chinese from very remote times. In the year 2640 BC, the empress Se-ling-she, wife of emperor Hwang-te, encouraged the cultivation of the mulberry tree, the rearing of the worms and the reeling of silk. The Chinese also credit her with the invention of the loom. The secret of the manufacture of silk was guarded by Imperial decree and he or she who disclosed the secret was threatened with death by torture. The silk industry thus remained the prerogative of the Chinese for something in excess of 2,000 years. Even the Japanese did not secure the secret until AD 300 by the process of hiring Korean men who succeeded in carrying off four Chinese girls who subsequently revealed all (as regards silk

Fig. 16

Metal *flabella* were of two types: the large-handled processional fan and the short-handled hand-fan. Shown here is one of the latter, illustrated from Butler's *Ancient Coptic Churches of Egypt*. This one is a circular metal disc decorated rather crudely with two figures of the Seraphim interspersed with Romanesque ornamentation.

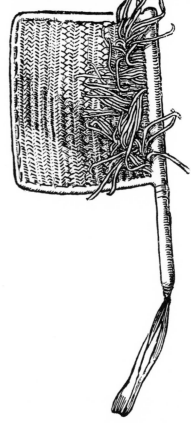

Fig. 17

The square or oblong flag-fan shown here is of the rigid type and was made by the natives of the Niger settlements of East Africa. Naturally-coloured plaited grass was frequently used or alternatively the grass would be stained red and black.

manufacture at least) and were thus instrumental in founding the Japanese silk industry.

Legend has it that, around 140 BC, silkworm eggs and mulberry seeds (one being useless without the other) were smuggled into border territory between India and China by a princess who concealed them in her head-dress. Sericulture in India was certainly first established in the area between the Brahmaputra and Ganges rivers, so its introduction was more than likely overland from China.

From the Ganges Valley, sericulture then moved slowly westwards into Persia and Central Asia.

The passage of Chinese culture, and thence the fan, into southern Europe may have in part been due to this wondrous fabric from the Orient, for at an indeterminate period shortly before the Christian era, raw silk began to be exported from the East into Rome. The route followed was largely overland and was most likely transported by numerous bands of itinerant traders bartering from one area to the next. Certainly, when silk first appeared in Rome its cost was enormous and it was quite literally worth its weight in gold. Rather surprisingly, its use by men at this time was considered effeminate.

From this evidence, we can see that some form of trade route between China and Rome did exist. And, analogously, word of the fan could also have come from China via the same trail.

This is pre-supposing something which might well be a false assumption, and that is that the fan did not emerge in Europe without outside influence. If this was so, and it would probably have begun in the southern part, it may have been in existence contemporaneously with the Egyptian fan.

Rhead asserts, but without producing evidence, that the fan reached the Romans via the Etruscans.* Since the country of Etruria or Tuscia (known by the Greeks as Tyrrhenia) was situated in central Italy, and since the last three kings of Rome were Etruscans, this brings us no closer to deducing the travels of the fan in Europe since we are still left with but surmise as to how the fan reached the Italian peninsula. The Etruscan period also tends to cast doubt on Rhead's suggestion since it only dates back to around 350 BC and received the Roman franchise in the year AD 91. Julius Caesar was involved with the Egyptians around 2,000 years ago where the ceremonial fan was surely better established than with the Etruscans to whom it was (in the words of Rhead) "a luxury".

These are all points upon which the truth may never emerge. Rhead records that ". . . the use of the fan as bellows appears to have been practically universal, and to have dated from a very early period of the world's history." The Greeks used a large flat fan for fanning the fire: this was called by them ῥιπίς and a smaller version, named ῥιπίδιον was used by males and females alike to keep away the flies. Portuguese fire-fans, the *abano*, are also of

* *History of the Fan*, London, 1910.

71

extreme antiquity (by European timescales). These are round in shape, and are coarsely plaited from straw or rush and attached to a rough wooden handle. The Egyptian fire-fan was made in the same manner as that of the Portuguese although, instead of being in the shape of a full circle, they were in the form of a major crescent. A measure of the versatility of this fan is revealed by the painted decoration of a tomb at Eileithyia which shows the interior of a storeroom with a workman using a fan of this shape to fan or cool the liquid which is contained in a number of vases or amphorae.

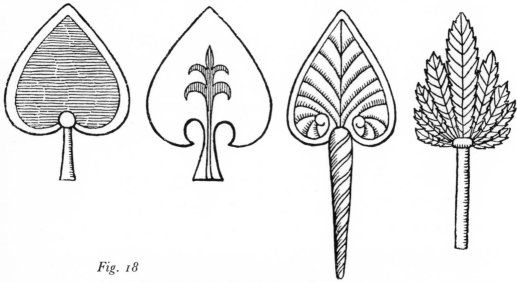

Fig. 18

A form of fan which is to be found in almost all the East is the single-leaf or heart-shaped fan. These, drawn by Woolliscroft Rhead, come from Greek terracottas. The earliest Greek fans were probably branches of the myrtle, acacia, the triple leaves of the Oriental plantain and also the leaves of the lotus which, together with the myrtle, were consecrated to Venus.

Similar fans were carried in funeral processions at Thebes along with the more ornamental semi-circular hand fans used by ladies to fan themselves as well as the long-handled fan carried by servants.

Another type of fan appears on a 12th-dynasty tablet in the British Museum depicting the Lady Khu seated with her husbands and receiving offerings from her children. Here is shown, resting against the seat, a hand fan which appears of rigid construction which seems to be intended for the use of the lady herself. The handles of these fans were made of ivory, painted wood or of sandal-wood.

The long-handled standard, banner and processional fans were usually formed of feathers of the larger birds. The feathers and the handle would then be dyed or painted in brilliant colours, the style of decoration following closely the meticulous care and sensibility characteristic of all Egyptian work. The tips of the feathers in some examples were surmounted by tufts of small fluffy feathers, a device common to several other countries including those fans made by the North American Indians.

Fig. 19

Part of the decoration from a Greek vase found at Kertsch and depicting Helen of Troy (enthroned) being tended. One of the attendants carries a feather fan. The piece dates from about 300 B.C.

Besides feather fans, many of these standard fans appear to have been formed of some material stretched upon a semi-circular frame and decorated in various ways. Not only were these in attendance on the King wherever he went, but they were also used as standards or colours in war, the royal chariot always being accompanied by at least two. Rhead points to the fact that all available evidence suggests that they were dedicated to the service of the Gods and a *stele* in the museum at Boulak depicts Osiris, the great deity of the Egyptians, enthroned with a flabellifer behind waving the long-handled fan. The radiating fans, wrote Professor Flinders Petrie, the archaeologist and expert on Egyptology, were used as sunshades and appeared in hieroglyphics as the determination of *Khaib* or shadow.

The connection between Osiris and the ceremonial fan may well have been of deeper significance than that which at first appears. Osiris, husband of Isis and son of Jupiter and Niobe, is said to have been the original king of Egypt and to have reclaimed his subjects from a barbarous life. He travelled widely, spreading the blessings of civilisation but on his return to Egypt, he was slain by his brother, Typhon, and his body divided into pieces. Isis recovered the surviving portions of her beloved and proceeded to render to each part all the honours which his humanity deserved. However, she failed to find the private parts of her husband's body and so to these she accorded honours more solemn and more mysterious than those bestowed upon the rest of him. Among the rites, was the representation of these portions in wood which were carried high during the sacred festivals she instituted in his honour.

These festivals of the *phallus* were imitated by the Greeks and introduced into Europe by the Athenians who made the procession of the *phallus* part of the celebrations of the Dionysia of the god of wine. Those whose task it was to carry the *phallus* at the end of a long pole were called *phalliphori*. Some of the Greeks believed that the ceremonies of the *phallus* were not derived from Egypt but that Pegasus of Eleusis first taught the Athenians how to worship Bacchus and that it was he who introduced the use of the *phallus* in the orgies.

The story of Osiris, as related by Plutarch, prompts us to take another look at the early Egyptian fan. The Italian Egyptologist, Hippolyte Rosellini drew several ceremonial fans from the Boulak museum and these display an unusual shape and proportion. Instead of the normal semi-circular palm surrounding the staff, the mount for the radiating feathers appears in phallic shape, heightened by the presence of the lotus bud shoulder, thereby implying a direct link between this form of ceremonial fan, the festivals associated with Osiris and the fecundity with which the lotus is

74

Fig. 20

The Greeks used feather fans extensively and they are frequently to be found
depicted on vases. This, from the Apulian Hydra in the British Museum,
evidently represents a conventional peacock-feather fan. The proportions of
the fan suggest that it was common to have a heavy-looking handle but in
fact surviving fragments indicate that this was made of a light wood.

allegedly endowed. The embellishment of the effigy of the *phallus*
with radiating feathers may thus be seen as one of the many forms
of worship of the reproductive powers of Man which were practised
in primitive times.

Representations of peacock feather fans are common on Greek
vases and many of these display a shape and form which is identifiable with similar forms of worship and symbolism. Rhead records a
vase in the British Museum (an oil-flask) which shows Aphrodite
seated in the lap of Adonis and an accompanying figure holds a very

75

large fan in the shape of a reversed heart. Here the fan is used to suggest the fecundity of Adonis. On the Apulian Hydra, also in the British Museum, a fan is featured which bears a more direct resemblance to the *phallus* and this includes a characteristic which is commonly associated with the Etruscans. This makes use of peacock feathers of different lengths arranged in a semi-circle as usual, but with longest feather in the centre thus producing an almost triangular form to the fan.

The fan of feathers which, according to Uzanne,* was used by the Vestal virgins to fan the flame of their sacrifices may be taken as having little connection with Osiris, even if only on the strength of the fact that, during the one thousand years during which the chaste ardours of their order were maintained (Numa, born on the day Romulus laid the foundations of Rome, is said to have appointed the first four), only eighteen had to be punished for incontinence.

The fans of the priests of Isis, when Isis, as the Minerva of Athens, was a Grecian divinity, are said to have been formed of the wings of a bird, attached to the end of a long wand. Rhead asserts that this thus resembled the caduceus of Mercury (the Greek Hermes). How the bird's wings could appear as the entwined serpents given by Apollo in exchange for Mercury's lyre he does not say, unless they depended from a cross piece at the top of the stick.

That the fan reached the Greeks from Egypt through the Phoenicians there seems little doubt, although it is probably wiser to state that there is no evidence to point to any other conclusion. When the sarcophagus of the Cyprio–Phoenician ruler, Amanthus, was found, it featured a representation of a train of horsemen, footmen and chariots, the horses' heads being adorned with a pleated fan crest which was similar to that used by the Persians.† A description given by Perrot and Chipiez of this relic says: "The parasol which shades the head of the great person in the first *biga* is the symbol of Asiatic royalty: the fan-shaped plume which rises above the heads of all the chariot horses, is an ornament that one sees in the same position in Assyria and Lycia, when the sculptor desires to represent horses magnificently caparisoned."‡ What is interesting

---

* *The Fan*, London, 1884.
† *The History of the Fan*, Rhead, p. 27.
‡ Lycia in the Persian Empire lies north-west of Cyprus and today is the peninsula forming the western seaboard of the Gulf of Adalia.

here is that this illustration contains a fan of the pleated form although in its realisation it was more than likely rigid and fixed to a short handle. The pleated form of fan has also been seen in both Egyptian and Assyrian monuments so indicating that this type of construction has been in use in Europe for a considerable time.

The Assyrian fan-shaped plume referred to here is the *anthemion* (Greek *anthos* meaning flower) which is an exceedingly characteristic Assyrian form. These forms are illustrated in Chapter 2. Widely used as an ornament in all forms of decoration, the description is used to describe many varieties of radiate forms. The anthemion design is sometimes called the honeysuckle ornament and in some Greek examples it is not unlike a cluster of the buds of that plant, although the honeysuckle is unknown in this quarter. However, like the *patera* or rose-form (Latin *pateo* meaning to lie open), the anthemion-form springs from the inherent beauty of radiate forms; the patera from the star; the anthemion from the fan.

The earliest Greek fans were most probably natural elements— the branch of the myrtle, acacia, the triple leaves of the Oriental plantain and also the leaves of the lotus. The lotus and the myrtle were both sacred to Venus, the famed goddess of beauty whose less endearing attributes included nymphomania, being an unfaithful wife, and a blesser of public licentiousness on a scale seldom encountered in classical times. There is also a reference to the fact that the myrtle bough also served the Romans both as a fly-flap and as a fan (*Martial*, iii. 82).

The single leaf or heart-shaped fan is also a recurring theme in Greek terracottas and numerous examples are to be seen in our museums. The circular fan of peacocks' feathers* was in use as early as the 5th century BC and even at this early date the device was established in Asia Minor. A slave in the *Orestes* of Euripedes (who was born 480 BC and died 406 BC) says: "After the Phrygian fashion I chanced with the close circle of feathers to be fanning the gale, that sported in the ringlets of Helen."

The Greek treatment of the heart-shaped fan is, from the artistic standpoint, extremely interesting. Stemming from the anthemion (where the central *folium* or leaf is the longest) this type of fan

* Grecian ladies are said to have preferred the feathers of the peacock, bird of Juno and symbolic of refinement, splendour and luxury.

followed the Greek doctrines of design. All the ornamental types of Egyptian decorative art are treated in a bold (and, in representations, diagrammatic) style. The arrangement of an Egyptian temple shows that whilst all the columns are similar, they are not identical and the preservation of symmetrical balance is followed only by the broad plan, not its detail execution. Of twelve columns, for example,

Fig. 21

The styles of Egyptian decorative art make a fascinating study. This representation of the lotus-flower, with its geometrically-generated form, was copied in the fan. It is significant that Moorish, Arabic, Persian and Indian ornamentation generally follow symmetrical patterns or constructions.

Fig. 22

A characteristic Assyrian decorative form is the anthemion, derived from the Greek *anthos*, a flower. The term is applied to radiate forms such as that seen here. It is also, erroneously, called the honeysuckle ornament. Its similarity to the early Egyptian peacock-feather fan and the later Greek feather fan with its longest member at the centre is most marked.

only the central two will be exactly the same. Those flanking them will have different capitals, similar to each other but not to the central ones; those extending outwards from these will again be matched in opposing pairs. By comparison, it is a feature of Moorish, Arabic, Persian and Indian ornament that exact symmetry should be followed. Chinese and Japanese art, on the other hand, delights in the violation of symmetry. And so the Greeks, in pairing either side of a central detail, often tended to prefer the heart-shaped fan rather than the segment of a circle.

Earlier I mentioned the introduction of the fan into Italy. Writing in the *Revue de l'Art Chretién* in 1883, M. de Linas wrote:

> The fashion of the fan was probably introduced into Italy in the 6th century BC. We learn from Dionysius of Halicarnassus, that Aristodemus, tyrant of Cumæ, and ally of Porsenna, corrupted the youths of this town by making them effeminate buffoons, accompanied by followers who carried the flabellum and umbrella.

This is a confusing reference since this particular Aristodemus had as his surname Malacus which means effeminate or delicate, and he was slain by Xenocrates (Plutarch). This could hardly have been the 6th century BC since Zenocrates died 314 BC in his eighty-second year.

In the previous Chapter, we saw the relationship between the fan and the umbrella in India and in this reference to Aristodemus we find flabellum and umbrella mentioned in the same context. On many Greek vases dating from the 3rd and 4th centuries BC, more particularly those from Attica, it is often very difficult to distinguish the fan from the umbrella. Sir George Birdwood (born 1832; died 1917) stated:

> Where it is distinctly an umbrella, it is either of the peaked Assyrian form, or of the dome- ("rondel" of Valentijin, etc., and "arundels" of Fryer) topped Indian form (*chhatra*); and when it is distinctly a fan, it is usually of the Indian type, determined by the fan palm frond and the peacock feather, and rarely of the Egyptian type determined by the date-palm and the ostrich feather.*

The Roman fly-flap (*muscarium*) comprised peacock's feathers often at the end of a long handle so that the fan could be waved by a servant (*flabellifer*) and compound references are to be found in Plautus (*Trinummus*, II. i.) and Propertius (II, xxiv. II), whilst Martial refers to the fly-flap (xiv. 67). The Romans also used the tail of the yak which appears to have been imported from India and was not so commonly employed as the *tabellæ* which was a species of fan of square or circular shape formed of precious wood or very finely cut ivory. A reference to the *tabellæ* is to be found in

* Woolliscroft Rhead, *History of the Fan*, p. 35.

Ovid in the third book of his *Amores*. He says "Wouldst thou have an agreeable zephyr to refresh thy face? This tablet agitated by my hand will give you this pleasure." Representations of fans such as these are seen on vases in the Louvre showing scenes of young Romans fanning their mistresses along the Via Sacra.

St Hieronymus, better known to us as St Jerome, father of the Latin church (born AD 331; died 420), endowed the fan with reverence, naming it as an emblem of chastity. The use of the fan in ancient Egyptian ceremony had not been overlooked by the early Christian church which had bestowed upon the object such a deal of importance. This utility device, venerated by Isis in Bacchanalian festivities, was thus launched on a new and pure path having been sanctified as a liturgical ornament. This appropriation has been claimed by the Apostles themselves but the earliest recognised notice of the *flabellum* in this connotation is in the Apostolical Constitutions which direct that after the oblation, before and during the prayer of consecration, two deacons are to stand, one on either side of the altar, holding a fan made of thin membrane (parchment), or peacock's feathers, or of fine linen, and quietly drive away the flies and other small insects, that they may not stick against the vessels; this use of the *flabellum* being derived, not from the ritual of the synagogue of the Jews, but from that of the Pagan temples.

Butler (*Ancient Coptic Churches of Egypt*) quotes a similar rubric from the liturgy of St Clement and refers also to *flabella* waved by the deacons in the Syrian Jacobite (and probably also in the Coptic) rite for the ordination of a priest at the laying-on of hands. It is significant that the Copts were the Christian descendants of the ancient Egyptians and their name is said to have come from Coptos, a once-great city in Upper Egypt situated about 100 leagues from Alexandria on a canal which led to the Nile.

Its early adoption by the Latin Church is demonstrable by the many references in various writings and in Smith's *Dictionary of Christian Antiquities*, the fan and its uses in the Christian faith are mentioned. The waving of the *flabellum* gradually acquired a deeper symbolism and was held to signify the wafting of divine influence upon the ceremony, the movements to and fro symbolising the quivering of the wings of Seraphim. For this reason, we find representatives of the Seraphim playing an important part in its ornamentation. The Book of Kells, which dates from the 7th century AD, contains a representation of the four evangelists in which the Seraphic symbol of St Matthew is figured by the crossed *flabella*, each having a pair of bells with triple hammers, the remaining three evangelists being represented by the usual symbols of the lion in the centre, and the bull and the eagle at the lower corners.

In these early *flabella*, two distinct types can be discerned. The first is composed of some yielding material such as vellum or peacocks' feathers and fitted with handles of ivory. The second is of

Fig. 23

A further variety of the anthemion is seen here from an Assyrian mural slab.
Here the chief elements are the stellate patera and the fan-like forms.

rigid construction and formed of metal such as silver or silver gilt, the latter being employed for the processional fan and both being used in ceremonial processions and the celebration of the mass.

Metal *flabella* also existed in two forms. One was the long-handled processional fan, and the other the short-handled hand fan. An illustration in Butler (see Fig. 16) shows an example of the latter in the form of a circular disc of metal somewhat crudely decorated with two figures of the Seraphim interspersed with Romanesque ornament.

Very few ancient *flabella* have survived and of these the most famous is that of the abbey church of Tournus on the Saône, south of

81

Chalon in France. This, according to Rhead, could be taken as a characteristic type. It is formed of a strip of vellum folded into a circular, pleated cockade painted on both sides with figures of St Philibert and other saints divided by conventional trees. The outer borders consist of a continuous scroll of Romanesque ornament interspersed with the figures of animals. The three concentric borders of the fan are inscribed with Latin hexameters and pentameters. The handle is formed of four cylinders of white bone, two being ornamented with semi-naturalistic vine foliage running spirally round the stem, and the two lower ones are fluted. These cylinders are united by nodes or pommels coloured green. The centre node is inscribed and the stem is surmounted by a capital with four figures of saints whose names appear on the node immediately beneath as S. MARIA; S. AGN; S. FILIB; S. PET. On the capital rests the guard or box which received the *flabellum* when closed and the four sides of this are elaborately carved in white bone which bears evidence of a different hand. One edge of this early folding fan is attached inside the box and the other to the detachable lid of the box, and, on opening, this lid is taken round, so opening the fan, to be attached to the back of the box with a cord. The fan dates from the 9th century AD.

In a singularly enlightening letter written *c.* 1098 by St Hildebert, Archbishop of Tours and accompanying the gift of a *flabellum* to a friend, we get an insight to its use and find some of the mystic import explained. The flies (whether real or now purely allegorical is unstated) represent the temptations of the devil and are to be driven away by the Catholic faith, the instrument of realisation being the *flabellum*.

Now this certainly sheds light on the true use of the church fan, for whilst it would no doubt have been disturbing to have the Holy Sacraments fly-blown, it seems an unnecessary involvement to introduce fans and fan-bearers into church ceremony unless both fan and flies have a hidden, deeper symbolism. This we now know to have been the case.

Both the British Museum and the Victoria & Albert Museum in London have a number of fragments of *flabella* and these instruments figure repeatedly in the inventories of church and abbey property. A Salisbury inventory makes mention of two fans of vellum or other material in the year AD 1214, whilst the Chapel of St Faith in the crypt of St Paul's in London possessed, in 1298, a *muscatorium* or fly-whip of peacocks' feathers.* Not only the cathedral and great church possessed the fan for we find in the churchwarden's accounts at Walderswick, Suffolk, in the year 1493, an entry for *ivd* for "a bessume of pekoks fethers".

Only occasionally was the *flabellum* represented in early illuminated manuscripts. Mention has already been made of the Book of Kells in which there are to be found miniatures of angels waving these instruments. In the Gospel of Trèves, which dates from the 8th century, is a conjoined evangelistic, symbolic figure holding a small *flabellum* in one hand and a eucharistic lance in the other. A few other references are to be found up to the 13th century.

Surprisingly enough, representations in printed books are even more rare. This is probably due to the fact that by the end of the sixteenth century the *flabellum* had fallen into disuse although as late as 1688 Randle Holmes (*Academy of Armory*) refers to "the flap or fann to drive away flies from the chalice". In Barclay's *Ship of Fools of the World* printed in 1509 there is a woodcut of a bespectacled bibliophile wearing cap and bells, seated among his books and holding in his hands a *flabellum* of feathers.

The use of the fan in religious ceremony throughout Europe then passed largely into obscurity. From the final dissolution of the Roman Empire (*c.* 3rd century AD) to that of the Crusades (the 8th and last in 1270), the general use of the fan was discontinued in Europe, its use probably only adopted by highly-placed personages. Even thus in its declining years, it still sufficed as a fly-flap or *flabellum*. Blondel infers from the circumstances of Étienne Boileau not referring to it in his *Livre des Mestiers* (1200) that even at this time the fan no longer served any domestic purpose except in very rare instances.

There is an interesting coincidence here in that the church fan declined as the bell came to play a greater part in religious ceremony. From the Book of Kells illustration, and other records, it is known that the small bell or *tintinnabulum* was in use in the 8th century AD. Since time immemorial, it has been the understanding of Man that silence encouraged the spirits of evil almost as much as darkness and therefore if one wanted to scare away evil, evil either had to be matched (the gargoyle being an obvious instance) or it had to be

* Dugdale: *History of St Paul's*.

83

 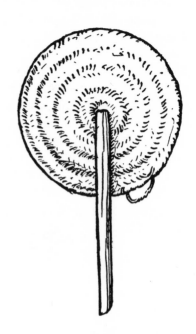

Fig. 24

Here, in a section of an Assyrian pavement, alternate rows of anthemion decoration is interspersed with the patera or rose form.

Fig. 25

The Portuguese fire-fan (Abano) is made of straw or rush, coarsely plaited and fixed in a rough handle. This type of fan has been made in many parts of the world for many centuries.

frightened by noise. The original bells seen in church were very small and formed tinkling ornaments on the robes of priests. This delicate sound was considered anathema to the allegorical flies.

By the 12th century, church bells of a type more familiar to us today were in wide use. Even as early as the year 750, they had become sufficiently common for Egbert, Archbishop of York (732–766), to order that all priests should toll them at appointed hours. The bell not only summoned, but it drove out evil and, to ensure that it did this to the very best of its ability, a ceremony was created whereby the bells were washed before being rung.

It would seem that as the church bell ascended in scope and

prestige, so declined the church fan. The evil carried by the flies could now be exorcised by the great bells high in the tower. Presumably at this time, the genuine flies reverted to a tolerated existence and their presence in church no longer meant that the Devil was abroad.

Whether or not there actually was a connection between the bell and the fan is uncertain but it remains an interesting coincidence. Now divested of its religious significance, the fan went into limbo.

We have seen how very few of these early Middle Ages fans have survived to this present day. Although the Tournus remains as a unique surviving example of a richly-carved and embellished folding cockade fan, another and much earlier Christian folding cockade fan is still in existence. This lies preserved in the Basilica of San Giovanni, Monza. It is made of pleated parchment, stitched at each fold, and contained in a sheath of finely-carved ivory. The fan was the property of the Lombardic Queen, Christian Theodelinda, who died in AD 628. Queen Theodelinda was largely responsible for the making of peace between the ruling barbaric race of Lombards (Longobardi) in Italy and the Catholic Church. She possessed a nail of the Holy Cross which was ultimately used as the setting to the Iron Crown of the kings of Lombardy. Upon the early death of her husband, the vicious Authari, she became more and more a mediator of the peoples and placed the Lombard nation under the patronage of St John the Baptist. At Monza, she built the first Lombard church and the adjacent palace wherein now lies amongst her surviving mementos her constant companion throughout all her endeavours—her pleated vellum fan. This has a beautiful purple hue of the same appearance as that of contemporary manuscripts and it is decorated with an alternating diaper of Romanesque ornament in gold and silver and round the outer border on either side is an inscription in Latin hexameters.* The form of the letters of the inscription, which are Roman with slight Rustic variations, and also the purple hue of the whole, are markedly similar to contemporary manuscripts of St Augustine of the end of the 6th century.

The case which forms part of the Theodelinda fan is constructed

* These are given in an article by W. Burges in the *Archaeological Journal*, Vol. XIV.

on the same principle as that for the Tournus *flabellum*, but it is not so long. It is made of wood covered with silver and it appears that the wood parts are probably restorations made to the original shape and the old silver used again. The length of the case, with the handle, is $15\frac{1}{2}$ inches and the diameter of the leaf is 10 inches. It should be stated that although this is a sacred relic and village maidens make pilgrimages to Monza, as the act of touching it is believed to facilitate and promote their marriage projects, there remains some measure of doubt as to its provenance. Whilst it cannot with substantiation be positively stated to have been the famed Theodelinda fan, there is also a lack of evidence to attribute it to anyone else. Much of this doubt centres on part of the inscription which bears a rather indistinct name "Ulfeda".

The fact that this fan has its handle terminated by a ring suggests that it was not a liturgic fan and this, coupled with its smallness of size, appears sufficient evidence to assign to it a secular origin.

The rigid flag-fan seems to have been in intermittent use in Europe from the early centuries A D. They were made either of plaited straw of various colours, of linen painted and embroidered, of parchment or vellum, or of silk, woven and embroidered, often with a lozenge-shaped diapering. The earliest examples which survive would appear to have Coptic or Saracenic origins. Two from the cemetery of Akhmin, the Greek Panopolis, are thought to belong to the period of the 4th to the 6th century A D. One of these is of finely plaited brown, red and black straw with a representation of four hearts encircling a cross, and the other is of a reticulated diapered pattern with a border of linen.

It was not just the flag-fan or the folding fan which was known in Europe, for the Indian *punkah* also had its following. The French writer Jean Louis Guez de Balzac (born 1594; died 1654) wrote during the reign of Louis XIV describing enormous fans in use in Italy which were suspended from the ceiling and worked by four servants. "I have a fan that makes enough wind in my chamber to wreck a ship." In 1791, they were introduced into the English residences of the East Indies and were subsequently used in all public places there.*

The earliest illustration of a *punkah* in Europe—this time a mechanically-operated one—is to be found in Georg Andreas

* *A Book About Fans* by M. A. Flory. Macmillan, London, 1895, p. 9.

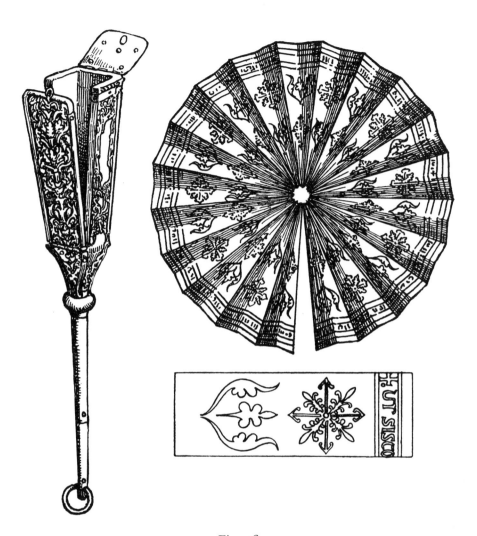

Fig. 26

The Theodelinda cockade fan or Monza flabellum showing the hinged top and front of the case in which the closed fan lies. The inset sketch shows in detail the recurring motif from the mount along with a fragment of the inscription, the letters of which are Roman with slight Rustic variations. The fan probably dates from the end of the 6th century AD and is contemporary with St Augustine.

87

Böckler's *Theatrum Machinarum Novum*, published in Nürnberg in 1673. Böckler's domestic air-mover was intended to be powered by the potential energy of a large weight via a system of pulleys and ropes. This is illustrated in Fig. 59.

In Chapter 1, I suggested that there was probably a connection between the fan as a means of identification, and the flag, banner, standard and pennant. In Chapter 2 it was shown how the Japanese war fan served both as a weapon and a representation of its owner. The fan would be used to display *colours* attributable to its user.

In the latter days of the Roman Empire, trumpet or bugle calls were used for manoeuvring troops and these rather primitive instruments would be embellished by the colours representing the particular battalion. The Roman *lituus* or cavalry trumpet and the *buccina* (the horn used in the infantry) were of sufficient length to serve as standard carriers without interfering with their use as musical instruments. It was not until the introduction of *zinken* or *cornetti* around the 13th or 14th century that much shorter wind instruments, bored with lateral holes, came into use. Even so, to this day on ceremonial occasions, military fanfares and calls are often made using an instrument carrying the standard.

The Royal standard, ceremonial colours and national flags may all thus be derived from one species of the early fan. (See also Chapter 1.)

The Romans were accustomed to bearing colours in battle and it is almost certainly due to the Roman influence that our warring ancestors adopted the self-same practice.

In spite of this apparent accession of one concept of the fan, the "conventional" fan in England appears to have been a late starter. Probably due to the fact that our climate did not at once suggest a need for its adoption, the earliest reference to the fan does not appear until the reign of King Edward I (born 1239; died 1307). This is quoted by Henry Thomas Riley in *Memorials of London and London Life in the Thirteenth, Fourteenth and Fifteenth Centuries,** who wrote:

> In the thirtieth year of King Edward I, precept was given to Nicholas Pycot, Chamberlain, of the Guildhall of London that he should cause to be sold all pledges for any debt whatsoever

* London, 1868.

then in his custody . . . In an inventory of pledges sold for arrears on the King's Tallage, 31 Edward L., 1303. One fan (value not stated) taken from Henry Gyleberd of the ward of Basseshawe for 2s. 8d. which he owes of arrears of the fifteenth.

This reference appears to indicate the importance and value set on the ownership of a fan. However, it should be borne in mind that personal possessions other than the necessary, utilitarian artifacts of life, were few indeed at this time in our history. Possession of a fan must indeed have demonstrated a measure of wealth and status.

On the face of it, it may seem surprising that the fan languished in Europe for so long without improvement, without flourishing and without a rapidly widening use. Other than the religious uses, largely abandoned by the 13th century, and isolated references such as that quoted above, two basic causes were responsible. Initially the fan as a utilitarian tool was generally not necessary. For blowing the fire, hand bellows later gave a less-dusty result. The second reason was that in its manufactured form, it was only available to the aristocracy and the gulf which separated the poor from the rich was of frightening proportions. As regards the growth of a fan industry, then, the opportunities were nil. The Dark Ages and the Middle Ages in Europe were conducive neither to art nor fashion and those who chose to follow either were few and far between.

CHAPTER FOUR

THE DEVELOPMENT OF FANS IN EUROPE

Fans have been known in Europe at least since the days of the Roman Empire. We have already seen how the Tuscans and the Romans used this ubiquitous implement. The story of Queen Theodelinda of the Lombards has also been told. From that time forward, however, a gap of several hundred years presents itself before the next direct reference to the progress of the fan can be found.

The widespread introduction of the folding fan in Europe is, as we shall see, directly attributable to the ascension of Portugal as a major trading nation possessing close commercial links with the Far East and Asia. There is, though, a remarkable account of an early folding fan in *Dictionnaire Raisonné du Mobilier Français* written by Emmanuel Viollet-le-Duc, the French architect and writer on architecture who lived from 1814 to 1879. In this work, he describes some thin metal fragments which were unearthed during excavations at the Château de Pierre. These fragments, considers the distinguished author, were found in the carbonised debris belonging to the time of the siege of 1422 and must therefore be assumed to come from some time before that time. The fragments are similar in a number of respects to a fan of the folding type of the form that we know today, and are made of an alloy of copper and silver. The fragment shown in Figure 27 as B represents one of the outside flats, and was fixed to a guard of wood or very thin metal to which was glued the stuff or vellum. The fragment shown as A represents one of the branch pieces or brins. Viollet-le-Duc inferred from the fact that the pieces were not pierced at the handle end but instead were finished in a cruciform shape, that the branches were formerly tied with a silken cord which would also be attached to the waist belt. In this description, he concludes with the very pertinent comment that "It is difficult to allow that the fan, which is merely a derivation of (the *flabellum* and cockade fan) was not in use until the 16th century, as several writers have contended."

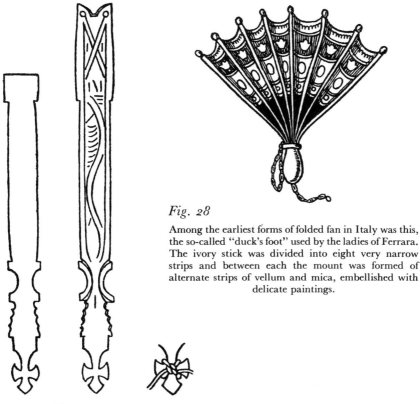

Fig. 28

Among the earliest forms of folded fan in Italy was this, the so-called "duck's foot" used by the ladies of Ferrara. The ivory stick was divided into eight very narrow strips and between each the mount was formed of alternate strips of vellum and mica, embellished with delicate paintings.

Fig. 27

The portions of Viollet-le-Duc's fan remains from the Château de Pierre. He believed that the piece A—the shorter of the two long pieces—was one of the sticks or brins, and the longer piece, B, one of the guards. He then suggested that the pieces might have been tied together after the fashion indicated in the small illustration at the right. Unless this knot were to be very loose, the fan would not have opened. A much more likely suggestion is that these parts were but the decorative metal pieces of a larger wooden fan.

In analysing Viollet-le-Duc's interpretation of the fragments, he appears to have failed to extend his deductions to a more satisfactory and practical conclusion. It is far more probable that the fragments he found were neither sticks nor guards, but purely the ornaments attached to such parts of a folding fan. This fan might then be made of ivory, wood or other material in the fashion later to be considered common. The burning of the original fan, preserving only the metal parts, appears to have been overlooked in his assumption that a silken cord might have tied the ends together. If we assume the fan to have been larger than the surviving fragments and if we assume that methods of construction similar to those which later become standard, then the fragment marked B identifies itself fairly clearly as the outer portion of the radiating guard from shoulder to tip, the missing piece extended from the cruciform portion downwards to a pivot point. This may indeed have been a thread but was much more likely to have been a metal pin: had iron been used, this pin would thus have probably disappeared in the intervening time.

Furthermore Viollet-le-Duc overlooks the fact that the cockade fan already existed at a period anterior to the sixteenth century. As Rhead says, the division of the cockade fan into two parts and the protection of the ends with some firm substance produces something similar to the folding fan which we know today. This we know was, in fact, done and the fan carried towards the close of the 16th century comprised a portion of a cockade inserted in a long handle similar to that of the plumed fan, thereby uniting the characteristics of both the folding and the plumed fan. The Venetian painter Cesare Vecellio, in his *Habiti Antichi et Moderni di Tutto il Mondo* (1590) depicts these small fans which are illustrated here.

It is thus fair to surmise that the small rigid fans shown by Vecellio were a form of interim device between the rigid fan of Asia and the folding fan proper. It is presented with a decorative development which is at one gradual and complete, and it is just possible that this fan form was conceived quite independently of Eastern influence. As for Viollet-le-Duc's fan remains, it is impossible to speculate as to how these came into existence since the fan type was certainly not new. Various Court inventories of the 14th century refer to fans under the curious name of *esmouchoir*, and miniatures of this same period represent ladies with long-handled fans made of feathers or rice-straw. The inventory of Charles V of France (born 1337; died 1380) contains the mention of a folding fan made of ivory with an ebony handle and bearing the arms of France and Navarre.* From the same source we learn that the Roman custom of employing servants to fan the King when at table still prevailed at that time. Reference to early pleated fan crests have already been made. A fan crest appears on the head of the

* *A Book About Fans* by M. A. Flory, p. 24.

horse in the Brétigny seal of Edward III, engraved as a result of the Treaty of Brétigny in 1360 by which the monarch renounced the title of King of France. The same motif—a fan crest on a horse's head—was used successively by Richard II, Henry IV (first seal) and Henry VI (silver seal), only the legend being altered.

An even earlier example is the large displayed fan crest in the centre of which is a lion *passant*, on the top of the flat helmet of Coeur de Lion (second seal of period 1197–9). This crest, which is the earliest authenticated instance of a regular crest* was used after his return from captivity and may thus possibly have been borrowed from or inspired by the East. Other fan crests are also to be found on the seal of Richard Fitz-Allan, Earl of Arundel (1267–1302); of Humphrey de Bohum, Earl of Hereford (1301) and others of the period. The common seal of the City of London (dated 1539) features a large fan crest charged with the cross of the city arms. Fox-Davies† writes that:

> In the course of time this fan, in the case of London, as in so many instances, has through ignorance been converted or developed into a wing, but the "rays" of the fan in this instance are preserved in the "rays" of the dragon's wing (charged with a cross) which the crest is now supposed to be.

Fox-Davies traces the origin of the fan crests back to the peacock popinjay vanity ingrained in human nature which much later lead to the decoration of the helmets of soldiers and even the Life Guards with horse-hair plumes and regimental badges, the cocked hats of Field Marshals and other officers with wavy plumes and similar exhibitions of embellishment right up until comparatively recent times. Fox-Davies suggests that all was but a combination of decoration and vanity.

The earliest records of the fan in England date from the year 1307. In the inventory of Isabella of France (born 1292; died 1358), daughter of Philippe le Bel who became Queen of England as the wife of Edward II, mention is made of *Due flagella pro muscis fugandis*. Note the use of the incorrect word for fan. During the reign of Henry VIII, two types of fan were in use: one for full dress and the other for walking. This latter was more a precursor of the parasol

* *Complete Guide to Heraldry* by A. C. Fox-Davies.
† *ibid.*

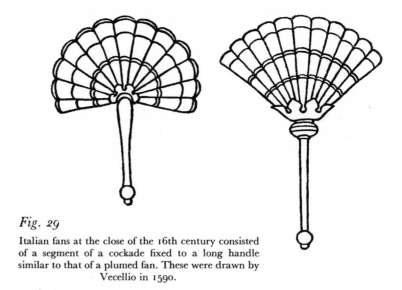

Fig. 29

Italian fans at the close of the 16th century consisted
of a segment of a cockade fixed to a long handle
similar to that of a plumed fan. These were drawn by
Vecellio in 1590.

since it had a handle about 18 inches in length and served to shelter
the bearer from the heat of the sun. Queen Elizabeth (see Appendix
C) considered the fan should be the only present which a sovereign
should receive from her subjects and left twenty-seven at her death
in 1660.

When Franco Fernando de Cordova, the Spanish explorer,
discovered Mexico in 1517 (it was subsequently conquered by
Fernando Cortez in 1519–21) he found that the fan was in use as a
symbol of authority. The two deities, Ometeuctli (God of Paradise
of the Tolteques) and Totec (military disciple of the founder of the
Mexican monarchy) were represented holding a feather *flabellum*
in their hands. Contemporaries of Cortez describe in their writings
that costly fly-flaps of feathers with handles encrusted with precious
stones were given as diplomatic presents. These were called
tleoatzehuaquetzalli. In the Hawaiian Islands from ancient times
forward, costly *kahilis* or fly-flaps have formed the especial insignia of
royal authority.*

Spain was noted as a manufacturing source of the leather fan
which, although not known for certain, was most probably of the
rigid or screen type as distinct from the folding fan. Many of these

* *A Book About Fans* by M. A. Flory.

94

were imported into France and in 1594 the statutes of the Master Leather Gilders (quoted by Rondot) contained the following reference:

> May furnish. . . . Fans made with outer lamb's skin taffety or kid enriched or embroidered—embellished as it may please the merchant and lord to command.

Perfumed leather fans were also imported from Spain and Mlle de Montpensier ("la Grande Mademoiselle", born 1627; died 1693)

Fig. 30

A French fan of around 1660 depicting The Character of Phoebus. Note the extremely wide mount and the treatment of the sticks.

wrote in her *Mémoires* that the Queen Mother (Anne of Austria, wife of Louis XIII, born 1601; died 1666) held one constantly.

Even though the folding fan may not have enjoyed any appreciable vogue throughout Europe until the 16th century, when it entered general use in Portugal, Spain and Italy, there is plenty of evidence to indicate that it was in intermittent use during these early periods. It may be suggested that it was the advent of the decorated folding fan which found fancy with the mass of the people and that as production increased and skills were channelled into its production, costs were systematically lowered, so presenting the fan to an ever-widening market potential.

When in 1497 Vasco da Gama, the Portuguese explorer (born 1460; died 1524), made his first expedition to the Far East, Portugal was set on the path to become the major trading link between

Europe and those far-off parts of the world. Just five years earlier, Christopher Columbus had set sail westwards across the Atlantic in an endeavour to find India and Cathay, and found instead America.

Vasco da Gama made three expeditions during the first twenty years of the 16th century and these, together with the successful operations of his fellow countryman Alfonso d'Albuquerque (born 1453; died 1515) in India, resulted in the complete supremacy of Portugal as a trading power with the East. Dr Birdwood in his *Report on Old Records in the India Office* (1898) describes how from Japan and the Spice Islands to the Red Sea and the Cape of Good Hope, the Portuguese were the sole masters and dispensers of the treasures of the East, a complete monopoly of the Oriental trade which continued throughout the 16th century. In 1502, the King of Portugal obtained from Pope Alexander VI sanctions constituting him "Lord of the Navigation, Conquests and Trade of Ethiopia, Arabia, Persia and India". However, it was not until 1516 that the Portuguese made their appearance in China where, according to Sir John Francis Davis, F.R.S., "at Ningpo, they succeeded in establishing a colony, carrying on a gainful trade with other parts of China as well as with Japan." From this intercourse of trade, the folding fan found its way half way round the world back to Portugal through its traders. Probably the first fans were carried back purely as mementos or gifts for the trader's own families. Soon news of the exciting new artifact from the Orient would have spread and demands made upon the traders for more fans.

The folding fan as introduced by this means marks the start of a new era of the history of the fan. Although both Chinese and Japanese fans exhibit identifiably characteristic styles, as an inspiration in the hands of European artists it ultimately developed a character and style quite its own.

Among the earliest types of folded fan in Italy was the so-called "duck's foot" used by the ladies of Ferrara. Here, the leaf, which opened to a quarter of a circle, was formed of alternate strips of vellum and mica and embellished with delicately-painted ornamentation. The ivory stick was divided into eight very narrow blades. This form of construction seems to have been fairly general for the leaves of folding fans following their first introduction around the middle of the 16th century. Two distinct styles can be traced: in one the decoration consisted of painting on the plain surface of the mica or vellum, or on both as in the case of a fan portrayed by Vecellio in the hands of a lady of Ferrara, and also in the Actaeon fan, shown in Fig. 28. The other is characterised by the elaborate piercing of the leaf to such an extent that it rivals for delicacy the most accomplished lace work. This came later to be known as *découpé* (see Glossary) and reached its peak of popularity during the latter half of the 16th century. It reached England probably about 1590 and is seen in portraits of Queen Elizabeth I of this time.

One style of découpé, demonstrated by a fan in the Musée de Cluny, features a leaf which is cut to an extremely refined geometrical pattern of circles and lozenges, with minute pieces of mica inserted at intervals, so imparting a richness and variety to the fan without destroying its lightness and elegance. The art of découpé originated in Italy and appears to have been practised widely at this period.

Mica itself was used for the entire manufacture of the blades: ivory sticks would carry a large number of perforated mica plates, each painted with arabesques of children, animals, birds and flowers.

Trade between the three nations of south-western Europe (Portugal, Spain and Italy) was so highly developed that once the folding fan had reached the shores of Portugal, its travels to the other two countries were both inevitable and speedy.

In Italy, the early folding fan mirrored the contemporary styles of Italianesque décor. Hence sticks exhibited great simplicity and reticence in keeping with the general grave character of the mounts. The brins, in a number of cases, comprised perfectly flat, plain pieces of ivory, relieved only by a little carving on the panaches which were ornamented in various ways, the most usual being by gold and silver piqué. The method of execution was to use a drill,* the tiny pieces of metal being pressed into the tiny reserves so created. Another method of decoration which was used was the delicate piercing of the surface of the stick which otherwise remained flat and devoid of carving. These pierced ivory sticks are occasionally alternated by sticks of another material such as light golden tortoise shell, horn or pierced cedar. Mother of pearl is treated in a

* A pointed drill would not have been used. The process called for the milling-out of a flat-bottomed recess, so a special flat-ended cutter would have been employed.

similar way as ivory and styles of working include flat-piercing; piercing and carving; piercing, carving and engraving; with, in some instances, the addition of painting and sometimes tinsel and silvering or gilding.

Various kinds of mother of pearl were used in the making of fans. These included the Burgan or Burgandine Pearl obtained from Japan; the white pearl known as *poulette* from Madagascar; and a black mother of pearl from the East. The shells being comparatively small, it was necessary to splice a number of pieces together to produce a suitably-sized whole. This was done so skilfully that extremely close examination is required in order to detect the splicing. The art of working mother of pearl in this manner has been practised in the east for many centuries. For the process of inlay and incrustation, the peculiar eastern pearl called "gold fish" is used. This was first introduced to Europe quite late in the history of the folding fan (around the middle of the 18th century) and the magnificent rainbow tints which it displays caused a complete revolution in the manufacture of *de luxe* fans. In the hands of the European *éventailliste*, the working of these materials and others such as tortoise shell built on the skills and techniques evinced by the work of the Eastern masters.

The earliest forms of the hand fan in Europe were both the type with sticks and a leaf or mount, and also the brisé type made of ivory, mother of pearl or wood. The earliest includes those which were imported in large quantities from the East from the latter part of the 16th century onwards. As part of the process of Westernization, though, the latter part of the 17th and early 18th century saw a trend towards less ostentatious decoration. Flat, pierced scrollwork supplemented by panels *en cartouche* painted and gilt, with portions of the ornament enriched with gold and colour replaced the more overt Eastern ebullience of artistry. The fans of this period opened out to a little less than a third of a circle. Later, low-relief carving was added, the ornamentation having assumed a rococo character.

With the fan firmly ensconced in Portugal, Spain and Italy, its progress into France was but a matter of time. The story is that it was taken there by or with the Italian perfumers who went there in the train of Catherine de Medici, Queen of Henry II of France (who reigned from 1547–59). Brantôme says that she made her first public entry into Paris as queen in the year 1549 and that she

Fig. 31

A bridal fan depicting Adelaide of Savoy, Duchess of Burgundy. The fan
dates from 1709 and the painting is after Watteau.

introduced into the French court the Italian feather fans which were
at that time in general use in Italy. In a half-length engraved
portrait in the British Museum, Catherine is seen with a plumed
fan with an elaborately ornamented handle garnished with pearls
whilst in another portrait she is seen with a plumed fan with a
mirror in the centre.

Flory,* on the other hand, suggests that it was the Italian round
screen fan which she introduced, adding: "This innovation,
manufactured and sold by perfumers who had followed the queen to
France, was greatly appreciated."

It is not beyond the bounds of possibility that Catherine de
Medici took with her several types of fan since a number of styles
was obviously in use at the time in her home country.

Brantôme records that when Henry II was accidentally slain in a
tournament to celebrate the wedding of his daughter,† the dis-

* *A Book About Fans*, p. 25.
† Henry II came to the throne in 1547, was wounded on 29th June, 1559,
and died on 10th July.

99

traught Catherine wore round her a "device" of broken fans with the feathers falling to pieces and the mirror cracked, symbolising the abandonment of worldly frivolities.

The first authentic evidence of the use of *l'éventail plissé** does not appear until the time of Henry III who reigned from 1574 until 1589, when he was stabbed to death by a Dominican friar. Fans were now in wide use and a French writer, Henri Estienne tells that they "were held so much in esteem, that, now the winter is come, the ladies cannot give them up, but having used them in summer to cool themselves against the heat of the sun, they make them serve in winter against the heat of the fire".†

Pierre de l'Estoile‡ describes the fan which was used by the effeminate Henry III which, evidently some form of cockade, "expanded and folded merely by the turn of the fingers". It was sufficiently large to be used also as a parasol, so serving the dual purpose of providing a cool draught of air and preserving the King's delicate complexion.

The fan was made of vellum, cut as delicately as possible, and trimmed with a lace of the same material. This elaborate art of cutting in vellum, paper or other materials, was a popular pastime of the period and it is supposed to have been practised by the King himself and Woolliscroft Rhead suggests that this method of découpé or découpé in association with other forms of ornamentation was employed in a large number of fans of this epoch, both of the cockade and semicircular form.§

The fan industry in France had become of such importance under Henry the Great (Henry IV who came to the throne in 1589 and departed, another assassination victim, in 1610) that it became necessary to regulate it by statute. Certain concessions were therefore granted in December 1594 to the several bodies of craftsmen engaged in the art of fan making. These were confirmed when fresh regulations added towards 1664.¶

After a petition was presented to Louis XIV in 1673 by the master fan makers of the city of Paris, they were constituted a corporate

* *Éventail plissé*—plaited fan.
† *Deux Dialogues du Nouveau Langage François*, 1570.
‡ *Isle des Hermaphrodites*, 1588.
§ *History of the Fan*, G. Woolliscroft Rhead, p. 146.
¶ *ibid.*

body by the edict of March 23rd of that year, and their privileges further strengthened by edicts of December 1676 and January and February 1678. The original number of masters was just sixty.* The edicts ordained that the company should be ruled by four jurors, two of whom were re-nominated every year in September by an assembly in which every master could participate, and no one could become a master without having first served four years' apprenticeship and having produced a *chef-d'oeuvre*. The sons of masters were exempted from this last requirement, as were the members who married the widows or daughters of masters. The widows enjoyed the privileges of their departed husbands so long as they remained single but were prevented from engaging new apprentices. The entrance fee to the company was four hundred livres.

The peak of development in the French fan-making industry was 1753 and in that year there were recorded no fewer than 150 master fan makers in Paris. The French fan makers were united with the wood polishers and the lute makers by the edict of August 11th, 1776, together with the painters, carvers and varnishers related to these crafts.

The type of fan which Catherine de Medici brought with her to the French court may have been but a bunch of feathers, but the fan was adopted by that nation and the burgeoning fan-making industry was not slow to develop its own styles of goods. Among the first fans which can be identified with France are those of the so-called *brisé* type.

This was composed of a large number of wide, continuous sticks or blades and was characterised by the absence of a mount as such. The continuous surface presented by the open blades which extended from outer edge to head gave artists the opportunity to do their very best paintings. It would appear that brisé fans were first made in the 17th century, but few surviving specimens are earlier than the second quarter of the 18th century and large numbers date from the early part of the 19th century. Of all made, those produced during the 18th century and finished in *Vernis Martin* are the most important. Whilst the paintings on these fans are almost European in style and character, the method of decoration was more than likely inspired by the widespread admiration for the highly polished surface of Oriental lacquer work.

* *ibid.*

Vernis Martin brisé fans are decorated with a delicate and usually highly finished painting executed in thin oil colours. The whole surface of the fan was covered with colour and gilding and finally was coated with an exceptionally fine and pellucid varnish devised by the Martin brothers who flourished in Paris from about 1720 until 1758. The ingredients of this outstanding varnish (see also Chapter 8) remained secret to four brothers, William, Simon-Étienne, Julien and Robert, the eldest, who was styled *Vernisseur du*

Fig. 32

A French fan of about 1740 depicting Jupiter and Callisto. The central motif is contained in a rectangular cartouche flanked by overlapping medallions and large pictorial cartouches of rococo style. It is interesting to note that the sticks are wider near the head than at the shoulder.

Roi. After his death in 1749, his widow and the other brothers continued the business which had three workshops, one in the Faubourg Saint Martin, one in the Faubourg St Denis and the third in the Rue Saint Magloire. The varnish was not applied solely to fans: coach panels, pieces of furniture, cabinets, even wall-panelling as well as many small objects such as snuff-boxes, *étuis* and suchlike were treated with the much-covetted finish.

Percival* comments that the firm would appear to have employed a number of painters since the styles in which the decoration is carried out are very numerous. In the case of fans, the majority of paintings were divided into two parts—an upper and a lower

* *The Fan Book.*

segment, so producing the effect of a painted mount and painted sticks. It was not uncommon for the two portions to display completely different themes and styles of execution although the two are always in harmony and the handle end is generally lighter in colour than the upper part. Predominating colours seem to have been rich dark greens and blues with few, if any, pastel shades. Although these were copied with varying degrees of success from the era of the Martin brothers onwards, none has equalled the beauty and quality of these valued and valuable fans. Only the Dutch ever approached the quality of these brisé fans.

The history of the French fan-making industry is bound up with the political strife which threw France into bloody conflict towards the end of the seventeenth century and from which, other than a few short intermissions of dubious peace, she did not emerge for almost a quarter of a century. The earlier revocation of the Edict of Nantes which forced so many craftsmen and artisans to seek refuge and a fresh life in England,* had depleted the ranks of the fan maker. Yet it was in the 18th century that, as a delicate rose drastically pruned, the fan trade revived to achieve its highest development from both an artistic and a purely commercial standpoint.

As the fan progressed in France, aiding, abetting and itself inspiring new fashions, it became associated with the finest craftsmen and craftsmanship. By the time of Louis XVI (Louis Seize), the brisé fan was smaller than in its previous period and was exquisitely fretted, a style more than likely inspired by the Chinese openwork ivory fans which figured among the admired curios imported in large numbers during the 18th century. However, these were no copies since the French ivory workers successfully adapted the style to suit their own masterful abilities. The designs were quite different and in many cases the openwork comprised a succession of fine perforated lines in the midst of which were silhouetted wreaths of

* The Edict of Nantes was decreed on April 13th 1598 and by which Henry IV of France granted toleration to his protestant subjects. The Edict was confirmed by Louis XIII in 1610 and by Louis XIV in 1652. It was revoked by Louis XIV on October 22nd, 1685. This act cost France 50,000 Protestant families, and gave to England and Germany thousands of industrious artisans. Some of the refugees settled in Spitalfields, others in Soho and St Giles's areas of London and here pursued their crafts which, besides fan-making, included the making of crystal glasses and the manufacture of silk and jewellery, subjects which were then little understood in England.

foliage and swags of flowers. The style and period are characterised by the three medallions, linked by garlands and festoons, which were sometimes carved in extremely low relief. These ovals would display either portraits or the caricatured heads of young people or children, village scenes, subjects such as bridal scenes, daintily painted landscapes or views of country seats.

The working of ivory to great nicety was exploited during this period and some fans were pierced in delicate diaper pattern so that their sticks were transformed into an almost leaf-like skeleton with, in some cases, no portion of the ivory broader than one thirty-second of an inch. Fans with sticks which, although similar in general shape, were each quite individual were introduced during this epoch.

Flat piercing was also the treatment used for horn at this time and was extensively practised during the whole of the 18th century. Many *minuet* fans of this style were produced, a number emanating from Italy.

For use on less formal occasions, this period also saw the making of fans of perforated wood such as cedar and satinwood in which the more delicate ornament was replaced by rather heavily executed paintings and applied engravings. Even so, the three-medallion feature was almost always maintained with the central picture often being a landscape or a group flanked by fancy heads and portraits. Percival* states that some of these displayed a political cast, showing a display of loyalty with portraits of the King and Queen of Bourbon, whilst others have more or less concealed paintings (for occasions when loyalty to the throne might have proved an embarrassment) hidden either by sliding portions of the guards or by the "puzzle fan" principle (see Chapter 7).

Other than brisé fans, the mounts of folding fans were sometimes single but the majority were double, having a separate leaf prepared for each side and then glued together, so sandwiching the sticks between them. The better fans had mounts of chicken-skin (a form of kid leather subjected to a special treatment), asses' skin, vellum, parchment, silk of various kinds, paper, lace and satin. The painting of the mount was either carried out in transparent colour or in gouache which had to be applied thinly to avoid the possibility of its cracking.

Silk as a substance for the fan mount appears to have been used as

* *The Fan Book.*

Fig. 33

This beautiful fan was made for Marie Antoinette and dates from about 1780.

early as the 15th and 16th centuries if one accepts the evidence of early inventories. These early silk fans were most probably simply a membrane of material stretched on a frame and decorated by embroidery and by the addition of a fringe of feathers. The handles were of precious metals, ivory or carved wood. Silk as a substance for the mount of folding fans was not widely used until towards the close of the 18th century. Some Louis XVI fans with silk mounts featured the three subjects painted on the material in conformity with the styles of the skin or paper fan mounts. Percival* believes that this type of silk was specially made for fans since it is very fine, even and light with the ability to take colour well. However, since earliest times silk weavers have produced several qualities of work including very fine fabrics, so I cannot agree that silk was especially woven for fans.

Silk mounts were sometimes decorated with round or oval spangles sewn on with fine stitches. Embroidery was seldom used although occasionally the simulation of a few small leaves, represented by broad, flat stitches of floss silk, are to be found. Fans of a

* *ibid.*

similar appearance, but produced by colour-printing the silk, were made in England about the same time.

The big drawback about silk as a medium for fan mounts was that, whilst the material and its decoration could be used to great advantage, it was only suitable for "one-sided" fans, the reverse being undecorated and displaying the untidy tangle of stitches which secured silk to sticks and held firm any decorative spangles and other desiderata. No second side could be added, because it would spoil the delicacy and thinness of the membrane and any fixative to hold two pieces together would have caused perishing and cracking. In fact, as a material for the construction of a fan mount, silk was a singularly unsuccessful one and fell far and away below substances such as chicken skin, lace and paper when it came to durability. Silk mounts tend to crack along the folds and are almost impossible to repair without spoiling their appearance.

Skin, however, did possess certain desirable qualities over silk. Properly prepared and applied, skin mounts proved very smooth and durable, and presented an ideal surface for painting. Its opacity meant that it could be painted on both sides or, as was to become more often the case, backed up with another mount. Besides the single mount, some fans, called *cabriolet* fans,* were introduced with not just one, but two and sometimes three mounts, the additional ones being relatively narrow.

Cabriolet fans appeared around the 1750s and are today quite rare. These were probably the most interesting specimens produced in an era when fans of greater complexity and novelty were being devised. There was, for example, the Lorgnette or Quizzing fan, with the aid of which a short-sighted person might stare as through an opera glass. There were fans incorporating peepholes so that the young and ladylike girl could be seen to shield her eyes from any scenes of immodesty which might offend against her purity, whilst maintaining an ample view through the aperture in the mount!

The latter years of the 18th century saw the introduction of the double or reversible fan which could be opened left to right or right to left, so exhibiting two different designs to each side. They were usually made of ivory with painted ornamentation although probably the most interesting were those made of sandalwood with

---

* Flory gives an alternative generic term for this type of fan as *éventail à galerie* (*A Book About Fans*, p. 49). See also Chapter 7.

three painted medallions on each side of the fan, giving a total of twelve subjects. These fans were common throughout most of the Western countries of Europe and indeed a large number were made in England with subjects after designs by Angelica Kauffmann and others.

After the French Revolution, the fan underwent a drastic change. The result, known as the Empire, was appreciably smaller than its predecessor, seldom exceeding 7 inches in length and quite often being smaller. The mount, however, was usually of large proportions relative to the radius of the fan. The mounts were made of silk, net, gauze, satin or lace, occasionally painted but almost always decorated with spangles. Besides round or oval spangles, new shapes appeared—crescents, stars, flowers and leaves. Some panels were stamped out of matted gilt metal which exactly fitted the fold of the fabric so that when the fan was opened, the adjoining metal-covered folds would butt together so accurately that the fan would appear to be made of fretted gold backed by net. The spangles were often worked into complicated patterns and enhanced by metallic thread embroidery.

On the subject of fan paintings, MacIver Percival* makes a curious although not unfounded observation:

> It is . . . curious that while fan leaves are often painted with much skill, and display considerable knowledge of design and composition, it is the rarest thing to come across one which possesses a really high degree of artistic merit or even any very pronounced originality. Actual copies of frescoes and pictures, *pastiches*—often very cleverly arranged—in the styles of popular painters, classical scenes executed in the conventional style of the day, and somewhat trite renderings of actual events, constitute the subjects of an overwhelming number of painted fans.
>
> Why we so rarely find the mastery of the art of painting minutely, yet broadly, which was possessed by the limners and the miniaturists who "painted in little" their marvellous portraits all through the period contemporary with the "Golden Age" of the fan is a mystery.

He continues by lamenting the fact that whilst other craftsmen

* *The Fan Book.*

and artisans saw fit to put their names on their works, the fan leaf painter almost always preferred to remain anonymous. Signatures which do appear on fans are seldom genuine, having been added either by the executant of a modern forgery or reproduction, or by some 19th-century collectors who, believing that they could detect the unmistakable characteristics (to them) of well-known masters, decided to rectify the careless oversight of the artist. These forged signatures always ascribed works to the better-known artists such as Watteau, Lancret or Fragonard. Whilst many fans are attributed to these masters, no authentic work of theirs is known on fans although fan leaves often portray pictures based on original designs, etchings and watercolours. "After Watteau" is usually a safer style of attribution than "By Watteau"!*

Even Honoré de Balzac was responsible for adding confusion when, in *Cousin Pons*, he brings in an episode concerning a fan supposedly signed by Watteau and which, in the story, was supposed to have been painted for the Marquise de Pompadour. Sufficient to say that, in reality, the fair Pompadour remained unborn until after the death of the illustrious artist.

Several real artists did, in fact, sign their works. One was Leonardo Germo who flourished in Italy during the early part of the 18th century, another was Francis Xavery who, according to Percival, dated one fan 1763 and another 1766.

In France, the approach to fan painting and the styles used was frequently very interesting. Whilst the details of classical costumes, armour and architecture are often lacking in historical accuracy, artistic licence was such that it did not fail to convey the desired impression that the personages represented belonged to the heroic age. As Percival comments, the artists never seemed wholly to have felt happy in confining their compositions within the space and shape dictated by the proportions of the fan. More often than not, the composition appears to have been based on the shape of an oval laid lengthways along the fan leaf. The oval is partially eclipsed by the lower edge of the mount which effectively removes the foreground from any picture conceived as a whole.

Faced with this limitation to a stylised art form, a new style

* Flory mentions "a fan signed by Watteau" which was formerly in the Bruzard collection sold in 1861. Watteau's designs were copied by many a young and no doubt needy artist.

materialised around the time of Louis XIV—a style which faced up
to these restrictions. Here, the subordinate groups of figures are
found on the left and right sides whilst the focal point of interest is

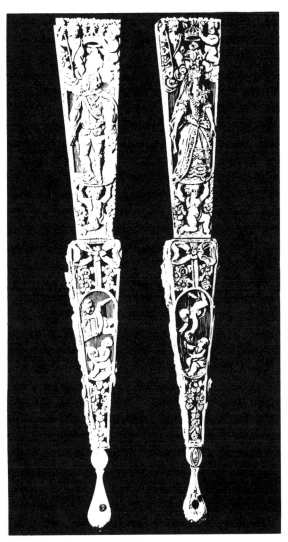

Fig. 34

A characteristic of the late 18th-century French fan was the extremely
beautiful working of ivory. These guards, which are from the same fan, are
carved with the subject of the Assembly of Notables, 1787. The fan is in the
Musée du Louvre.

concentrated on the central portion of the leaf which is also the principle part of the painting. From the standpoint of accuracy, though, this portion of the fan mount picture is in truth the middle distance. For this reason, fan painting demands some form of breaking up of the picture into three views in this way otherwise an unacceptable breach of the elementary laws of perspective and proportions will be apparent. The difficulty was usually overcome by presenting the three pictures (one central and two flanks) as vignettes but occasionally the central painting (and rarely the other two as well) would be in a cartouche. An idea of the aesthetics of fan artistry can be gained from examination of a Chinese "hundred faces" or mandarin fan (see Plate 7) where the extraordinarily busy scene is sustained from one side right across to the other with the inevitable perspective clash mentioned. Oriental art, though, has always been far more tolerant of such foibles and indeed it might be germane to cite the formal Italian fan mounts as the antithetic form.

Of course, there existed exceptions. Some fan leaves were of such proportions that one large picture could be displayed with the edges of the picture bordered by floral decoration. And those lithographed fans which were so prolific in the latter part of the 18th century often featured designs which were à la pastiche.

The rather sober designs of the time of Louis XIV, albeit executed in brilliant colours, gradually gave way to the *Conversation galantes*, *Pastorelles*, *Dejeuners sur l'herbe* and *Moments musicales* which were the theme of so many pictures of the day. The leaves, formerly of either paper or a rather stout, open-grained chicken skin, now depicted somewhat more charming subjects. Whereas the early fans tended to show people in dignified and rather stiffish poses (even when they were supposed to be enjoying themselves), subjects inspired by Watteau, Boucher and Fragonard now reigned supreme. Not that any identifiable work of any one painter was copied, for the artists were pastmasters at producing an acceptable design by combining a figure or a group from one work with the landscape from another, and ringing the changes. The classical subjects of former days were still to be found, but the reigning influence was for more freedom of lines. The classical drapery was not so voluminous in these Louis XV period fans. Another difference was that the figures were generally smaller in size than in the earlier examples and a more circumspect approach was made to the historical accuracy of the costumes displayed.

Frequently French fans bore decoration based on the Oriental style. Indeed both in England and France, Chinese decoration had a strong following and from the late 18th century onwards this type of subject was quite widely employed.

The last decades of the 18th century were marked by the widening use of the fan as a means of commemorating some event in contemporary history. Among the most popular of these events was the first ascent by Man into the air by hot-air balloon. The Montgolfier brothers made their first ascent at Annonay on June 5th, 1783 and within a year, ballooning caught on as the fashionable achievement of the time. Fans appeared in great numbers showing the Montgolfiers and their rival *ballonauts* and when, in August 1785, Jean Pierre Blanchard made his first descent from a balloon by parachute, yet another spectacle was added to the aeronautical scene. Within a few short years, baling out of a balloon and descending by parachute was a popular diversion and this, too, was depicted on fans although, let it be said, these are nowhere as common as ballooning fans.

One of these fans, depicting "aerial navigation" shows what is obviously Blanchard's balloon (it has rudders) and beneath this the words *Vive la Physique*. Around the central picture are various verses in praise of the conquest of the air written in flowery language and containing the interesting prophecy that soon all the world would journey by air instead of by a coach. And this was printed in 1783! Remarkable though it is, its progenitor could not have foreseen the heavier-than-air flying machine, and what worse chaos would air transport support today if flying had progressed no further than the hot-air balloon!

As with so many of these printed fans, all ballooning fans were of the etched type with the colouring rather roughly added by hand. Many fans were produced during the time of Louis XVI and the mounts depict a strange taste for decoration. The Revolution produced many bitter scenes shown on fans whilst the birth of the ill-fated Dauphin in 1781 was commemorated by the issue of fan leaves. Even the sacking of the Bastille in 1789 formed the subject of many a fan mount. Aquatint or stipple engraving was much in use as well as etching and hand-colouring. All were media used for the several fans issued with the theme *Liberté, Égalité, Fraternité*.

To the French of this period, the fan had assumed what can only be termed a political significance. Today one may if one so wishes, acclaim ones beliefs or ones loyalties by wearing a badge carrying a printed slogan saying "Vote for so-and-so" or "Down with such-and-such a thing". In this time of the recrudescence of what we can today identify as the French doctrine, Royalists were still catered for and fans showing portraits of Louis XVI and Marie Antoinette with the motto *Lache qui t'abandonne* were made. Another and more popular type* was the *Testament de Louis XVI* with a portrait of the King in the centre and with portraits of his son and daughter to left and right. The whole was executed in stipple engraving. To carry such a fan, though, was a risky business.

A change was coming over the French fan as the 18th century drew to a close. Perhaps the first hint of future mass-production was rearing its ugly head. Or perhaps it was just that demand could not be matched by available skill. Whatever was the cause, quality began to fall and fan paintings displayed little more than, as Percival† says, perfunctory transcripts carried out with fatal facility but showing little or no thought or effort on the part of the painter.

By the Directorate and Empire periods, painting as a means of decoration for fans had been almost entirely superseded by the use of sequins and spangles. The major output of the French fan industry comprised "sparklers" and the painted fan, where it remained in production, was the exception to the ruling norm.

The coming of the printed fan leaf revolutionized the production of fans. The mount could now be produced far quicker than by earlier methods and, even in the case of the painted or hand-coloured lithograph, the deftness needed to colour these was of a lower order than that required of the fan leaf artist proper. As techniques of manufacture improved, production increased and prices lowered. The result was a greater demand and thus it comes as no surprise to find that printed fans, introduced in the second half of the 18th century, together add up to a very large percentage of all fans ever made. The output of French printed fans alone was prodigious, particularly of those with a political theme. Of those which deal with Napoleon alone, Percival* relates that there are

* *The Fan Book.*
† *ibid.*

said to be nearly a thousand. Bouchot* states that in one year, over a hundred were issued bearing as their subject the glorification of the mighty conqueror of Europe.

The sticks and handles were generally accepted as being the most valuable parts of the early European fans. They were often of precious metals or of a material so ornamented by carving or other means that it merited great value being placed upon it. Being far more durable than the remainder of the fan, these parts could be re-used if and when the mount was damaged. There are many references to the silver handles of fans in Elizabethan plays and writings.

When the folding fan came into being, precious metals were not so suited to use for the sticks and so artisans searched for a replacement substance. They found it in ivory which remained, from earliest times, the commonest material. It had all the right qualities —lightness, strength, flexibility and the ability to take carving, piercing, staining and painting as well as inlaying with metals and dry enamels. And so the material of the Orient came into European use.

Both guards and sticks formed the ground for lavish decoration, reaching its peak during the period of Louis XV. At this time the sticks, instead of each being treated as separate elements, were considered as one continuous ground for decoration. Elaborate designs were carried over from one stick to the next as if they represented an undivided surface. This depended for its success on the sticks being broad at the shoulder and virtually square-cut. Sticks with rounded shoulders usually denote a much later period.

As distinct from sticks which together form a continuous surface, many fans were produced which had sticks which bore no resemblance at all to one another. Each stick presented a totally different shape and form of enrichment so much so that no continuity or regularity can be detected. Nevertheless, the balance of the whole was usually so skilfully engineered that the total lack of symmetry is not apparent at first glance.

Mother of pearl was also often employed in the making of sticks and guards as was tortoise shell inlaid with gold and gold incrustations. The selection and matching of materials and their decorative

* *L'Histoire parles Éventails Populaires*, 1883.

working reveals the enormous skills of the master craftsmen who engineered them. The sensitivity with which these workers handled their raw materials and worked them into exquisite end products has survived the intervening years and to hold and examine one of these fans is to see into the mind of a man long since dead. Artistry, whim, humour, subtlety and an appreciation of fashion and taste— all are to be found in the fans of this period.

Ivory and tortoise shell sticks were frequently decorated with piqué, large numbers of tiny metal "dots" inlaid into recesses which were "blinded" into the material. For pale or blond tortoise shell, gold was commonly used whilst silver or gold would be used for the darker shells. This, combined with the technique of laminating pieces of shell of differing colours to produce one stick of the right length (one piece of shell being far too small) produced a very beautiful effect. The skills called for can best be illustrated by instancing that the sticks for a fan, which might number twenty-two, when closed do not measure more than ¾ inch thick, yet with such thin sticks of shell these could be (and often were) thinned down to reveal details in relief.

The carving of the ivory sticks for French fans was principally done at Dieppe.* Here many ivory carvers and turners had established family businesses, skills being handed down from father to son. Only carving and piercing was done here, painting and other decoration being applied at other specialised centres throughout France. In this way, the components of a fan went from master craftsman to master craftsman, each being responsible for just his own individual part of the fan-making process.

An extremely rare book called *Le Journal du Citoyen* was published at The Hague in 1754. This is quoted by Uzanne† and gives an insight into the cost of fans at this time:

Fans in gold wood (gilded wood?) 9 to 36 livres the dozen; those in palisander wood only 6 to 18 livres. For fans in wood, half ivory, that is, the chief sticks (guards) in ivory and the gorge in bone‡ one had to pay as much as 72 livres; for those entirely made of ivory, 60 livres, and even 30 to 40 pistoles a

* MacIver Percival.
† *The Fan*. English translation, 1884, p. 79.
‡ MacIver Percival misquotes this as *wood*.

dozen; the mounts were of perfumed leather or paper, and the frames were often enriched with gold, precious stones and painted enamels.

Besides these, there existed cheap fans at prices from fifteen to twenty deniers which had a frame of wood encrusted with ivory and a coarse paper mount liberally decorated with flowers, trophies or cartouches containing songs, in what must have been poor taste.

With the death of Louis XV and the accession of Louis Seize, fans again underwent a change in decoration. The discoveries made at Herculaneum had inspired the classically minded along new lines. Symmetry and style now ruled supreme; decorations were arranged in matching pairs, irregularly-shaped cartouches gave way to the purity of the oval or circle or, occasionally, the hexagon or other regular outline. Fan mounts now displayed unashamed conformity although the style of painting lacked little of the delicacy and subtlety of the former *genre*. The style of ivory working also changed to what was known as *oeuvre mosaique* in which the design would comprise two parts—the background and the reserves. The ground would be pared away to extreme thinness and then pierced. As a rule, the perforations would assume the form of closely-spaced slits or a diaper pattern which formed a background to the reserves which might take the form of medallions or subjects such as trophies, festoons, amorini, busts, figures or groups. These would be left in silhouette slightly raised about the thinner pierced background and would then often be carved very finely.

The French Revolution had far-reaching effects and not un-naturally one of these was to deprive the fan maker, particularly the maker of delicate fan sticks, of his market. With the Court no more and the surviving aristocracy now poor and unable to indulge in the delicacies of life which had mattered so much in former times, the craftsman fan makers found their declining market dictated retrenchment. No apprentices were taken on and the making of fine sticks and mounts virtually ceased. In their place came the Republic fan with coarsely-printed and painted mounts and roughly-made sticks of bone or wood. The few short years until the formation of the First Empire under Napoleon Bonaparte I in May, 1804, had seen an irrevocable change in the trade of the fan maker. Although there was now a resurgence of some of the pomp, ceremony and dress of the pre-Revolution days, tastes had differed. The *nouveau riche* now preferred show rather than delicacy and so the fan increased in size, decreased in quality, and became a tool for the *braggardocio* of the ex-plebeian.

These Empire fans had one general characteristic to commend them. The sticks were usually in perfect harmony with the mount.

Fig. 35

Another of the Parisian-made fans exhibited at the Great Exhibition in 1851 by Duvelleroy. Notice the large sticks of mother of pearl carved and pierced with a central reserve which is provided with a painting.

The simpler style of the stick, usually embellished with small plaques of highly-burnished steel let into the bone or ivory, probably led to the construction of the fan being carried out in entirety by one workshop. Because the mount was very deep, and in consequence the sticks were quite short, there was also little space for involved ornament. The top of the shoulder is rounded—almost always a clear indication of a late period, the exception being the sticks of the Vernis Martin fan and those with flat sticks painted with ornamentation. The material was generally ivory, bone or horn, pierced but seldom carved. For the guards, it was usual for the ornamentation to take the form of piercing and then a metallic foil backing would be applied, either matt or gold or silver. Sometimes, in cases where steel inlays were used on the inner sticks, steel guards with small facets would be employed.

Amidst all this rather tasteless work, some extremely expensive fans were made for Court use at this time. The finish and workmanship remained mediocre, and the cost accrued solely from the gold and gemstones used as decoration.

Some measure of resurgence of the quality fan came about in an interesting way according to Charles Robin, author of *The Illustrated History of the Exhibition of 1855*. It seems that a ball was given at the Tuileries in 1829 at which three quadrilles were to be danced in costume. The Duchesse de Berry was anxious to have fans suitable for the period of her Louis XV quadrille and secured some specimens collected by a perfumer called Vanier. The fans were admired by the court ladies and so suddenly there was a demand for the fans of past grandeur. In order to supply the increasing demand, skilful painters and carvers set to work and reproduced examples of the time of Louis XIV, XV and XVI.

By the spring of 1830, the old style of fan was back in production with the work of the goldsmith, enameller, sculptor and artist combining their talents—at copying. It is truly to be regretted that during this period, when craftsmen and artists still abounded, they saw fit, through public caprice, not to exhibit their contemporary creative skills but rather to resort to the cunning of the imitator. At best, after all their labours, they had nothing new to show for it and, for the student of sociology who sees the contemporary art form of a period as a looking glass portraying contemporary fancy, costume and fad, these fans are entirely a disappointment. For the collector today, their authenticity (or rather that of the originals) must often be suspect, so cleverly executed were many of these copies. However, I do not consider them to be forgeries, for it is my contention that you cannot "forge" or counterfeit a work of art without possessing the same talent as the original artist. All you may truly deprecate is the copyist's absence of originality.

The return of the old style of fans was widespread. Ostrich feather fans appeared with plumes never choicer. Chantilly, Duchesse and Point à l'Aiguille lace were worked with marvelous skill and the French fan started out once more on a short-lived crest of vainglory. By the 1870s it was spent and the fan embarked on its final decline.

Scented fans made of wood and scented paper were a late 19th-century invention, reaching the peak of their popularity about the mid-1890s. Rimmel's scented fans, painted with groups of flowers whose individual perfumes they gave out, were known to all ladies of the time. During this same period, a discovery was made by one of the French fan manufacturers concerning the transferring of brilliant-coloured and reflective particles of dust which covered the wings of butterflies to the surface of parchment. Countless butterflies were sacrificed to produce these very expensive little fans, a small specimen of which apparently cost from £20 upwards.

A feature of the French fans introduced in the mid-19th century and sustained through to its end was the attachment of small glass mirrors into recesses in the guards. Tiny vinaigrettes were also fitted in the guards of some and before the fall of the Second Empire in 1870, the transfer of looking glasses and perfume from the *chatelaines* worn around the waists of 19th-century ladies to their fans was complete.

In the early days of the folding fan in Europe, Italy was renowned for the excellence of manufacture and the decoration of the fan leaves. The long association between the Italians with the precursors of the folding fan may have had something to do with this but be that as it may, from the earliest times Italian fans have been decorated in an elaborate manner. The early fans made of mica and cut vellum (découpé) were extremely ornate. They remained in fashion for a very long time. Sometimes the cut vellum fans featured uncut reserves within which miniatures of extreme delicacy were painted. Lace being at that period in wide use for the ornamentation of garments and bed furniture, the fan maker set himself the task of trying to emulate the delicate tracery of lace in his work.

The respect which the Italian fan makers gained for their work extended beyond their national boundaries and their wares were sought by nobility and by the courts of Europe. However, during the 18th century when France was in the ascendant, this encomium passed into French hands and from that time forward, the painted fan leaf of France set the standard for all others. The strong French influence in Italian fan leaf decoration which followed did not

Fig. 36

Duvelleroy of Paris was a famous maker who produced many quality fans over a long period of time. This one was specially made by him for show at the Great Exhibition held in London's Hyde Park in 1851. Note the proportions of the mount to the sticks and also the very free treatment of the mother of pearl sticks. Compare this fan with The Royal Fan, also made by Duvelleroy for the Great Exhibition, and illustrated in Fig. 41.

altogether obscure Italian individuality.

Again Percival makes an apposite comment:

It is perhaps because Italy was during the 17th and 18th centuries the Mecca of so many pilgrims bent on the pursuit of pleasure or the acquisition of learning, that there seems to have been more self-consciousness among Italians as to their treasures, both of nature and art, than was prevalent among other nations. The number of fans of Italian provenance which are ornamented either with copies of celebrated paintings, or with paintings or well-known buildings and scenery, far exceeds that of French fans dealing with similar subjects.

Whilst it was a comparatively simple matter to take an existing frescoe or painting which was suitable for a fan leaf, and then copy it on to a fan, it did not automatically follow that because the original was a fine work of art it would make a good subject or design for a fan leaf. A certain amount of rearrangement was inevitable if it was required to fill the required space. Whereas the French artists went to considerable trouble to compose their designs using figures and other details from different works, the Italian painters seldom went to such lengths and generally contented themselves with deleting portions that could not be adapted or by re-spacing and re-positioning groups and decorations where necessary. It is possible to trace the trends in Italian fan painting from the earlier specimens where, as a rule, the painting would cover the entire leaf with the addition of very little extraneous material. Certain subjects proved very popular and appeared time and time again. One was the Aurora of Guido which was used, with slight variations, on a large number of fans. Some of these early period Italian leaves were never mounted and survive as arc-shaped paintings which have been framed or mounted in albums.

Of all the Italian mounts, the most distinctive are those which have the whole field occupied by subjects usually taken from classical mythology. These are either direct copies or rearrangements of the works of the later Italian masters such as Guilio Romano (better known as Guilio Peppi, born 1492; died 1546) the Bolognese family of Carrachi (Agostino, born 1557; died 1602: Annibale, born 1560; died 1609: Francesco, born 1595; died 1622: Lodovico, born 1555; died 1619), Reni Guido (born 1575; died 1642); Giovanni Francesco Barbieri (better known as Guercino, born 1591; died 1666), as well as many French artists who either work in Italy, or whose works found their way there such as Nicholas Poussin (born 1594; died 1665) who spent the greater part of his life in Rome, and Charles Le Brun (born 1619; died 1690). The mounts of these early Italian fans are usually very deep (i.e. they cover a large area of the sticks) and are generally of skin although occasionally of paper. The paintings are either in pure water-colour or in gouache. Again, some of these mounts were never made into fans at all and have survived just as curved paintings, whilst others have been removed from the sticks and framed as a picture. It is a tantalising fact that none of these can with any degree of certainty be attributed to a master hand.

Another form of characteristically Italian mount—certainly Italian in origin, is that which comprises rather elaborate compositions finely drawn in Indian ink, either with pen or brush, on skin mounts, usually vellum. From the absence of colour, one assumes that these were fans of mourning. The sticks are invariably of ivory, piqué or carved. The subject is gloomy and, although delicately executed, often displays a pervading sombreness. One, described by Rhead, features Bacchus and Ariadne after Carrachi, and another has a crowded composition of the Triumph of Alexander (after Le Brun) and, on the reverse, the Death of Actaeon.

Production of this style of fan was not the sole province of Italy and, according to Duvelleroy, were made in other parts of Europe. He himself owned a Dutch example with ivory sticks carved *à jour*, a vellum mount displaying on one side an embarkation with numerous figures and on the reverse a dance of peasants with musicians.

Of all the European countries, it was in Spain that the fan was in widest use. Both men and women considered it part of their costume and any thoughts of effeminacy attached to its masculine use should be tempered by the fact that the Spanish soldier (according to Disraeli in *Contarini Fleming*) would not mount guard in the scorching sun without its solace. Indeed, as in China and Japan, there was a fan for every occasion in Spain. Normal, street use called for the cheap paper fan whilst the silk fan was pre-eminent at the bull-fight and the theatre or on feast days.

Generally, Spanish fans followed closely the tastes and fashions of France. This is at once understandable when it is realised that the Parisian-made fan was highly valued in Spain and, in fact, large numbers were imported from France to be finished by local artists. Because of the dearth of skilled ivory carvers, from the Renaissance onwards, Spain appears to have imported carved ivory fans from France and Italy.* Even so, the fans imported into Spain appear to have been made with just this market in view and they display

---

* See *The Industrial Arts of Spain* by Juan F. Riano, 1879, which contains the statement:
"Notwithstanding, however, the numerous examples of ivory carvings which are still to be met with in Spanish churches and cathedrals, I find no information which enables us to affirm that this artistic industry existed in Spain during the sixteenth, seventeenth and eighteenth centuries . . . I am led, therefore, to suppose that . . . it is necessary to end at the Renaissance the history of ivory carving in Spain".

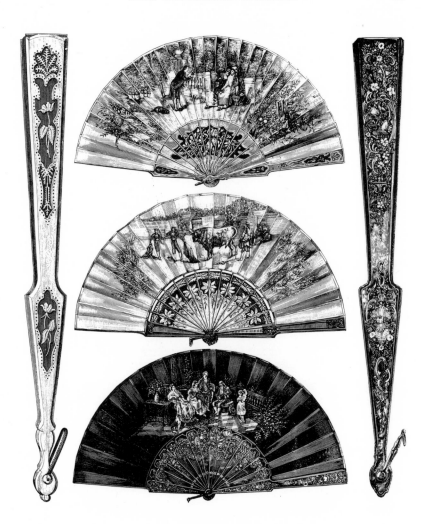

Fig. 37

Although Madrid was not the centre of the Spanish fan-making industry, it was there that Bach had his premises. At the Paris International Exhibition of 1878, three fans were exhibitited. Afterwards, they were bought by Eugéne Rimmel and distributed in England.

decorations to suit Spanish tastes.* The subjects displayed on the mounts were, not surprisingly, similar to those of the French fans and indeed the same scene or view was frequently to be found on fans of both nationalities. The treatment of the sticks was similar, although it may have been the Spaniards who first treated these as a ground for piecemeal decorative treatment. A number of fans exhibit this characteristic of involved and complex design extending right across the sticks in such a way that every individual stick is quite different from any other stick in the fan. An unusual style is evinced by a fan illustrated in Rhead† wherein the sticks are inversely tapered, actually being wider at the head than at the shoulder. This 10-stick fan, opening to 180 degrees, is of almost battoir shape. Indeed it was the battoir which was most highly favoured in Spain. Characterised by its narrow mount, the painting usually featured numerous subjects in small medallions and its richly-ornamented but rather coarsely-worked sticks—seldom more than eight— often worked into unusual shapes, being broadened in parts to look almost like a figure eight.

The bull-ring scene on a fan mount was a natural and popular one and these are almost all of undoubted Spanish origin. One of the better-known Spanish makers was Bach of Madrid whose fans were shown at the 1878 Paris International Exhibition and are illustrated here as Fig. 37.

Spain did not escape the influence of the classical revival which progressed through Europe in the middle of the 18th century and so fans appeared which bore paintings of subjects from Greek mythology. Towards the middle of the 18th century and onwards a new style appeared. In this the sticks numbered between eight and ten and were usually of tortoise shell, although ivory and other materials were also used. They were elaborately carved and pierced between wide, gold and silver encrusted guards. These fans always featured narrow mounts, representing three-sevenths of the length of the stick. Although Spanish in origination, this style was probably copied by other countries as well.

In spite of the Parisian influences, the Spanish never quite

* In 1823, Spain levied a protective duty on French fans but even so, the sale of Gallic fans to the Peninsula increased during the years which followed. (*Vide: The Illustrated Exhibitor*, Cassell, London, 1851.)

† *History of the Fan*, illustration facing page 130.

ascended to the same heights of workmanship and perfection as regards the treatment of the stick. As the end of the 18th century approached, even this mediocrity began to deteriorate. Just as the early Spanish fans were strongly influenced by Titian who painted a number of pictures for the Escurial, so the fans of the latter half of the 18th century were similarly influenced by the work of Francisco Goya. Many representations of his work are to be found and his inspiration revitalised Spanish fan painting as a whole.

In spite of the existence of a large retailing trade in Madrid and the operation there of a few well-known makers such as Bach and Pedro Martin, the centre of the fan-making industry of Spain was not, as one might expect, the capital, but Valencia on the Mediterranean coast. Here fine fans were made for the Spanish monarchs Fernando VII, Carlos III and IV, and others. Many of these survive today in the Mares Museum in Barcelona and in the Municipal Museum in Madrid. Among the large number of Valencian makers was Don José Mario Prior Sanchis who flourished during the second half of the last century and who was still in business in 1900 when in his sixties. His factory was in the Paseo de la Pechina and José Prior was at one time elected president of the Industria Abaniquera in Valencia. His workrooms produced a prodigious quantity of fans for although only he and his two sons, José II and Salvador, made fans; they employed painters and carvers all over the town and all worked very long hours. It was said that "this was the place where the tree trunks entered whole and came out as a completely finished fan ready for the home and overseas market." Spanish fan makers suffered greatly from the importation of vast quantities of cheap Oriental goods and Prior's greatest achievement came in 1905 when the King of Spain visited him. Taking advantage of the undoubtedly fine impression which his work had made on the king (who had shown his appreciation by immediately appointing Prior purveyor to the Royal household), Prior asked if he would ban the importation of Japanese fans into Spain. This the king did and as a result Spain's fan-making industry has survived to this day —modern Spanish fans are still in production.

Ever since the Middle Ages, the people of the Netherlands have been famous for the splendour of their costume. Fans were widely used by the Dutch during the 16th and 17th centuries. In the *Omnium pene Europae, Asiae, Aphricae, atque Americae Gentium habitus* engraved by A. de Bruÿn and published at Antwerp in 1581 (nine years before the earliest edition of Vecellio), the long-handled plumed fan appears with a Belgian lady whilst the shorter-handled tuft-fan is also to be seen. The rigid feather fan was also to be depicted in the works of the great Flemish painters Vandyck and Rubens. In the engraved work by de Bruÿn, the large folding fan appears constantly, though not always in the hands of Netherlandish ladies.

The history of the fan in this quarter of Europe did not exactly follow either French or Italian tastes and influence. Painted mounts appeared early and were of large dimensions. Découpé fans were also produced but in these the skin was punched rather than cut, this operation naturally being performed before mounting. Embroidered fans with tortoise shell sticks which together produced a rather heavy fan both in weight and appearance, were in use from the middle of the 17th century. But it was the decoration of the brisé fans in which the Dutch really excelled. There is some doubt as to whether the Dutch equivalent of the French Vernis Martin did in fact predate the famed French product but it is certain that Dutch fans of this type were being produced at the same period as that of the Martins. Opening out to a little more than a quarter of a circle, these fans usually employed lighter colouring and more pastel shades than the French ones. The most characteristic of the Dutch ivory fans are those in which the blades are cut in fine open work with a border of from $1\frac{1}{2}$ to 2 inches, delicately painted with flowers, fruit, birds and butterflies. Sometimes, the main parts of the decorations were cut separately from thin ivory, painted and then applied. The connecting ribbon in these fans is usually of white fabric and is placed immediately below the painted border instead of being on the extreme tip.

The Dutch very frequently chose Oriental designs for their brisé fans. However, the style of execution, whilst being fine, is so very definitely Western that these cannot be mistaken for the Chinese product. Again, the Dutch ones were painted in oil colour, a material not used on Chinese fans.

Lace, gauze and spangled fans were all produced by the Dutch. A particularly unusual feature of some Dutch fans is the carving of the sticks when closed. The closed sticks were formed into figures, heads or ornament. Although this feature is sometimes found on fans from other nations, it was widely practised in the Netherlands where it was brought to a fine art.

The fan in Germany was not destined to develop any worthwhile or beneficial national characteristics and in fact demonstrated a Teutonic heaviness, lacking the dainty touch of the French fan. Some did reach a commendable standard and compared favourably with the products of Western Europe. One type, apparently peculiar to Germany and common during the 18th century, featured painted subjects cut out and laid on lace or net. The results of this form of appliqué decoration were extremely effective.

The fan in Russia followed the classical style to the extreme and fans from that country display perfect taste without the excess of ornamentation associated with the French and, to a lesser extent, German fan. Carl Fabergé is credited with the manufacture of some extremely expensive fans, one being that presented to the Grand Duchess Olga Alexandrovna by the Tsar Nicholas II on the occasion of her marriage to Prince Peter of Oldenburg on July 27th, 1901. The mount, with a surround of swags and wreaths, has a central cartouche painted by the miniaturist Solomko which shows the ancient custom of the couple receiving gifts of bread and salt. Below this cartouche is a second, much smaller rectangular cartouche showing a view of Oldenburg Palace in St Petersburg. Two medallions containing the initials of the couple in Cyrillic characters, flank this, the intervening spaces being taken up by decorative medallions of smaller size. The guards of this interesting fan are of gold overlaid with translucent yellow enamel and surrounded by diamonds.*

Another very unusual fan and one which is in the same class as that described above, is a gold, red-enamel hand-painted fan with pearl-studded guards. Possibly from the Fabergé workshop, this fan has a small quarter-repeater watch in one guard and a small musical movement within the other guard. This movement plays on bells and it is thus likely that this was made in the second half of the 18th century (the much more compact tuned steel comb was

* This fan is illustrated in *Peter Carl Fabergé* by H. C. Bainbridge (Spring Books, London, 1949).

invented in 1796).* The style of painting is French.†

The spread of the fan across Europe was thus total and complete. Paris has established fad and fashion for hundreds of years and, within limits, what the Parisians have adopted has, within a few short years, been mirrored by society elsewhere.

Even further north, the fan has had its uses if not its manufacturing industries. A confusing reference attributed to *Nature and Art*‡ and quoted by Salwey relates that the Order of the Fan was instituted by Louisa Ulrica, queen of Sweden in 1744, for the ladies of her court, which gentlemen were afterwards allowed to join (the punctuation here is as used by Flory). Unfortunately, I can trace no reference to Queen Louisa Ulrica. Ulrica Eleanora came to the throne in 1718 but, under pressure from the aristocracy, her consort, Frederick I, assumed the throne in name only. I imagine that the reference refers to Ulrica Eleanore.

In concluding this Chapter on the fan in Continental Europe, it is worth turning to the pages of Tallis's *History & Description of the Crystal Palace* to observe his words on European fans, with particular reference to those exhibited at the Great Exhibition of 1851:

> In the works of the middle ages references are made to the two forms of the fan: to that employed in winnowing the grain, and that used in the service of the church, alternately to court the breeze or wave away the flies, till we hear of the fan as brought to France by Catherine de Medici, when it was no longer stiff and unyielding, but light and pliable. In the early part of the seventeenth century, it was so constructed that it could be folded in the manner of those used in the present day. Formed of paper and perfumed leather, it became the delight of the French court; and attracting the attention of artists, fans, in the luxurious reigns of Louis XIV, and Louis XV (in the latter under the name of "Pompadours") shone with gilding and gems, and at length glowed with the pictures of Boucher

---

* *Vide* p. 11 of *Collecting Musical Boxes* by Arthur W. J. G. Ord-Hume (Allen & Unwin, London, 1967).

† This fan is illustrated in *The Curious History of Music Boxes* by R. Mosoriak (Lightner, Chicago, 1943).

‡ *Nature and Art*, vol. I, p. 62.

and Watteau, until at length no toilet was esteemed complete without a fan, the cost of which was frequently in those days as high as from £12 to £15 sterling. In Italy, on the contrary, in the early part of the seventeenth century, even painted fans were of a very moderate price, and of universal use. "The first fans," says Coryat, in his Travels in 1608, "that I saw in Italy, I did observe in this space between Pizighiton and Cremona; but afterwards I observed them common in most places where I travelled. These fans both men and women of the country do carry to cool themselves with in the time of heat by often fanning of their faces. Most of them are very elegant and pretty things. For whereas the frame consisteth of a painted piece of paper and a little wooden handle, the paper which is fastened into the tops is on both sides most curiously adorned with excellent pictures, either of amorous things, having some witty Italian verses or fine emblems written under them, or of some notable Italian city, with a brief description thereof added thereto. These fans are of a mean price, for a man may buy one of the fairest of them for so much money as countervaileth an English groat." England must have been a great buyer of fans in the last century, as a lady of that period would have felt as awkward without her fan as a gentleman without his sword.

FRANCE

The collection of fans in the French department was most complete, and contained several specially decorated in honour of the Exhibition, and of her Majesty and Prince Albert. Among these the "Royal Fan," by Duvelleroy, attracted general admiration. It comprised a pleasing group of the whole of the royal family, with a rich emblazonment of the arms of England. Besides these and others painted by first-rate artists, it also comprised most of the descriptions manufactured for exportation, and which possessed distinctive characters, accordingly to the market for which they were destined. For instance, some displayed great differences in the length of the ribs and the portion of the circle occupied by the fan when open; other fans, intended for Turkey and

1. Flag fan woven on narrow strips of bamboo about $\frac{1}{8}$ inch wide using cotton coloured orange, salmon pink, grey, green, black and white. The fringe is of green and white cotton. The handle and the top and bottom edges are bound with sap-green cotton cloth. African, early 20th century.

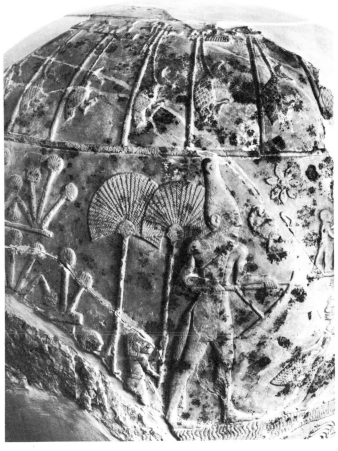

2. Egyptian ceremonial fans depicted on the mace-head of the Scorpion King, a sculpture dating from the end of the predynastic period, about 3200 BC. This was found at Hierakonpolis and is now in the Ashmolean Museum at Oxford.

Picture: Ashmolean Museum

3. Side-mounted circular flag fan of plaited coloured grass. Indian.

4. Square shaped plaited straw fan with revolving hollow wooden handle. Indian.

5. Plaited straw fan with coloured woven design finely executed in coloured grasses. The whole woven on a rigid grid provided by narrow strips of bamboo. Edged in feathers, some of which are dyed. Probably West African.

6. Pair of flag fans made of plaited straw with woven coloured design attached to wooden handles dyed red. West African.

7. Fly-whisk made from a zebra tail with a handle formed from a hippopotomus tooth. East African.

8. Plaited straw fan, halberd shape, embellished with appliqué shapes of coloured felt. Probably Indian.

9. Palmeletto leaf fan with bamboo handle. The rim is of very thin strips of bamboo laminated. To this is sewn leaves of broad grasses glued edge to edge and then varnished. This mount is sewn to the bamboo rim using alternate sections of white and black cotton. The bamboo handle is slotted to take the circular leaf and is decorated with burned-in pokerwork designs. The attachment of the leaf is by two rivets and the rim of the leaf, where it passes through the handle, is reinforced by a small U-sectioned metal clip around which is bent a U-sectioned plate of tortoise-shell.

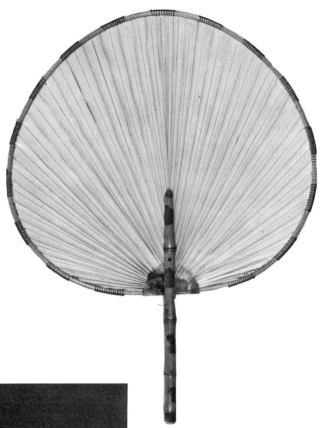

10. Modern African fan made of finely-plaited straw with coloured designs worked in. The whole is 11 inches (28cm) in diameter with feather fringe. The handle is of wood and is encased in the weaving of the mount, itself woven into a geometric pattern with coloured straw.

11. Painted and decorated découpé fan, the mount extensively pierced. Subject depicts Chinese figure bearing a yoke and containers. Sticks of wood, guards ivory with simple burned-in pattern, upper parts of guards made of grey-painted wood with delicate floral pictures. Chinese, c. 1775. 11 inches (28cm).

12. Asymmetric or spiral-mount mandarin fan, carved and pierced sticks and guards in wood. Carved and painted ivory faces and brocade robes. Chinese, c. 1880. 14 inches (35·5cm).

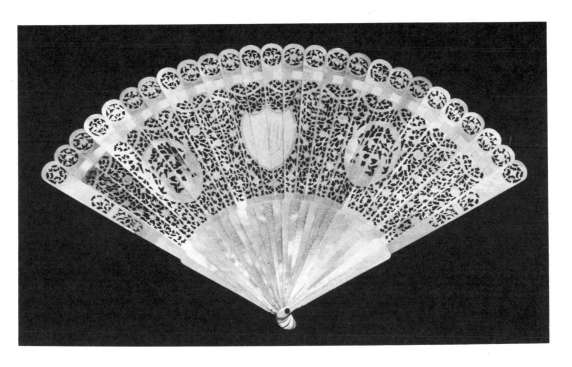

13. Mother of pearl brisé fan. Sticks with carved gorges, carved and pierced mount portion, rounded blade tips and threaded tape, the centre shield reserve with the initials "J.M." Chinese, 19th century. 10½ inches (26·5cm).
14. Below: Two black and gold lacquered brisé fans, both fine examples of Chinese lacquered work. Left: 8 inches (20cm): right: Painted monogram "P". 10½ inches (26·5cm).

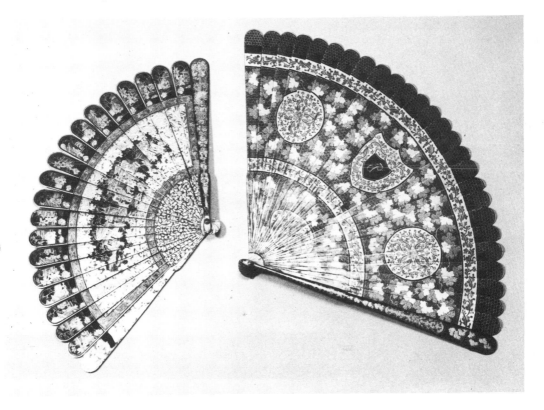

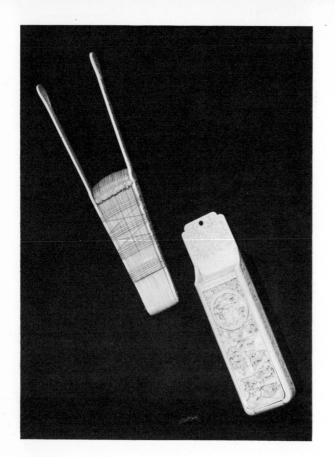

15 and 16. Chinese circular fan made of ivory finely pierced and carved with overall design. The extended guards form the handle of this very delicate cockade-type fan which is 16 inches (40cm) in diameter. The case is built up of carved ivory panels and has a hole in it. It is possible that this fan was made to be fixed on the wall by its case.

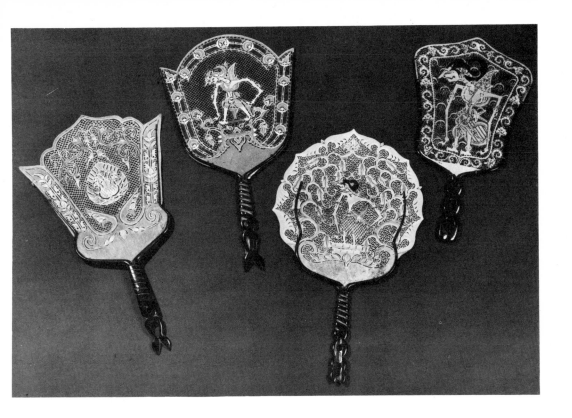

17. Four Javanese shadow fans with mounts of finely-cut water buffalo hide and unusual carved handles which extend at each side into a partial frame.

18. The reverse of a Chinese mandarin fan similar to that in *Colour Plate 4*. Three paintings in vignettes, the left showing a white horse, the centre seven figures, each with a fan, and the right one showing two Pekinese dogs. Mid-19th century. 10½ inches (27cm).

19. Silver filigree brisé fan with blue and green enamel design. Chinese, *c.* 1860. 7½ inches (19cm), below 20. Three cabriolet-type fans. That at the top right has ivory sticks and guards and is decorated with scenes from Chinese life. The plain ivory reserves between the two mounts bear the name "Maria". 8½ inches (22cm). Top left: Black lacquered sticks and guards inlaid with silver. The mount again shows Chinese domestic scenes and the faces are of carved and painted ivory, rather like the "hundred faces" mandarin·fan. 8½ inches (22cm). Bottom: Modern paper cabriolet-type fan with 32 sticks. 8¼ inches (21cm). All are Chinese.

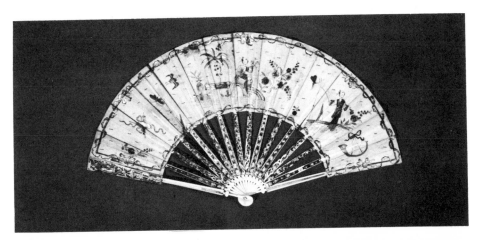

21, 22 and 23. Trick fan which displays four different pictures, depending which way it is opened. In Plate 21, the fan has been opened from right to left, showing a scene of Chinese life. On the reverse (Plate 22) is a small picture of what could be a monument. If the fan is now opened in the usual manner from left to right (Plate 23), a completely different picture is displayed and on the reverse of this is a different picture of the same monument seen on the reverse before. The sticks and guards are carved and pierced in ivory with silver and gilt ornamentation. Chinese, c. 1790. $10\frac{1}{2}$ inches (26·5cm).

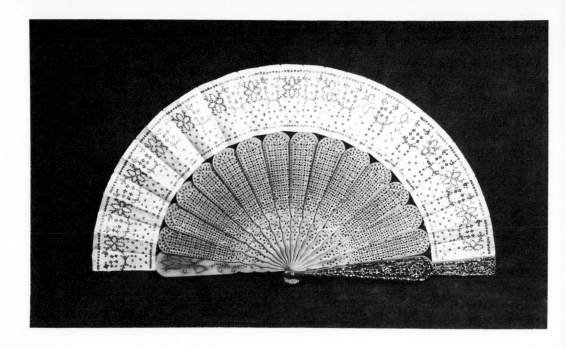

24. Finely pierced sandalwood sticks embellished with silver piqué, the guards decorated with heavy cut steel. The narrow mount is patterned in silver sequin design. Probably oriental, late 19th century. 10½ inches (27cm), and below 25. Spanish mid-18th-century fan painted with scenes in the lives of monks and friars. Note the very slender sticks and guards. 11½ inches (29cm).

26. The reverse side of the fan illustrated in Plate 25 reveals a valley scene, a shepherd boy seated by a tree and two nuns with rosarys being offered refreshments by an old woman, and below 27. Aphrodite reclines in a boat surrounded by water nymphs and garlands, cornucopia and dolphins. Lower left is seen Pan approaching a maiden on a bank; lower right Pan is entwined in a net by two maidens. The sticks and guards are of mother of pearl and neo-classical in design. The gorges are paired in the design. French, *c.* 1820–40. 10½ inches (27cm).

28. A fine example of a Brussels needlepoint (Point de Gaze) lace fan. Sticks of carved and overlaid mother of pearl pierced overall with design. Fine iridescent pierced and carved guards with square shoulders. English or French, *c.* 1860. 12 inches (30cm).

29. Painted trompe-l'oeil mount showing Naples Harbour by day and Vesuvius in eruption by night. The painting is dated 1776. Sticks and guards of carved ivory. Probably Italian. $11\frac{1}{2}$ inches (29cm).

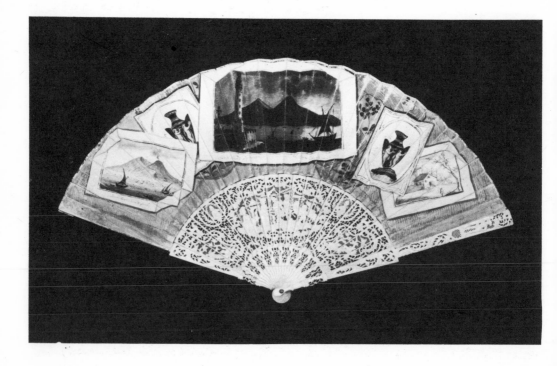

30. Battoir fan with painted vellum mount with three medallions decorated with garlands of roses vignettes. The sticks of mother of pearl with putti and urn ornamentation. The guards with a circlet of rose diamonds. German, *c.* 1750, and below 31. Four ivory brisé fans. Top left: finely carved and pierced ivory, the upper part of the sticks showing various birds, the centre depicting Chinese domestic scenes. *c.* 1830–40. 7½ inches (19cm). Top right: Carved and pierced ivory, the tips of the sticks with birds and animals; beneath the ribbon Siamese fighting fish, the centre portion a floral design with a plain reserve for a monogram. Chinese, *c.* 1830. 7½ inches (19cm). Lower left: Small ivory brisé with gilt medallions along the top of the sticks, monogram in central oval medallion "C.F.W." English, *c.* 1810. Lower right: Pierced and carved ivory with initial "L" in the centre. Chinese, *c.* 1790. 9½ inches (25cm).

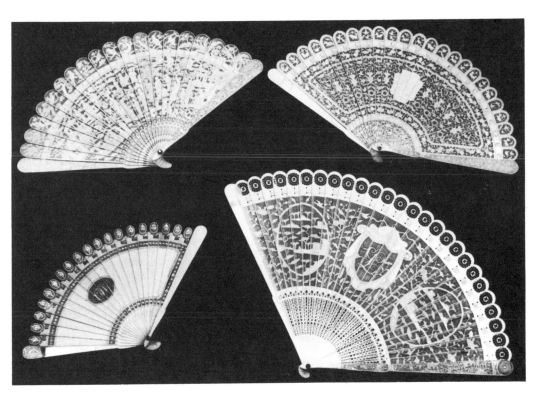

32. Four brisé fans. Top left: Black and gold lacquered wood, monogram "M.B." *c.* 1840. 7½ inches (19cm). Top right: Blonde tortoise-shell with garlands and floral decoration with silver clouté, *c.* 1820. 6½ inches (17cm). Lower left: Horn fan with small spy glass set in the head, sticks and guards decorated with silver piqué, Possibly Dutch. 6 inches (15·5cm). Lower right: Blonde tortoise-shell with pierced sticks and guards decorated with cut steel. English. 6¼ inches (16cm), and below 33. Pierced ivory sticks and guards, vellum mount with gilt spangled ornamentation. Three vignettes, the central showing Britannia placing a laurel wreath on Cupid, flanked by ovals containing birds. The whole in gilt decorated glazed case. Probably French, mid-18th century. 8½ inches (24cm).

Morocco, were composed entirely of feathers, and, in conformity with the Mohammedan doctrine, no living object was
painted on them. The principal foreign market for fans made
in France are the South American States. In the decoration
of such fans as were intended for Buenos Ayres, blue and
green were carefully omitted, these colours having political
significance, and being prohibited from use on pain of death.
All the exhibitors were of the class called "Eventaillistes," as
none of the manufacturers of the department of l'Oise sent
their productions.

SPAIN

There were two exhibitors of fans in the Spanish Court,
one of who contributed painted, and also printed "Feuilles"
and the other both feuilles and complete fans, some of which
were copies from French models. The examples, although
they bore no comparison in point of taste or execution with the
splendid fans from France, were good of their kind; and it
would appear that the attention of their exhibitors had been
directed rather to the manufacturer for an article of general
sale, than to the production of works of art. But it is remarkable
that no finer specimens should have been sent from a country,
in which the use of fans is so prevalent, that they are commonly offered for sale outside the arena of the bull-fights, and
other places of amusement. The fans in the Tunisian Court
were ten in number, and in some cases ornamented with rich
embroidery. From Turkey, the only specimen was an embroidered fan, made at Constantinople. Wurtemberg contributed several bone and ivory fans, reasonable in price, but
very inferior to the ivory fans exhibited by the French makers.
The number of exhibitors of fans was twenty-three; of these
two received a prize medal, and one obtained honourable
mention.

M. Duvelleroy and M. Felix, both of Paris, were the
holders of the prize medals; the former for a display of fans,
ornamented with artistic paintings, and remarkable for the
beauty of the inlaying and the pierced ivory and mother-of-
pearl frames. The most elegant fan in this collection was one
painted by Roqueplan; the ribs were of richly-pierced, and

sculptured, mother of pearl, inlaid with gold; it was valued at £40. Besides the above, others intended for foreign markets were exhibited, the prices of which varied from 5d. to 40s. per dozen.* M. Felix obtained his for a collection of fans, for the most part copies of the best examples of ancient fans: these were such remarkably beautiful specimens of vellum-painting, that they fully entitled this manufacturer to the award, and were moreover the richest of any exhibited.

* Cassell's *Illustrated Exhibitor* mentions "elegantly painted" fans being sold in London for threepence-halfpenny, and relates that Duvelleroy was able to compete with low-cost Eastern imports and even to supply Parisian ladies with superior goods at "an almost ridiculously low price", thereby implying that *c.* 1851, Eastern makers were exporting good quality fans to the West.

CHAPTER FIVE

THE FOLDING FAN IN ENGLAND

In the previous Chapter, I mentioned that the fan crest was used in England as early as the year 1197 and its popular use in a similar context expanded during the 14th century. Similarly we find the *flabellum* is mentioned in many inventories, references including one to a silk fan at Salisbury in the year 1214, and one of peacock's feathers at St Paul's Cathedral in 1295. It would seem that sometime before the end of the reign of Richard II (1367–1400), fans were known and used by Royalty and the Court. By the time of Henry VIII (1491–1547), fixed feather fans were carried not only by ladies but, according to the essayist George Steevens: "Even young gentlemen carried fans of feathers in their hands, which in wars our ancestors wore on their heads."

It is interesting here that the writer identifies the feather fan with the fan crest and is evidence of the design of hand-fans during this early history period.

The carrying of fans by men in England, even in contemporary times, was considered effeminate in some quarters. Hall's *Satires*, published in 1598, mentions dandies chalking their faces and peering into looking glasses "Tir'd with pinn'd ruffs and fans." Nineteen years later, Green wrote: "We strive to be accounted womanish by keeping of beauty, by curling of hair, by plumes of feathers in our hands which in war our ancestors wore on their heads."

The overt effeminacy of men so decked out did not pass unnoticed by William Shakespeare who alluded to it as "those remnants of fool and feather that they have got from France." In his notes on the fashions in the early part of the seventeenth century, John Aubrey mentions: "The gentlemen had prodigious fans and they had handles at least half a yard long, with these their daughters were oftentimes corrected."

The antiquary F. W. Fairholt (1814–66) states that the first appearance of the modern fan is to be seen in a print of the early part of the 17th century. The long handle, he says, is still retained and the fan, although arranged in folds, does not appear to be capable of being folded. Fairholt does not identify this print but Woolliscroft Rhead identifies the fans as being those depicted by Vecellio (in 1590) and earlier engravers (see Fig. 29). Either Fairholt's print was subsequent to the execution of the original or Rhead is incorrect in making this attribution. However, this must be purely a point of detail since there is no reason to doubt that fans of this period were similar in general to those rather stylised representations by Vecellio.

It was not until the last decade of the 16th century that the folding fan appeared in painted portraits, among the earliest of these being that of Queen Elizabeth* at Jesus College in 1590 in which the Queen is shown holding a découpé fan with pointed edging. This type appears to have enjoyed considerable popularity at this time and découpé fans are shown in many subsequent paintings. The treatment of the outer, curved edge of the fan varied from the triangular points of Queen Elizabeth's fan to a more semi-circular form and the patterning of the mount often resembling lace. Lace itself was also used for fan mounts; usually lace mounts were of expensive Flanders or Brussels origin.

A curious statement that to Madame de Maintenon is attributed the introduction of the folding fan into England is contained in several writings on the fan, including Salwey.† No doubt Frances d'Aubigne Maintenon, virtuous second wife to Louis XIV and who was born in 1635, was well-acquainted with the folding fan but to claim that she introduced it into a land whose queen had been portrayed with such an instrument 45 years before her birth can be nothing but grossly inaccurate.

An event which was of considerable significance to the development of the fan in England was the marriage of the thirty-two-year-old Charles II with twenty-eight-year-old Catherine of Braganza, Infanta of Portugal, in 1662. The Queen and her retinue of Portuguese ladies introduced the gigantic green shading fans of Moorish origin which, in the absence of parasols (at that time unknown in England) served to shield the complexions of the ladies from the sun. Through this marriage, England had direct access to the benefits to be accrued from Portugals' position as a leading

* See Appendix C.
† *Fans of Japan.*

world trader. In fact it is quite possible that, whilst no doubt King Charles II's public eye was on the charm and beauty of the young Queen, his private thoughts dwelled on less chivalrous matters such as the political and trading benefits which could come his way. The formation of the East India Company in December, 1600, had marked the establishment of that Oriental trade which was to assume vast proportions during the succeeding century. So it was that, as part of the King's marriage treaty, Portugal arranged for India to begin trading on an increased scale with England. Indian fans soon reached England and, by virtue of their lightness and elegance, they lent themselves to use by ladies for the first time in England as a weapon of coquetry.

Agnes Strickland* comments that in most of the early engraved

Fig. 38

This fan which dates from 1668, is said to have belonged to the daughter of Gilbert Burnet, the historian and theologian who became Bishop of Salisbury in 1643. Two characteristics worth observing are first of all the narrow, wavey sticks, and secondly the proportions of the mount with its simple decorative treatment of one main subject.

portraits of Catherine of Braganza, the Queen is represented with a folding fan, in each instance closed; in one instance (that of an equestrian portrait) a large fan is depicted. By this, I interpret her meaning to be one of the large Portuguese shading fans.

It would appear that there were few fans made in England before

* *Lives of the Queen of England*, London, 1840–48 (an illustrated edition appeared in 1851–52).

the close of the 17th century. As well as quantities of Oriental fans and Portuguese shading fans, large numbers of mounts were also imported from Italy—an aspect of the so-called English fan which can make fan identification into a farce. In Chapter 8 is related how, in 1709, the Worshipful Company of Fan Makers was established largely as a result of the influx of fan makers following on the revocation of the Edict of Nantes twenty-four years earlier. It was through this now-accepted persecution of the Protestants that the French Huguenots were obliged to seek refuge in England and other countries where, because of their skills in crafts hitherto prized and imported, they were welcomed with open arms. Along with jewellery workers, glass artists and *ébénistes* there were numbers of *éventaillistes* who rapidly established an industry which could not be termed indigenous. They brought with them across the Channel not only the money to finance their work (in most cases the meagre savings of their lives) but what was even more valuable—their skill as craftsmen and their habitual thrift and diligence. H. M. Baird wrote:*

> The countries whether they went were enriched by the arts and trades which the French refugees introduced, and still more by the examples of industry, probity, and sincere piety which they exhibited in their own persons.

These early years of the English fan-making industry were not easy. The trade during the 17th century had been in its infancy with the manufacture of fans carried on in a desultory manner devoid of recognition and organisation. Within the space of a few years, though, matters changed. The immigrant fan makers settled in London, took on apprentices and began teaching other workpeople their trade and its associate crafts. With the responsibilities imposed by such an establishment, it is not surprising that the importation of foreign fans and the whole operation of the old nefarious trade in fans now came under close scrutiny. When in 1702 an advertisement appeared announcing: "For sale, by the Candle, at the Marine Coffee House in Birchin Lane. Forty Thousand Fans of Sundry Sorts",† the fan makers began to con-

* *The Huguenots and the Revocation of the Edict of Nantes.*
† *Social Life in the Reign of Queen Anne*, John Ashton, London 1882, Vol. 1, p. 176.

sider ways of uniting for the protection of their own trade. So came about the formation of the Fan Makers' Company and, in 1710, there were no fewer than between two and three hundred persons sufficiently involved in the business to apply for membership. Since these were men "living in London and Westminster, and twenty miles round, and who had served as Apprentices to the said Art and Mistery by the span of seven years", there must also have been others who were excluded by geographical detail from this assignation.*

From that time forward, the trade was an increasing one and in spite of the competition from overseas, the first half of the 18th century saw a steady increase in the numbers of fan makers and fan painters. All, though, was not well in the camp. Printed fan leaves were at the root of the trouble.

An insight into the state of the industry is contained in an article which appeared in the *Westminster Journal* for February 23rd, 1751. It is interesting inasmuch as that it shows not only the number of genuine fan-makers, but also the enormous number of printed leaves which must have been issued in order that the suggested small tax could have been calculated as producing the sum of £30,000. The article was quoted by the *Gentleman's Magazine* for that year:

> A writer in the *Westminster Journal* . . . proposes a tax upon plain and printed mounts. Printed ones not coloured to pass free as before. A sixpenny stamp to be affixed in the midst of a plain or printed fan mount, and a shilling stamp on a leather one. This may produce a revenue of ten, twenty, or thirty thousand pounds per annum, encourage a very ingenious branch of business, and only hurt about half a dozen paltry plate printers who are enriching themselves and starving hundreds.

If "hundreds" were to have their livelihood affected by the printed mount, then obviously there must have been a very large number of painters who practised the painting of fan mounts.

The competition afforded by these printed fan leaves (which, by

---

* See Chapter 8, p. 195.

the way, were of London manufacture), was not the only occurrence to blight the existence of the *évantailliste* in London.

Throughout the latter half of the 17th century and the first half of the 18th, considerable numbers of fans were imported into England from India, China and the Far East which, together with the importation of Italian mounts already mentioned, posed a very serious threat to the home industry. The extreme cheapness of the imported fans was largely due to the introduction of the printed mount because, although they were very much inferior to the hand-painted ones, they had the advantage of being so cheap that they found a ready and voluminous sale on the market.

In the following year, it was stated in an advertisement in the *Daily Advertiser* (also quoted in the *Gentleman's Magazine*) that there were nearly a thousand "poor unfortunate artificers in the several branches of the fan trade". It continued: "The home-made fans are in every way preferable to foreign; and that by encouraging the latter, they will relieve a number of unfortunate families from the most grievous distress and despair."

The fan makers took their case to Parliament and demanded prohibition of these foreign fans.* The result was that in 1627, during the reign of Charles II, it was decided to impose a protective duty of forty shillings a dozen on all wooden and feather fans and also to place a temporary embargo on the importation of all painted fans.

Even so, foreign merchandise continued to enter Britain and numerous different statutes were invoked to stem the flow of this business. Much of the early records of the Fan Makers' Company

---

* The petition to the House of Commons read as follows:

The Fann-makers' grievance, by the importation of Fanns
from the East Indies.

That the manufactures of Fanns and Fann-sticks, though it may seem slight to some, is certainly at this time of very great consequence to a very considerable branch of the trade of England, for that it employs multitudes of men, women, and children, in making the sticks, papers, leathers, in ordering the silk (which paper, leather, and silk is manufactur'd in this nation); likewise great numbers employ'd in painting, varnishing, and japanning; and further until there be put a stop to the importation of Indian Fanns and Fann-sticks, of which it can be proved that 550,000 have lately been brought over, great numbers of poor people, continually employed in the work must inevitably perish.

has been lost but the question of imported fans recurs. At the beginning of the Minute Book opened in 1775 someone penned some summary notes on the subject as follows:

Observations of the Importation of French or Foreign Fans. Calpins for Fans (Mounts). By the 11th George the First Chapter the Seventh Calpins for Fans are rated in the Custom House Books at Seven Shillings and sixpence a Dozen the Duty paid on Importation is one shilling five pence seven eights per dozen. And besides if made of leather and the leather be the most valuable part. For every twenty shillings of the real value upon cash the Duty upon importation is six shillings.
By the 12th of Charles the 2nd Chapter the fourth fans for women and children (French making) are rated in the Custom House Book at £2 per dozen and the Duty paid on importation £1.5.0. per dozen.
BUT if the Fans are painted they are prohibited to be imported and are seizable as *painted wares*.

The prohibition of embroideries under various statutes is also noted and the penalties stated, and the statutes relating to the importation of gold and silver fringes and lace are given. These were liable "to be forfeited and Burnt, and £100 paid by the importer of every parcel so imported".

The Minute Book contains other comments which are of interest in piecing together the environment of the fan maker in these far-off days:

By the Act of the 6th of Ann Chapter 19th. Silks wrought or made with gold or silver or materials clandestinely imported are forfeited with £200 by every importer and £100 by the Receiver Seller or Concealer.
Upon which Act it appears that either Mounts or Fans that are painted are seizable and that Fans or Mounts Embellished with Gold or Silver are Prohibited under very severe penalties Particularly under the Acts of the 4th of Edward 3rd and the 15th and 22nd of George II.

On July 1st, 1779, a member of the Company named Robert

Clarke, represented to a meeting of the Court of Assistants that the "importation of French and Foreign fans daily increased" and it was decided that "advertisement should be inserted in the Public Papers and Hand Bills delivered setting forth the pernicious tendency of such proceedings." It was intended to defray the expenses of this campaign by subscription.

The Peace of Versailles with England, signed on September 3rd, 1783, served only to make the situation worse. The outcome of the free trade practices for all which followed, led to the establishment of a commercial treaty with France. Once more we turn to the Minute Book:

> Observations on the Commercial Treaty with France which took place the 10th day of May, 1787.
> Schedule D in the Book of Rates. It is expressed Paper Hangings for Rooms for every £100 imported there shall be paid £75 per cent.
> Paper not otherways particularly enumerated or described for every £100 value £55 per cent.
> Toys for every £100 value £33 per centum.

Fig. 39

The famed Bartholomew Fair in London is featured on this printed fan published by Setchel during the period 1730–50. Note the plain, extremely wide shoulders to the sticks.

Query as plain fans may be imported do they not come under the Denomination of Toys?

Schedule D all other goods, Wares and Merchandise whatever not being particularly enumerated or described or otherwise charged with Duty not prohibited to be imported or used in Great Britain and not being exempted from Duty, for every £100 value thereof £27.10.0 per cent.

By which it appeareth Paper Fans Mounts plain cannot be imported without paying a Duty of £55 per cent. And that Plain Fans cannot be imported without paying a Duty of £27.10 per cent.

Or if they are Imported as Toys £33 per cent.

It comes as no surprise to discover that the English style of fan painting was influenced strongly by contemporary French and Italian styles and Percival considers that some of the more successful representations of French and Italian originals may have been executed by artists of those nationalities because there are comparatively few fans of the early years of the 18th century which can positively be identified as being of English origin. Of those that can be identified, Percival comments that they vary a great deal in character and the artistic treatment is heavy and rather crude with the colours thickly applied and the details added in a "liney" style. Generally the portrayal of figures shows them in stiffish poses and the colouring and arrangement is rather childish.

A style of fan mount fashionable in the 1730s was the tinted drawing which, as with so many water-colour paintings of the time was executed mainly in Indian ink partly by pen and partly by brush. The result is somewhat dull in colour but a good specimen reveals a great deal of delicate detail. An artist named José Goupy excelled in this media in which the colour is of secondary interest and comprises washes over the ink. The style of the arrangement looks very similar to that of the Italian fans which were so popular during the 18th century except that whilst Goupy and others like him worked in water colour on paper, the Italian paintings were far fresher and brighter and were often painted in gouache on skin as well as paper.

It must be said that, as regards execution and composition, these early 18th-century English fans were a poor match for the French and Italian products and it is small wonder that the industry wallowed in a period of decline. The reason for this is hard to explain since the mainstay of the London fan industry was the Huguenot artisans and their apprentices. The probability is that these craftsmen centred mainly on the manufacture of the fan frame and were forced through circumstances to use, in the majority of instances, fan mounts from whatsoever sources they were available. Economics may also have entered into it since by the early part of the 18th century, fans were no longer in use only by the wealthy and the noble. The middle classes now carried fans and some were almost two feet wide.*

Matters must have improved, though, by the time Horace Walpole wrote to Sir Horace Mann in Florence on January 27th, 1761. Here he refers to sending: "Six of the newest fashioned and prettiest fans I could find. They are really genteel, though one or two have caprices that will turn a Florentine head."

During the last quarter of the 18th century, the fan mount showed certain changes in format. Whereas in former times the principal side portrayed one scene across the entire leaf together with its various embellishments, the focal point was shared between three different subjects each of which was contained within a medallion or cartouche. Although this style can be traced back to Italy in the middle 18th century period, it would appear to have reached this country through France where a similar arrangement was in vogue (see Chapter 5). Aroused by the works of the brothers Adam, a renewed interest in the classical and in architecture caused many Italian artists and craftsmen to come to this country and among them were some who painted fans. One of these was A. Poggi who held an exhibition in 1781. He worked from the designs of Sir John Reynolds, Angelica Kauffmann, Bartolozzi, West and Cipriani.

Throughout the closing decades of the 18th century, fan paintings were often painstakingly finished and quite well designed and executed. Compared with French mounts though, the decoration and ornament were conceived on too small a scale and appear somewhat thin and wiry when compared with the best French specimens which combined a light and airy effect with the filling

---

* *The London Magazine*, 1744, said: ". . . a lady will soon screen herself and her family against all the inclemencies of the weather." The umbrella was unknown at this time.

of the space available. Percival comments that the subjects in the medallions are frequently too minute, and the whole too precise and tight in execution. The English style of fan at this period, in being so very exact and organised in appearance, had moved yet further from that coveted characteristic of the French fan—a freedom and spirited flow of the brush stroke which was at once subtle and purposeful.

Spangles were also used in conjunction with painting, more particularly where the ground was of silk which was a favoured material during the mid-Victorian era and onwards. Inlets of lace and gauze were also introduced, those of the latter substance often being painted with floral emblems, musical instruments and such-like.

Percival comments on the very chalky appearance of the body colour used at this time and queries whether this was due to the material being insufficiently ground up, or the use of an inferior medium.

The painted fan continued in use in England for some while after its French counterpart had generally been superseded by products of a coarser variety. The style of three medallions remained in fashion until it faded into obscurity before the rising vogue of the silk or gauze fan, the decoration of which, after a transitional period (as related further on) during which medallions and spangles were used, stabilised as a total execution in spangles.

Other than the painted fan, England produced its share of printed fans. These are not to be despised from the collector's point of view for they were immensely popular fans even though they were, by the very nature of the topical scenes which they depicted, destined to be nothing more than ephemeral. They were made to celebrate a season, as souvenirs of a special event—some even for just one week or even a day—and for the student of social events they record tastes and fashions which may barely have endured longer than the day in which they were created.

A feature of English printed fans which is of particular interest and value to the collector is that it was required by law, under the provisions of the Act of 1735, that they should bear the date of their issue and the name of their publisher. Unfortunately, this information was almost always printed on the lower part of the mount and here it was quite often trimmed off during the operation of fitting the mount to the sticks.

From this information, it is a simple matter to form some idea as to the principal publishers of printed fan leaves and a great number appear to have been published by M. Gamble at the Sign of the Golden Fan in London. He advertised his fans over a considerable time in the pages of *The Craftsman*. Theatrical fans, printed from etched plates and hand-coloured by girls, were produced in large numbers and depicted scenes from both contemporary short-lived stage productions and the time-tested classics such as *Romeo and Juliet*. Other fans included those which recorded the arrangement of the boxes and seats at the opera. This notion was no doubt thought up for the benefit of the élite among the clientele so that they might quickly locate their friends (and enemies?). It no doubt served an equal purpose for the *hoi polloi* to whom the sight of the famous and wealthy was of more consequence than the activities the other side of the footlights.

It was Gamble who advertised, as early as 1732–33, the "Church of England Fan, being an explanation of the Oxford Almanac for the year 1733". This must have been among the very earliest of this class of fan. These fans frequently depict Biblical scenes whilst others have Psalms and other portions of Scripture set out with a surround of garlands of flowers and scroll work. It comes as rather a surprise to find that some of these fans display particularly rough, crude work and would hardly seem a match for the well-dressed lady in her Sunday finery.

As the 18th century passed, the printed fan played a declining part in the history of the fan in England. Indeed, it was not until around the 1840s and 1850s that the lithographed fan emerged in quantity. These were coloured in imitation of the valuable hand-painted French originals. Whilst these were but very cheap impersonations of quality fans, some were of tolerably high standard.

Whereas in the case of painted, printed, folding and other types of fan, tastes vacillated through the centuries; feather fans, the oldest and most primitive of all, appear never to have fallen from fashion. Throughout history we find references to this simple device either in the arranged layout of the ancient Egyptian peacock's feather fan (variations of which were still in use in the 1900s) or in the form of gathered feathers which may or may not be folded about a rivet through ferrules on the quills.

Fig. 40

As a means of recording fragments of history, the fan was without equal, for it had the facility and ability to chronicle contemporary events in a way which was quite beyond the means of any other form of published media. On this fine English fan is depicted Mrs Fitzherbert and the Prince of Wales, later to become George IV. Maria Anna Fitzherbert (née Smythe) entered into a morganatic marriage with the man whose name she might never take on December 15th, 1785. On April 8th, 1795, the prince married his cousin, Charlotte Sophia who, twenty-five years later, became Queen of England.

The first silk fans in England appeared during the closing decades of the 18th century and to begin with these followed the three-medallion style of decoration. The spangle with its brilliant facet of glossy silver, though, was literally catching the eye and its use on fans was initially as a border to the medallions. This border was sometimes a single row of closely-set spangles, sometimes a double row and quite often the border of the fan itself was rimmed with them. Generally the spangles were round or oval in shape and superseded embroidery which was either completely absent or present only as a few flat stitches of floss silk.

Colour-printed silk fans are most probably particular only to England. Many charming subjects were depicted in this way at the end of the 18th and the beginning of the 19th century and, as regards both appearance and execution, are preferable to the hand-painted fans of the period. Other than the printed and coloured main motif, the rest of the fan would be decorated with arabesques and wreaths, garlands and other devices which would either be printed or worked in sequins. The sequins were either silver or gold and, coupled with the rich and varied colour of the prints on the silk ground, the effect was both harmonious and charming.

A particularly attractive class of fan appeared during the period of the Regency and remained very fashionable right through to the end of the reign of William IV. These are not necessarily of great artistic merit but they are to be admired for their attractive colouring and dainty finish. Among the most charming of these are semi-transparent brisé fans which were made of extremely thin sticks of horn and decorated in rather vivid colours with tiny flowers in body colour. The favourite floral decoration comprised forget-me-nots, roses and heartease, all blossoms being drawn somewhat incongruously to the same scale. The horn is usually pierced in the parts which are not painted and the result is extremely pretty. The horn from which these fans were made is a tough substance and, in spite of the dainty appearance presented by these fans, they are among the toughest of all made and thus are frequently found to have survived in perfect condition. They are sometimes referred to as "whalebone fans" but this is a misnomer.

Of the same period are fans in bone or wood and decorated in much the same manner and style, usually with a reserve, unfretted, upon which is a rather crudely painted landscape, a rustic scene or a floral decoration. There is, according to Percival, a strong probability that these fans were in truth, of Dutch origin and were imported in large numbers or, alternatively, made especially for the English market. Some of these fans have been found with the 19th century paintings washed off and a fresh painting after the style of Watteau added in their place. In this form, they have been seen described as "18th century minuet fans".

Painted ivory brisé fans of the latter part of the 18th century were all derived from the Italian style and are usually easily identifiable by their delicate piercing with fretwork pattern, the presence of one principal medallion and usually two smaller flanking ones, and gilt which was applied with a brush. These fans opened out to about a third of a circle.

At this time, a number of rather odd brisé fans were made in England. Percival relates how the guards of one were ornamented to resemble a quiver, each stick being carved and painted in imitation of an arrow. These fans were more curious than pretty and another had its edge cut into battlements and the painting on the sticks was a view of a castle wall. Fans such as these were produced in the first quarter of the 18th century to cater for a demand for the unusual and novel and with them went those fans which today we would identify as burlesque fans—that wide range of fans which were caricatures, parodies and comic comments on contemporary affairs which were almost Hogarthian in their approach. These, of course, were invariably printed fans. The burlesque design was as much part of the fan's artistry as the classical, rococo and *art nouveau*.

Following the Louis Seize period in France, the Empire fan, so much smaller than the fans of the previous times and seldom exceeding 7 inches in length, became fashionable in France. Not surprisingly, by the opening years of the 19th century, the Empire fan had a measure of following in England. Many were imported, but no doubt the fan-makers responded to the challenge and London manufacture followed. It is, though, almost impossible in most cases to decide whether an Empire Fan is French or English: it is most probably French in origin although it might well have spent its "working" life in England. Spangled Empire fans were in great demand and occasionally the guards would be pierced and inlaid with small pseudo-Wedgwood cameos of jasper, glass or jet.* Cut steel stars and ovals were also forms of ornamentation commonly used, but probably the majority were simply pierced and fretted and a backing of metallic foil applied.

Throughout the 18th century, England possessed a great number of skilled craftsmen who specialised in the making of sticks. The quality of their work is difficult to reconcile with that of the leaves since the printed or crudely-painted mounts were of far from comparable quality. The ivory sticks used for many fans were almost always extremely well finished and well made. The only form of ornamentation which many of these sticks had was the use of a different material for the head; wooden sticks had an ivory head;

* Wedgwood perfected his jasper process by 1777 and painted Wedgwood medallions were extremely popular from thence onwards until the early 1880s.

ivory sticks one of tortoise shell; tortoise shell would be combined with pearl shell.

Stick making was considered to be at least as important a part of the manufacturing processes of a fan as the painting. At the time of the grant of Arms to the Worshipful Company of Fan Makers the words "or Fan-Stick Makers" were added in the description of the Arms as recorded in the Company's Minute Book. The crest of the Company shows a complete fan, and a complete fan is included on the shield, but the tools shown are all those which were used by the stick makers—the shaver for thinning down the ivory, the piercing saw for fretted designs and the bundle of finished sticks. None of the necessities of the painter is shown.

The welter of engraved fans and a gradual change to the use of plain gauze, silk or taffeta fans during the early Victorian era heralded the decline of the fan in England. To set the scene, though, it is necessary to look at England in the light of events in France. It appears obvious that the remaining demand for quality fans was for those made in France. It must be admitted that this had always been the case and the French fan had the reputation of being the very best. In the same way that young ladies were expected to finish their education in France, the implication was that whilst the British were the ebullient Empire-builders, the best of things did not automatically herald from "old Albion".

England was not alone in her prizing of French fans. When Rondot compiled his report on the 1851 Great Exhibition, he recorded:

> The revolution of 1848 would have crushed the French fan industry if it had not been for the orders for exportation. The production, which in Paris amounted to the value of three million francs in 1847, was reduced to half in the disastrous year that followed; of 565 workers of both sexes, 315 were thrown out of employment. At the time of writing (1854) the industry was in a flourishing condition. Paris is still the only city where a fan may command the price of a hundred pounds.

The Paris Exposition of 1867 showed still greater proof that the French fan was holding its own. Duvelleroy* commented that the

* *Exposition Universelle. Paris 1867, Rapports du Jury International.* vol. iv.

number of artists and workers employed in Paris and the Oise was 4,000, the annual value of the production being ten million francs of which threequarters was for the foreign market.

Paris et la Chine ont seuls le monopole du commerce des éventails, mais c'est aujourd'hui, en Europe, une industrie toute française, pour laquelle le monde entier est notre tributaire.

Lady Bristol* wrote that:

Spain, who for thirty years had tried to organise her industry, has only arrived at the production of the commoner classes of fans. Italy, who uses fans greatly, does not make them; Portugal being only the third in the European market. In the Great Exhibition of 1851 there was not one single fan of British manufacture exhibited.

In his notes to the Catalogue of the Fan Exhibition at South Kensington in 1820† Redgrave stated: ". . . that there were no English fanmakers living except those who made cheap and coarse fans, is substantially correct today."

If one examines the fans which were produced at the time these caustic comments were made, we can see just how right they really were. To return, though, to the Great Exhibition of 1851, this great overt display of industrial development and wealth mounted a display of many fans, albeit not of English manufacture. Great Britain still had a great empire of which it was justly proud. Talliss's *History of the Crystal Palace* tells us a little about the fans produced by the members of this empire, and describes some of those shown before our wide-eyed predecessors who visited Paxton's great palace of glass in London's Hyde Park:

BRITISH COLONIES

The colonial dependencies of Great Britain contributed many examples of fans, some of which were interesting on account of their simplicity, whilst on the other hand, those from India

* article in *Queen*, Christmas number, 1890.
† Redgrave, S.: *Preface: South Kensington Catalogue of the Loan Exhibition of Fans*, London, 1870.

presented most striking proofs of the luxurious splendour of
the Indian princes. There were, for example, two fans contributed by H. H. the Rajah of Kota, one with an ivory handle,
the other with a gold handle; but as the names of the various
manufacturers were unfortunately not ascertainable at the time
the Jury examined these specimens, no prizes were awarded

Fig. 41

Engraved by P. Duvelleroy in Paris and published in London by Tallis was
this, the Royal Fan, made expressly for the Great Exhibition of 1851. It
depicts Queen Victoria, Prince Albert and their children. The shoulder of
the sticks is virtually non-existent and the guards are practically wedge-
shaped.

in their favour. The Indian fan differs from that of Europe
and China in not closing, and likewise in its form, and it is
usually kept in motion by an attendant. Besides the fans affixed
to central handles, all of which were most gorgeously enriched
with embroidery and jewels, there were exhibited others
resembling a curtain suspended from a silver rod, which is held
horizontally by the attendant, and waved backwards and
forwards over the head of the wealthy Hindoo: and there was
also the circular standard-fan; the handle being a silver staff,
crooked at the top, to which the fan is attached on the opposite
side to the crook. The attendant stands by the side of his
master, and placing the end against his foot, inclines it away

Fig. 42

The autograph fan was usually of the brisé type, plain ivory sticks being provided for the acquisition of signatures. This one, dating from about 1882, has the tips of each blade decorated with small coloured paintings.

from his body, and slowly swings it to and fro. There was also a beautiful peacock-feather fan from Assam, and a fan, or *punkah*, composed of China beads and pearls, and made in the city of Delhi. The most simple, however, were those made of the entire or the divided leaf of the *Borassus flabelliformis*, manufactured at Calcutta, and commonly used both by natives and Europeans. The other examples comprised a punkah made of khuskhus grass (*Andropogon muricatus*) which, when wetted, emits a fragrant perfume; fans made of sandal-wood, from Calcutta; a fan made of bamboo, from Moorshedabad, and several of a similar description, from other parts of India; and lastly, from Bengal, large hand-fans, made of the palmyra-leaf. The inspection of these beautiful productions of Indian workmen, naturally suggested the idea that their skill and remarkable taste might be turned to profitable account, if directed to the production of fans suitable to the European and American markets. Nova Scotia sent an example of a very simple Indian fan. From Trinidad, Lord Harris, the governor, sent examples of fans for ladies. And from Western Africa, Mr R. Jameson, of Liverpool, exhibited several fans from the banks of the Niger, one of which was made of a species of grass. A few specimens were exhibited in the collection from Egypt, to which much interest was attached, as coming from a country in which, possibly, the fan was first devised.

In 1859, a Frenchman from Sainte-Geneviève (Oise) named Alphonse Baude invented a machine which, along with the printed fan mount, removed the last vestige of human artistry and creativity from the fan. His mechanism was a device for cutting and carving fan sticks automatically. Ordinary fans now literally became "run of the mill" products. Quality articles were still made, but in decreasing numbers and at ever higher prices. Rondot mentions one fan carved in mother of pearl and signed by Camille Roqueplan for Duvelleroy which sold for one thousand francs. Other exceptional fans were made, usually for royalty and to mark special occasions.

The art was not furthered by the revival of the découpé style of mount in imported Chinese fans. These fans comprised two leaves with a simple ornamental painting on one side and either a plain reverse or an even simpler motif. The leaves were then pasted in the usual way to form the mount into which slotted the plain wooden sticks. After all was done, the entire fan was put under a press which, in the same manner as pierced paper doily mats are made, punched tiny piercings over the mount. Those parts of the mount which formed full folds between the sticks were fully pierced; those carrying the sticks pierced only at the top. All the aspects of fan making had now been mechanised—painting, printing, colouring, carving, folding and now punching. That uneven battle, expressed simply as art *versus* avarice, had been lost by the craftsman.

During the latter half of the 19th century, three prominent fan-makers from Paris, Duvelleroy, Alexandre and Aloys van de Voorde, made efforts to sustain the declining interest in high-class fans and exhibited work by leading painters. The Worshipful Company of Fan Makers in London also did its best to revive the dying craft, and in 1870 at the instigation of Queen Victoria organised an exhibition at what was then the South Kensington Museum (now the Victoria & Albert Museum). The Queen herself offered a prize of £400 for the best fan and the display presented 413 examples of the fan-makers' art from the finest collections both here and abroad. The exhibition was a great success and the interest shown in it encouraged the Company to arrange a competitive exhibition at the Drapers' Hall in 1878, again under the patronage of Royalty—this time HRH Princess Louise, later to become the Duchess of Argyle. One thousand two hundred and eighty-four fans were shown and medals in gold, silver and bronze were offered, together with a total of £172 in cash, as prizes. Prizewinners were also awarded the Freedom of the Company.

In 1889, the process was repeated, this time sponsorship coming from private individuals and newspapers. One hundred and sixty fans were entered this time, and the venue was again Drapers' Hall. One of the sponsors was *Queen* which commented in its editorial pages:

> Considered as a whole, the exhibition did not come up to our expectations. The liberal prizes offered ought to have brought forward finer and more original work in a branch of minor art which is to be considered as the special province of lady artists,* and presents so many opportunities for fanciful composition and refined taste in arranging and grouping.

The following year (1890) yet another exhibition was staged, this time with prizes totalling £275 and with the proviso that the pieces should be the exclusive work of British subjects. The number of fans shown now reached six hundred but once more work of true quality was absent. There was, however, novelty. Some enterprising engineer had the temerity to present a development of the fan which fitted somewhere between the small, battery-powered electric hand fan seen today (which rotates an aircraft-type propeller of plastic) and the classic wrist-moved fan. His "butterfly fan" sprouted two large gauze wings, speckled and veined to simulate the real thing, and reciprocated after the manner of Lawrence Hargrave's flapping-wing flying machine of seven years earlier. The user pressed on a small lever in the handle whereupon the wings fluttered in a manner which must have been certain to have caused amusement in public places, and chaos at the opera.

Another novelty to be seen at the Drapers' Hall that year was

* Fan painting is not necessarily so: most of the early workers were men.

Fig. 43

A fine example of a lace fan, this one was presented to Queen Alexandra for use on Coronation Day, 1902, by the Worshipful Company of Fan Makers. The free treatment of the shoulders is especially beautiful as is the Greek influence on the formation of the design.

the dressing-case fan which was a fan and entire toilet case. Said to have been the idea of Mrs Kendal (later Dame Madge Kendal) the actress (born 1848; died 1935) it allowed its fortunate owner the opportunity of performing those beautifying rituals which might otherwise be denied to her through lack of facilities. Originally, the mount was of black gauze with a black velvet mask in the centre so that the owner could keep an eye on all about her as she pursued her toilet. The broad guards contained all her needs behind hinged panels. A tiny mirror, a container for pins, a glove-hook, needles, thread and a pair of scissors. The lower end of the fan contains a miniature powder box and puff, while the tassel opened to reveal a tiny thimble. It was produced in various forms around the 1890s by its London manufacturers, W. Thornhill & Co.

Lace from Honiton in Devon remained the only aspect of the art of fan making in England which was sought after and at the

Paris Exposition of 1900, Devon lace fans were seen. Already at this time, though, fans were no longer of any consequence. The fan, from both the aesthetic standpoint and that of the collector, had passed many years earlier. And Europe was approaching a war which, in the space of four years, took the world aeons beyond the first decade of this century.

There were, though, one or two outposts of the fan which remained for a while. Feather fans, for instance, returned to the fashion scene in the years which followed the First World War and London's large Army & Navy Co-Operative Society Limited advertised:

Real Ostrich Feather Fans.

Mounted on Single Handle	9/- and upwards
Ditto, 5 sticks	24/- do
Ditto, ditto, with Diamante added.	50/- do
Mounted on 8 sticks	67/6 do
„ 10 sticks	75/- do
In stock, or to order.	

This advertisement, from the giant 1,184-page 1924 catalogue, was then followed by a cryptic announcement which read:

Member's own Feathers Cleaned and Dyed and made up into fans.   Prices on application.

CHAPTER SIX

THE LANGUAGE OF THE FAN

The transmission of messages between two people using pre-concerted code is of great antiquity, the earliest system, alluded to by the prophet Jeremiah writing six centuries before the Christian era, was the beacon fire. Polybius (*c.* 210–*c.* 128 BC) writes of a far better method of telegraphic communication which, he says, was invented either by Cleoxenus (the historian of Persia) or Democritus (*c.* 460–357 BC) wherein the alphabet was divided into five portions of nominally five letters each. Ten torch bearers were then used to signal, successively, the column on which the required letter stood, and then the letter itself, both achieved numerically. The coming of the electric telegraph and the semaphore, the first of which was erected on the roof of the Admiralty Office in London in 1816, set the seal on more than 2,000 years of masculine endeavours to get a message across distance without recourse to the indelicacy of voice. The ladies, however, cultivated their own subtle means of communication which did not require the ignition of hay-bales on hill-tops, nor concentration on the wavering needles of the electric telegraph. They used the fan and, in skilful hands, there could be no finer means of what we could call "close-proximity" communication.

The expression "language of the fan" is most probably of Spanish origin for it was Fenella who published in that tongue a guide comprising no less than fifty directions for the operation of the fan as a means of communication. This *vade mecum*, emanating from the country which one may assume was responsible for the invention of the language, was subsequently translated into German by one Frau Bartholomäus and based upon this the Parisian fan-maker J. Duvelleroy, published an English variant.

It must at once be said that, although the initiator of the message was almost always the woman, the intended recipient was not necessarily also female and for this reason the understanding of the signals conveyed by the movement of the fan had to be equally familiar to both sexes. Furthermore, as Disraeli wrote,* "We should remember that here (Cadiz), as in the north, the fan is not confined to the delightful sex. The cavalier also has his fan; and, that the habit may not be considered an indication of effeminacy, learn that in this scorching clime the soldier will not mount guard without this solace." Indeed, the Spanish fan, be it in the hands of male or female, was never still, its perpetual motion portraying the feelings and thoughts which passed through the mind of its owner. The toreador used his fan to excite the bull, whilst the dark-eyed beauty used it as a screen—perhaps but a tantalising, partial screen—to her loveliness in order to excite her man.

The use of the fan and the eye together were cunningly employed by the adept dames and demoiselles, and M. Louis Énault commented shrewdly that "either one alone would suffice for a man's destruction".

Spanish custom precludes lovers and those engaged from being alone together and from this intensely frustrating environment there developed the system of specific communication by code so that the lady-love might enjoy some measure of intimacy with her sweetheart. From these conditions of necessity, it seems likely that the code was developed to the point where a potential suitor might instantly detect an unattached lady and also learn whether or not his attentions were welcomed.

Looked at today, some of the signs and their interpretations may seem terribly naïve but it must be remembered that the customs, privacies, restrictions and morals of times past were totally different from those accepted today and the opportunities for young people to meet and get to know one another were very limited. And it was in the ballroom in the presence of other potential suitors, parents, guardians and chaperons that introductions and love-play had to be acted out as effectively as possible, and quite possibly at an extended range.

Here are some examples of the language of the fan which, by its very complexity, is far more expressive than that of the flower and shows the fan purely as a love-medium:

Carrying in the right hand in front of the face—Follow me
Carrying in the left hand in front of the face—Desirous of acquaintance
* *Contarini Fleming*

Placing it on the left ear—I wish to get rid of you
Drawing across the forehead—You have changed
Twirling in the left hand—We are being watched
Carrying in the right hand—You are too willing
Drawing through the hand—I hate you
Twirling in the right hand—I love another
Drawing across the cheek—I love you
Presented shut—Do you love me?
Drawing across the eyes—I am sorry
Touching tip with the finger—I wish to speak to you
Letting it rest on the right cheek—Yes
Letting it rest on the left cheek—No
Open and shut—You are cruel
Dropping it—We will be friends
Fanning slowly—I am married
Fanning quickly—I am engaged
With handle to lips—Kiss me
Open wide—Wait for me
Carrying in the left hand, open—Come and talk to me
Placing behind the head—Don't forget me
With the little finger extended—Good-bye
The shut fan held to the heart—You have won my love
The shut fan resting on the right eye—When may I be allowed to see
    you?
Presenting a number of sticks, fan apart opened—At what hour?
Touching the unfolded fan in the act of waving—I long always to be
  near thee
Threaten with the shut fan—Do not be so imprudent
Gazing pensively at the shut fan—Why do you misunderstand me?
Pressing the half-opened fan to the lips—You may kiss me
Clasping the hands under the open fan—Forgive me I pray you
Cover the left ear with the open fan—Do not betray our secret
Shut the fully-opened fan very slowly—I promise to marry you

Woolliscroft Rhead instances certain differences between Duvel-
loroy's code and the original Spanish but emphasises that the
principles remain the same. Once the basis was understood, it
is easy to imagine that there could be some considerable measure
of latitude in actual use as indeed would be dependent upon, say,

the relative positions of the two people concerned.

Excepting the use of the fan by the male referred to above as a means of keeping cool, the environment in which the language of the fan would be practised remains unique in the annals of communication. In no other mode of parlance is the very wherewithal of contact the prerogative of but one of the parties.

The English poet and essayist, Joseph Addison (born 1672; died 1719) saw the lady with her fan as a force to be reckoned with and in No. 102 of *The Spectator* for 1711 he published an amusing satire worth quoting just once more:

Mr Spectator,—Women are armed with fans as men with swords, and sometimes do more execution with them. To the end, therefore, that ladies may be entire mistresses of the weapon which they bear, I have erected an academy for the training up of young women in the exercise of the fan, according to the most fashionable airs and motions that are now practised at court. The ladies who carry fans under me are drawn up twice a day in my great hall, where they are instructed in the use of their arms, and exercised by the following words of command: "Handle your fans," "Unfurl your fans," "Discharge your fans," "Ground your fans," "Recover your fans," "Flutter your fans," By the right observation of these few plain words of command, a woman of tolerable genius, who will apply herself diligently to her exercise for the space of but one half-year shall be able to give her fan all the graces that can possibly enter into that little modish machine.

But, to the end that my readers may form to themselves a right notion of this exercise, I beg leave to explain it to them in all its parts. When my female regiment is drawn up in array, with every one her weapon in her hand, upon my giving the word to "Handle their fans," each of them shakes her fan at me with a smile, then gives her right-hand woman a tap upon the shoulder, then presses her lips with the extremity of her fan, then lets her arms fall in an easy motion, and stands in readiness to receive the next word of command. All this is done with a closed fan, and is generally learned in the first week.

The next motion is that of "Unfurling the fan," in which are comprehended several little flirts and vibrations, as also gradual and deliberate openings, with many voluntary fallings assunder in the fan itself, that are seldom learned under a month's practice. This part of the exercise pleases the spectators more than any other, as it discovers on a sudden an infinite number of cupids, garlands, altars, birds, beasts, rainbows, and the like agreeable figures that display themselves to view, whilst every one in the regiment holds a picture in her hand.

Upon my giving the word to "Discharge their fans," they give one general crack that may be heard at a considerable distance when the wind sits fair. This is one of the most difficult parts of the exercise; but I have several ladies with me, who at their first entrance could not give a pop loud enough to be heard at the farther end of a room, who can now discharge a fan in such a manner that it shall make a report like a pocket-pistol. I have likewise taken care—in order to hinder young women from letting off their fans in wrong places or on unsuitable occasions—to show upon what subject the crack of a fan may come in properly. I have likewise invented a fan with which a girl of sixteen, by the help of a little wind which is enclosed about one of the largest sticks, can make as loud a crack as a woman of fifty with an ordinary fan.

When the fans are thus discharged, the word of command in course is to "Ground their fans," This teaches a lady to quit her fan gracefully when she throws it aside in order to take up a pack of cards, adjust a curl of hair, replace a falling pin, or apply herself to any other matter of importance. This part of the exercise, as it only consists of tossing a fan with an air upon a long table—which stands by for that purpose—may be learned in two days' time as well as in a twelvemonth.

When my female regiment is thus disarmed, I generally let them walk about the room for some time, when, on a sudden—like ladies that look upon their watches after a long visit—they all of them hasten to their arms, catch them up in a hurry, and place themselves in their proper stations upon my calling out, "Recover your fans." This part of the exercise is not difficult, provided a woman applies her thoughts to it.

The "Fluttering of the fan" is the last—and, indeed, the

masterpiece of the whole exercise—but if a lady does not mis-spend her time she may make herself mistress of it in three months. I generally lay aside the dog days and the hot times of the summer for the teaching this part of the exercise, for as soon as ever I pronounce, "Flutter your fans" the place is filled with so many zephyrs and gentle breezes as are very refreshing in that season of the year, though they might be dangerous to ladies of a tender constitution in any other.

There is an infinite variety of motions to be made of in the flutter of the fan. There is the angry flutter, the modest flutter, the timorous flutter, the confused flutter, the merry flutter, and the amorous flutter. Not to be tedious, there is scarce any motion of the mind which does not produce a suitable agitation in the fan; insomuch, that if I only see the fan of a disciplined lady I know very well whether she laughs, frowns, or blushes. I have seen a fan so very angry that it would have been danger-ous for the absent lover who provoked it to have come within the wind of it, and at other times so very languishing that I have been glad for the lady's sake the lover was at a sufficient distance from it. I need not add that a fan is either a prude or a coquette, according to the nature of the person who bears it. To conclude my letter, I must acquaint you that I have from my own observations compiled a little treatise for the use of my scholars, entitled, "The Passions of the Fan," which I will communicate to you if you think it may be of use to the public.

So far we have been dealing with the transmission of whole sentences by the movement of the fan. A form of fan existed which allowed a slower but infinitely more precise and useful dialogue to take place. This was the conversation-fan or speaking-fan and the first reference to it appears in *The Gentleman's Magazine* for 1740 which printed a twelve-line piece of doggerel to commemorate the subject.* The interesting point here is that the *modus operandi* of the speaking fan was exactly the same as that described by Polybius 2,000 years ago. The alphabet is divided into five sections, and I can do little better than to quote Rhead's description:†

Five signals are given, corresponding to the five divisions of the

* Woolliscroft Rhead *History of the Fan*, p. 253.
† *ibid.*

alphabet, the different letters, omitting the J, being capable of division into five, the movements 1 2 3 4 5 corresponding to each letter in each division. 1. By moving the fan with the left hand to right arm. 2. The same movement but with right hand to left arm. 3. Placing against bosom. 4. Raising it to the mouth. 5. To forehead.

Example.—Suppose *Dear* to be the word to be expressed. D belonging to the first division, the fan must be moved to the right; then, as the number underwritten is 4, the fan is raised to the mouth. E, belonging to the same division, the fan is likewise moved to the right, and, as the number underwritten is 5, the fan is lifted to the head and so forth. The termination of the word is distinguished by a full display of the fan, and as the whole directions with illustrations are displayed on the fan, this language is more simple than at first might appear.

As might be inferred from the method of use, the conversation-fan was not intended to play any direct part in communication with the male of the species and was reserved for those intimacies which women alone may share, although we might justly assume that the topic of conversation would be not totally unconcerned with the male sex.

Here, though, comes the only disenchanting part of the story. In the same way that today women's fashions in clothes and accessories almost always emanate from the masculine brain, it was a man who recognised that feminine chit-chat could be turned to his advantage. Charles Francis Badini invented *The Original Fanology* or *Ladies Conversation Fan* which was engraved and published by William Cock of 42 Pall Mall, London on August 7th, 1797. The fan bore the legend:

> The telegraph of Cupid in this fan
>> Though you should find, suspect no wrong;
> 'Tis but a simple and diverting plan
>> For ladies to chit-chat and hold the tongue

and with directions as to its use on the flanks, a central medallion showed Venus robbing Cupid of his bow.

So the fan silently served as a method of soundless speech and was probably instrumental in fostering countless *affaire de cœur*. But it also had use as a messenger in its own right. An intriguing procedure took place at certain dances—a variation of which has survived to this day in certain quarters and with a somewhat different end in view. The fans of the ladies present were placed in a hat. The gentlemen, assures *Chambers's Encyclopaedia*, would then select their partners by drawing a fan, for whoever owned the fan which was drawn became the partner—for the dance. This led to careful observation, and after a time a lady became known in society by the fan which she carried.

CHAPTER SEVEN

TYPES OF FAN

When compiling any listing of the many types of fan, one problem at once arises and that is to determine the difference between the contemporary names of different types, and the names by which that variant came to be known either contemporaneously or subsequently. The chicken-skin fan, for example, defines that the leaf or mount is of so-called chicken-skin (see Glossary) and the name "chicken-skin fan" would never have been applied to this genre at the time they were offered for sale. However, this is a term which is now in common usage amongst collectors to define a fan with this type of mount. As another example, the balloon fan was just another type of printed fan, the decoration of which was enlivened by the depiction of a contemporary scene. The fly-whisk, on the other hand, whilst probably not the contemporary name, served no other purpose than that of keeping flies away.

What I have attempted to achieve here is to list all these names, including the names by which the fan or types of fan are known. Those names which have been given that apply to various *genres* are shown in italics. The listing is in two parts—first of all a concordance and then a detailed description of each item.

Advertising	Broken, or Trick
Aide Mémoire	Cabriolet
Assyrian Plaited	Camp
Autograph, or Inscription	Cartographic
Balloon	Ceremonial
Bamboo	Chicken-Skin
Battoir	Chapel
Biblical (see *Church*)	Children's
Botanical	Church
Bridal (see *Wedding*)	Clock
Brisé	Cockade

Commemorative
Conversation
Court
Dagger
Dance
Découpé
Dolls'
Dominotier
Double, or Reversible
Double-Entente
Dressing Case
Dutch
Ecclesiastical (see *Church*)
Egyptian
Empire
Entertainment
Expanding
Feather
Figaro
Filigree
Fire
Flabellum
Flag
Fly-Whisk
Folded, or Pleated
Fortune-Telling, or Gipsy
Giant
Gipsy (see *Fortune-Telling*)
Hundred Faces
Inscription (see *Autograph*)
Ivory
Javanese Shadow
Lace
Lorgnette, or Quizzing
Mandarin
Medallion
Minuet
Modern
Mourning

Mystery, or Puzzle
Neapolitan
Necromantic (see *Fortune-Telling*)
North-American Indian
Opera-Glass (see *Lorgnette*)
Palm
Panorama
Parachute (see *Balloon*)
Peacock Feather
Pompeian
Punkah
Puzzle (see *Mystery*)
Quizzing
Reversible (see *Mystery; Double Entente*)
Revolving Fan, or Roll-up
Rubber
Rush
Sandalwood
Scented
Screen
Shaker
Shovel, or Scoop
Speaking (see *Conversation*)
Swinging (see *Punkah*)
Tea
Telescopic (see *Expanding*)
Theatrical
Thousand Faces (see *Hundred Faces*)
Topical
Tortoise shell
Trick (see *Broken*)
Trompe-L'Oeil
Turtle-shell
Vannus
Ventilabrum
Vernis Martin

163

Grass	Wallpaper
Gun Sen, or War	War
Hand-Screen	Water
Hide	Wedding, or Bridal
Historical	Widowhood
Horn (see *Tortoise shell*)	Winnowing
Humorous	Wooden

ADVERTISING FAN

This was usually a simple, printed fan contrived as a "give-away" to carry a message from its sponsor. These were often presented to ladies at theatres, fetes, trade shows and similar functions and are of little other than curiosity value to collectors. See also SCENTED FANS.

AIDE MÉMOIRE

This encompasses a particular class of fan which relies for its embellishment on the printing of information of a practical kind upon its mounts. Percival* postulates that these may have been intended for use in young ladies' seminaries at dancing lessons, enabling unoccupied moments to be profitably employed. Although they were no doubt both cheap and plentiful at the time of their publication (they are all printed with occasional colouring by hand), they have not survived in quantity and are thus quite scarce. For examples of the aide mémoire, see under CARTOGRAPHIC, HISTORICAL and BOTANICAL. There were many others such as those providing the words and music of songs, the rules and scoring for a game of cards, directions for the figures of country dances and even as parochial as showing the names of holders of boxes at the opera. The greater majority appeared in the second half of the 18th century; and most of these during the last twenty years of it.

ASSYRIAN PLAITED FAN

The Assyrians used a similar type of fan to that used in Egypt which was crescent-shaped, square or triangular. This was a primitive rigid fan woven in grasses. On a relief found at Nimrud near Nineveh on the River Tigris, now in the British Museum, there is a circular arrangement divided into four compartments representing

* *The Fan Book.*

Fig. 44

An autograph fan made of plain, smooth ivory sticks. Dame Adelina Patti
is said to have had one of vellum upon which all the monarchs of Europe
signed their names below some lines of praise and compliment.

the interior of a castle with towers and battlements. A eunuch is
seen waving with his right hand a square, flag-shaped fan which is
almost certainly of this variety. In his left hand is what appears to
be a fly-whisk.

AUTOGRAPH or INSCRIPTION FAN
Originally a rigid plate of ivory or stiff paper, and later made
rather like a normal brisé fan of ivory. Autograph fans were popular
in ancient China as during the period of the Emperor Chien Wen of
the Liang dynasty AD 550. They were used as autograph albums
and were revived during the latter half of the 19th century. Of
necessity, the early ones were plain, relying for their decoration on
the message written upon them. These are rare and valuable today.
More recent specimens were sometimes supplied printed with the
signatures of famous painters or musicians, the latter type being
illustrated with a few bars of music. The ivory surface was prepared
with pumice stone so that the ink would "take".

BALLOON FAN

This is truly a commemorative fan but, because of the immense flights of public fancy which the knowledge that man could cast off the surly bonds of earth was greeted, so many fan mounts depicted various ballooning scenes that they deserve a separate classification. Two brothers in the paper-making business, Joseph Michel and Jacque Etienne Montgolfier made their first successful balloon ascent at Annonay (Ardêche), Southern France on June 5th, 1783. News of the achievement spread far and wide like wildfire and Louis XVI commanded a repeat performance before the entire Court at Versailles. This was the start of a "ballooning cult" which was reflected in a large number of fans depicting balloons. The ascent of MM. Robert and Charles on August 27th, 1783 is also pictured on fans which generally show them looking over the edge of the basket, each holding a flag. Almost all balloon fans are of the etched type, coloured by hand and are not generally of high quality. One prophetic fan depicts Blanchard's balloon of 1784 embellished with verses in flowery language praising the conquest of the air and asserting that soon all the world would journey by air instead of coach. A variety of the balloon fan which we can include here is the "parachute fan" commemorating the first descent by parachute made by Blanchard on August 20th, 1785. Several are to be seen in the Science Museum, London.

BAMBOO FAN

Fans made of bamboo leaves are of great antiquity and date back at least 2,000 years. The split bamboo has been used for making folding fans for a long time and is still used today. The number of sticks in this form ranges from sixteen to thirty-six although the former is the usual number. The bamboo handle for screen fans is also extremely old and was in use in Japan and China. The first folding fans, as invented by the Japanese in or about AD 668–71, were made of folding bamboo. Probably the oldest material for the manufacture of fans and thus as old as the invention of the fan.

BATTOIR

The battoir fan, named after the French for tennis-racquet, is one of the more unusual types of fans and it is immediately recognisable whether open or closed. This type of fan, which was most highly prized in Spain, has far fewer sticks than any other type of fan of the same size. When the fan is open, this paucity of brins is at once noticeable. Usually, the battoir has no more than eight sticks. When the fan is closed, it is obvious that the leaf, having fewer folds, will be disproportionately broad. For this reason, the guards are very wide (hence the allusion to a racquet in the name) and are spade-shaped. Percival* implies that these may have been made in Spain but comments that since they demonstrate considerable skill and craftsmanship, this does not align with the large importation of French fans into Spain.

BOTANICAL FAN

This is one form of a particularly unusual and, today, comparatively rare type of fan believed to have been intended as an AIDE MÉM-OIRE (q.v.) for use in young ladies' seminaries so that they might profitably employ their otherwise unoccupied moments. The botanical fan shows the names of the various parts of a flower on the mount. It is a printed fan.

BRISÉ—See in Glossary, page 32

BROKEN or TRICK FAN

A Chinese invention this is to all intents and purposes an ordinary, often plain, folding fan. When opening from left to right it presents no uncommon feature. However, when handed to another person, the unsuspecting recipient finds to his embarrassment that his attempt to open the fan has somehow separated the mount into many pieces and the sticks just fall apart about the rivet. The secret is in the folding of the mount which is in truth made up of as many pieces as there are sticks and folded in such a manner that when opened one way, the sections engage one with its neighbour and open in a regular fashion. But when the fan is reversed or opened from right to left, the folds no longer engage and each falls free. An American manufacturer was advertising these trick fans for 20c each in the 1880s. They were sometimes used by conjurors in order to amaze their audiences.

CABRIOLET

The cabriolet fan appeared as one manifestation of *la fureur de*

* *ibid.*

cabriolets as Horace Walpole described to his friend Sir Horace Mann in a letter dated June 15th, 1755. It was in this year of the reign of Louis XV that one Josiah Childs, brother of the Earl of Tilney, introduced a light, two-wheeled, one-horse chaise fitted with a large hood and a covering for the legs and lap. The *cabriolet* (the name is still with us today, only it has been shortened to "cab") was an instant success with the Parisians. In the same way that today the supersonic aeroplane is not an infrequent decoration on head-scarves and boy's shirts, and in an earlier generation the symbol of progress and manhood and thus decoration was the motor-car; so Paris went *en cabriolet*. Walpole wrote "men paint them on their waistcoats have them embroidered for clocks to their stockings, and to the women, who have gone all the winter without anything on their heads, are now muffled up in great caps, with round sides, in the form of, and scarce less than, the wheels of chaises." The *cabriolet* also inspired not just a new subject to be depicted on the fan, but also a new type of fan. These fans, which are scarce, are readily identified by the fact that they always have more than one mount; the majority have two mounts representing segments of concentric annular leaves, and very occasionally three leaves. The outer or superior mount always has the greater chord. Most, but not all, cabriolet fans are decorated with the vehicle after which they are named. However, these mid-18th century fans are sometimes to be found with other subjects. The inferior mount is usually less than half the width of the superior and as a rule the separation between the two is approximately equal to the width of the narrower mount. That portion of the sticks which extends between the two leaves is carved or otherwise decorated to match the shoulder of the stick. Flory* gives an alternative name for the cabriolet: *éventail à galerie*.

CAMP

The so-called Camp fan or *Ha uchiwa* (*jin sen*) is a Japanese fan originally introduced from China in the 7th century. It is made of the feathers of the eagle, pheasant or peacock and the handle is usually lacquered red, black or blue, and made of bone or wood.

CARTOGRAPHIC

The cartographic fan is another example of the AIDE MÉMOIRE

* *A Book About Fans.*

(q.v.) group and appears in two forms: either with a complete map of the whole of England, or of particular counties. It is probably dated from the end of the 18th century.

CEREMONIAL FANS

The fan as used in ceremony goes back to the days of ancient Egypt (see Chapter 1) and many special fans produced since that time can lay claim to being designated ceremonial fans of one sort or another. Rhead* relates how the Indians of the Great West used ceremonial fans on the banks of the Lower Mississippi in 1682. A Taensas chief visited La Sieur de la Salle at his camp and was preceded by six attendants to clear a path and prepare the meeting place. The chief then advanced, preceded by two men bearing white fans while a third displayed a disc of burnished copper, probably in representation of the sun.† Its use in far earlier times, its use in the Latin Church and its interrelation with the *flabellum* is described in Chapter 3.

CHAPEL FAN

The chapel fan was published in 1796 and depicted in its centre a group of "The Resurrection of a Pious Family" after a picture by the Rev. W. Peters. This is stipple-engraved, uncoloured and mounted on plain wooden sticks. See catalogue of Fan Leaf Subjects, Chapter 12.

CHICKEN SKIN—see Glossary, page 33

CHILDREN'S FANS

Fans were made for children in Italy and most other European countries during the 18th century. They were both painted and printed and frequently served also some educational value in having the numerals one to ten printed on the leaf. The Dutch also produced small, well decorated and spangled fans for children and although these are noticeably smaller than the general size of fan, they display excellent craftsmanship and beauty. They exist as Vernis Martin brisé as well as chicken-skin and paper specimens.

* *The History of the Fan.*
† *La Salle and the Discovery of the Great West* by Francis Parkman.

CHURCH

The church fan first appeared late in the 1720s and was intended
to be used by church-goers. They received the special sanction of
the Bishop of London and the decoration was usually moralistic.
Not to be confused with CHAPEL (q.v.) fans. See Chapter 12 under
"Gamble".

Fig. 45

A cabriolet-type fan of the Louis XV period shows scenes in French life and,
at the top of the fan, a cabriolet itself.
Picture by courtesy of The British Museum.

CLOCK

Britten (*Old Clocks and Watches and Their Makers*) provides details
of a form of fan which, although in no sense a fan in the accepted
meaning of the term, is sufficiently fan-like to warrant inclusion
here (see Fig. 46). This is, in fact, a timekeeper and is therefore
not intended to be carried but rather to be mounted on a wall.
The earliest fan clock seems to be that described by Britten as
appearing in an engraving of the tutor to Charles, son of King
Philip II of Spain who reigned from 1556 to 1598. The dial comprises
a double fan of white and black slats which expanded and contracted to suit hours of varying length in day and night throughout
the year. From this rather imprecise account one assumes this to be
a semi-astronomical clock which indicated the varying hours of

daylight and darkness through the seasons. The engraving is said to date from about 1570. Other forms of fan timekeepers have been constructed and the general form comprised thirteen very light sticks, *à la brisé*, pivoted in the manner of an ordinary folding fan to a backing covered with velvet. At six o'clock in the morning and in the evening, the fan would be wide open and a serpent, fixed by its tail to the velvet, would point to the hour with its tongue. Immediately after six o'clock, the fan suddenly closes, the serpent still pointing to six, but it would then be the figure on the right hand side of the fan (see Fig. 46). The pivot of the fan was rotated by clockwork driving a rack and pinion controlled by a snail-shaped cam, so allowing the fan to open gradually as the hours progressed, and then suddenly close. Such a fan clock was illustrated in *Harmsworth London Magazine* in 1901. The clockwork motion of this novel clock fan (the sticks of which were delicately decorated in the precise manner of a brisé fan) is very similar to that of the semi-circular clock whose hands move through 180 degrees and then fly back to start over again. One of these clocks is to be seen in the Ilbert Collection (British Museum).

Fig. 46

The fan clock. Each stick was numbered according to the hour and the fan gradually opened, the correct hour being indicated by the small serpent, seen at the lower left stick.

COCKADE FANS

The cockade fan comprises a long handle, the upper end of which forms the centre of a circular fan. When closed, the pleated fan shuts up against the handle. Some examples have, in effect, two guards which, when the fan is fully open, come together as one handle. A folding, telescoping cockade fan is shown in Fig. 61.

COMMEMORATIVE

The fan as a means of commemorating some event was introduced around the early 18th century. These are usually printed or lithographic subjects (particularly during the early 19th century) and serve as contemporary records of some historical event. Percival* mentions an early one representing the coronation of George II in 1727 which shows the King and Queen seated under a canopy with a lion and unicorn above. There were also several fans printed to commemorate the marriage of Princess Anne (daughter of George II) to William, Prince of Orange, in 1734. Battles and naval victories were also subjects for these fans. A number were published depicting persons and events connected with the Peninsular War which were intended for the Spanish market.

CONVERSATION FAN

Also known as the speaking fan, this type is used for the conducting of a silent conversation. The movements of the fan are made to correspond with the letters of the alphabet. A detailed description is given in Chapter 6 (page 153).

COURT FAN

The Japanese court fan dates from the invention of the folding fan in the seventh century. Two main types exist, the thirty-eight-blade *Akome ogi* and the twenty-five-blade *Hi-ogi*. A ceremonial fan carried by the ladies of the Japanese court, this is a brisé-type of fan having long trailing tassels from the guards, these being of such length that in some cases they reach to the ground (see Fig. 14).

DAGGER

The dagger fan deserves inclusion only because by connotation it is

* *The Fan Book.*

considered to be related to our subject. This, however, is not so much a fan but a potentially lethal weapon of Japanese origin which the Chinese subsequently saw fit to forbid. It looks like a folded fan in a case and is made to be kept in the belt of a kimono. The harmless looking accessory is, though, a broad-bladed knife with a seven-inch blade.

DANCE FANS

The *Mai ogi* is literally a fan of a dancing girl. Japanese, it dates from the beginning of the 17th century and is characterised by having ten ribs and a mount made of a very thick paper which is painted with a family crest. The rivet also secures a small piece of lead in the eye of both guards which, in adding weight to the base of the fan, permits more graceful movements of the fan to be made.

DÉCOUPÉ

The earliest European folding fans included the découpé or cut vellum fan, first seen towards the end of the 16th century and throughout the 17th century. They were generally made of vellum or occasionally of tough paper and were pierced and embossed with extreme delicacy to resemble the embroidery of the cut linen and stitching which was so fashionable during this period. Available evidence in the shape of contemporary portraits in which they were featured indicates that this type of fan must at one time have been extremely popular. No doubt due to the extreme friability of its materials, comparatively few have survived. They were sometimes adorned with insertions of mica sticks which passed through slits in the vellum leaf. These mica sticks sometimes formed the ground for delicate paintings and occasionally the leaf would be provided with reserves (uncut, unworked areas of vellum) which would be the base for finely-painted miniatures. The rarity of the découpé fan, whilst it is not always as ornate as those which were to follow, makes it a choice item for the collector and for this reason has been the subject of the counterfeiter's attention—see Chapter 10.

DOLL'S FANS

The beginning of the 19th century saw the rise to perfection of the doll and, by the time of the Great Exhibition, the wax doll with its exquisitely reproduced features was being made in increasing numbers. The dress of these dolls was a microcosm of the real thing and with Victorian and Edwardian finery had to go the dress fan. Fans for dolls are usually no more than two to three inches long and both brisé and paper-mount fans were made. Simple, punched ivory sticks make these tiny objects effective replicas of those found in the adult world.

DOMINOTIER or WALLPAPER

The manufacture of a cheap decorative wallpaper in France to replace expensive Chinese imported papers began in the 1600s. Called *dominos* these measured about 16 inches × 12 inches and were printed from carved wooden printing blocks. The monochrome prints were then hand-coloured by illuminators who often added freehand touches. These printed sheets were used to ornament many objects, to line chests, screens, to make book covers and to make fans. Dominotier or wallpaper fans were made during the 18th century and early 19th century.

DOUBLE or REVERSIBLE

This type of fan will open both ways, i.e. from left to right or from right to left, and show two different pictures on each side, thereby making four pictures visible, two per side, depending on the way it was opened. Brisé by construction, these were fashionable throughout Europe during the latter years of the 18th century and many were made in England. Usual materials were ivory or sandalwood and the effect was achieved quite simply. The fan comprised approximately twice the number of sticks which one would normally expect for a fan of its proportions. Each stick, however, was arranged on its ribbon so that only half of its width was exposed when opened in either direction. Each stick thus carried a segment of two pictures, one to be visible one way, the other for opposite opening. Sometimes called Double-folding. See also MYSTERY.

DOUBLE-ENTENTE

This type of fan is exactly on the principle of the DOUBLE, MYSTERY or PUZZLE (q.v.) fan. The apparent decoration is harmless enough such as a flower, a bird or a landscape. However, by reversing the opening of the fan, a different picture is presented, this time of either a ribald or amorous nature. Although these fans have always been considered an offence to decency, like so many automata of this type they are at once rare and display an exactness and delicacy of workmanship which commands the respect of any collector— even if he has to choose his audience with great care!

DRESSING CASE FAN

Around about 1890–5, Messrs W. Thornhill & Co. produced their "dressing case fan" which was a fan and entire toilet case in one. The sticks were silvered and the mount of black gauze with a black velvet mask set in the centre. Behind this mask, the owner could conduct repairs to her make-up whilst at the same time watching what was happening about her. The broad guards were hollowed out and provided with swivelling, concealed covers. Turning them back revealed behind one a small mirror; behind another a receptacle for hair-pins, scissors, glove-hook and so on. There was also, at the lower end of the fan, a silver box containing a small powder-puff.

DUTCH

The Dutch were great imitators in the design and decoration of their fans. The earliest appear to have been rigid feather fans and frequently are depicted in the masterpieces by the great Flemish artists Van Dyck and Rubens. Painted mounts and folding fans were introduced probably contemporaneously with France and the treatment of the mount closely followed the practice of French and Italian styles. During the 18th century, the Dutch were very fond of using Chinese designs on small ivory brisé fans in the Vernis Martin style. However, the Dutch never matched the artistic finesse of the Oriental execution of the human face and their paintings were in oils, a process never used on Chinese fans. Dutch brisé fans, like those of the French, were small in size, usually about one quarter of a circle, and the elements united by a narrow white silk ribbon placed a short distance from the ends of the sticks which were rounded in profile. The Dutch also made embroidered fans, the execution of which tended towards being rather heavy in appearance.

ECCLESIASTICAL—See CHURCH

EGYPTIAN

The plaited hand-fan (see also under FIRE), the rigid fan and the feathered, non-folding ceremonial fans were all among the earliest of fans made (see Chapter 1). The variety was wide, ranging from the long-handled, semi-circular ceremonial fan to the single ostrich plume used most probably as a fly-whisk.

EMPIRE

Painting as a form of decoration for fans was largely abandoned during the so-called Empire period (1804 to *c*. 1814) in favour of sequins and spangles. These fans were much smaller than those that preceded its introduction, rarely exceeding 7 inches in length and frequently less. Contrasting with this, though, the mount occupies a far greater proportion and the distance from the head to the shoulder is very short. The mount was generally of fabric; silk, gauze, satin and net all being used and the decoration was most commonly stamped metal spangles of various shapes such as flowers, crescents and geometric shapes. Metallic threads were also used to outline designs. The variety of Empire fans is almost endless and they are frequently very dainty, colourful and attractive. Silk specimens appeared in all colours, the most popular being a rosy red and a deep bluish green. In some cases, the mount was further embellished by appliqué either of a different textile material or by mica and gelatines. The guards of Empire fans were often pierced and inlaid with imitation cameos of Wedgewood, glass, jet or jasper. Besides cut steel ornaments, the greater number were simply fretted and backed with a metallic foil, either gilt or coloured. Horn guards were sometimes embellished with tiny imitation stones or pastes fixed into shallow depressions in the surface. One feature of the Empire-style fan is that the stick is generally in perfect keeping with the leaf, thus suggesting that the entire fan was made in one workshop.

ENTERTAINMENT

This somewhat loose term is given to those fans which portrayed on their mounts illustrations of popular and fashionable resorts, entertainment and such like. Typical subjects were Bartholomew Fair (last held in 1855 after seven centuries of existence), Ranelagh (the public garden opened in 1742 and terminated in 1804),

Vauxhall Gardens (opened *c.* 1661 as the New Spring Gardens, and closed in 1859), the famed Crescent at Buxton and similar attractions. The Pump Room at Bath was featured on one, the Parades at Bath on another. These all appear to have been published by speculators rather than the *entrepreneurs*.

EXPANDING

The invention of the expanding fan appears to be closely tied up with the changing custom of ladies' dress which saw the introduction of the small *reticule* or hand-bag for this fan was made to be telescoped into a sufficiently small size to fit inside. The *reticule* was carried by ladies of polite society during the first half of the 19th century. The fan was simply engineered, the telescoping being effected by the simple expedient of not attaching the leaf to the sticks. The sticks were very short in relation to the mount which was generally doubled and starched to provide radial rigidity. The short sticks were located in full-radius pockets. With the fan closed, the mount could then be slid down towards the head, so effectively shortening the length of the closed fan. When opened, the mount was retained by the angle of the sticks. There were several varieties, including a more conventional fan, the guards and sticks of which were each in two pieces, pin-jointed at the shoulder so that the fan could be "broken" back on itself in the closed position.

FEATHER FAN

The ancient Greeks used fans of peacock feathers as did the Pharaohs. Fans made of ostrich feathers date back to the 16th century when feathers were first imported from Venice. This trade continued for many years and in no country were they more extensively used than in England. The Chinese used the feathers of the Argus pheasant in the early 19th century and peacock feathers have been used both for the main portion of the fan and also for decoration to chicken-skin and paper fans. Feather fans are both rigid and folding.

FIGARO

The success of Beaumarchais' comedy *Le Mariage de Figaro*, first performed in Paris in 1874, inspired the publishing of fans bearing a scene from the play plus stanzas of verse from its text. Whilst the true Figaro fan naturally relates to this comedy, the term is loosely applied to those other fans which were produced bearing scenes and texts from contemporary operas, such as *Tarare* (again by Beaumarchais with music by Salieri, first performed on June 8th, 1787 and later renamed *Axur, Re d'Ormus*), Grétry's *Richard, Coeur de Lion* (1784), Dalayrac's *Nina ou la Folle par Amour* (1786) and *Raoul de Créqui*, and numerous other operas and plays, the titles and authors of which are no longer familiar to most of us.

FILIGREE

The first filigree fans were of Chinese origin, the Orientals being greatly skilled in this art. Sometimes they were of gold but more often of silver gilt, the gilding serving the dual purpose of preventing tarnishing and of decoration. The filigree of finely-pierced ivory and horn, and of filigree lace are both quite different and of much later origin. Filigree was often used with, or formed the basis of, Chinese enamel work.

FIRE

The fire fan was a plaited hand fan used by the Egyptians (see under EGYPTIAN) which also had other domestic purposes. Its use was to fan up the flames.

FLABELLUM

Flabellum (plural=*flabelli*), neuter. The diminutive of *flabrum* (meaning blasts of wind or a breeze) and meaning a small fan. The true Latin name for a fan and one later used to describe the ECCLES-IASTICAL fan (q.v.).

FLAG

The flag fan was common to the whole of the East and a greater proportion of the West and is of great antiquity. Its ancestry can be brought right up to date with the small hand flag. During its historical period, it was made of plaited grasses and in some cases was loose on the handle to allow it to be swung round and round like a rattle.

FLY-WHISK

The earliest fly-whisk fan was the single ostrich feather. Again, this is of great antiquity being known in the major part of the East and parts of the West. The whisk and fly-flap were made of horse-hair, peacock feathers, grasses, palm leaves and numerous other similar materials. The yak-tail was also used.

FOLDING or PLEATED
The general term given to a fan which folds up as distinct from a rigid fan. The leaf is thus pleated into superimposing folds.

FORTUNE TELLING
The fortune-telling fan appeared during the period 1790 to about 1810 although isolated examples were made outside these dates. The leaves were almost entirely devoted to the printed word. A variant, the Gipsy fan, appeared in quantity during the 18th century. This featured a central medallion showing a gipsy telling fortunes, and the different cards for telling fortunes, together with their significance, arranged in four rows over the general field of the fan. These cards and explanations extended over both sides of the leaf. One type, called the Oracle, was published in London in 1800. Another, the Wheel of Fortune, appeared about the same time and showed on its mount the faces of four gipsies, one of them being a Norwood Gipsy. This followed the breaking up of the vast gipsy settlement at Norwood, then just outside London, in May, 1797. Yet another variety, called the Necromantic fan, appeared as early as 1734 and depicted a necromancer being consulted by ladies.

GIANT
The *Mita ogi* or giant closing fans were featured in the pageantry at Ise in honour of the Sun Goddess, the traditional originator of the Japanese dynasty. It was six or seven feet in length and was made of six sheets of painted *Hi-no-ki* (wood of the yew family). In the ceremonies, five men would each be appointed to carry one of these huge fans.

GIPSY—See FORTUNE-TELLING

GRASS
The most primitive of all fans includes the switch of grasses, no doubt originally just gathered loosely and held in the hand, but

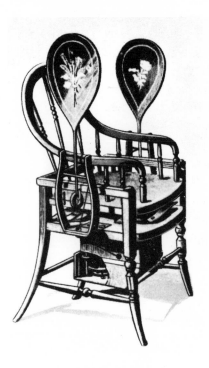

Fig. 47

The air-conditioned armchair was another attempt to overcome the stuffi-
ness of Victorian homes. Above the arms two large fans were arranged in
such a manner that as soon as anyone sat on the seat, the weight of the
person acted on a clockwork mechanism which caused the fans to flap to
and fro. Any slight lateral displacement of the head was no doubt rewarded
by a painful entanglement in the mechanism.

later conjoined with a wooden handle. Grasses, of which rush and
bamboo are types, were initially employed whisk-fashion or loose,
but were woven or plaited into semi-rigid shapes.

GUN SEN
This is the name of a folding iron battle fan introduced by the
Japanese during the 12th century. It was used by generals, court
nobles, *samurai* and court officers.

HAND-SCREEN

These are generally rigid fans, early ones being woven from vegetable materials or of painted wood. Later examples were of thin cardboard, shield-shaped and sometimes printed with a line-engraved design which was afterwards coloured, these being early 19th century in origin. See also HIDE.

HIDE

Screen fans were occasionally made of leather or hide. These were usually round or oval in shape and were the product of more primitive peoples. The majority of these seem to be of African origin and some are decorated, in addition to the natural pattern of the leather, by appliqué designs in different coloured leather.

HISTORICAL

The historical fan belongs to the AIDE MÉMOIRE (q.v.) group and has printed upon the leaf a synopsis of the history of England. First published in 1793, the fan is printed in a very plain style and provides dates and basic facts.

HORN—See TORTOISE SHELL in Chapter 8

HUMOROUS

Lithographed or engraved fans published during the first half of the 18th century and on into the 19th often took as their subjects either the humorous treatment of topical events, or gave advice of a whimsical nature on such subjects as love, success, wealth and health.

HUNDRED FACES

Of Chinese origin, this type of fan, also sometimes called Thousand Faces, is painted with large numbers of figures each of which has a face carved and painted on ivory and separately attached. The belief, held in some circles, that these faces are human fingernails is without foundation. These are very unusual and strangely attractive pieces. The French later produced copies but these lacked the Oriental sensitivity of the ivory working and painting. See also MANDARIN.

INSCRIPTION—See AUTOGRAPH

IVORY—See in Chapter 8

JAVANESE SHADOW
A rigid Javanese hand screen of finely-cut water-buffalo rawhide upon which is a design often featuring dancing girls embellished by gold and colours. The handle was generally of shaded or brown water-buffalo horn.

LACE
Fans with lace mounts first appeared during the second half of the 19th century and the medium was thoroughly exploited up to the early years of the present century. Brussels lace, Chantilly, Batenburg, Italian Burano, Carrickmacross, Reticella and Duchesse have all been used to make often very beautiful fans. Usually the fineness of the lace and its embellishment is enhanced by the use of plain wooden sticks, or sticks with but modest decoration. Devon's Honiton lace and the flat needle-point of Ireland's Youghal lace have also been much sought after by fan-makers. There are exceptions to this approach to stick decoration such as the exquisite fan presented to Queen Alexandra in 1902 by the Worshipful Company of Fan Makers. (This is shown in Fig. 43.) Again, some of the products of M. Duvelleroy in Paris featured the finest lace decoration with richly-painted and pierced ivory sticks.

LORGNETTE
Made at the end of the 18th century and the beginning of the 19th, the lorgnette fan first appeared during the 17th century in Paris where it was known as an opera-glass fan. A small spy glass was set in the principal sticks, either at the top of the panache or at the rivet or head so that a magnified view of some object (or person) of interest could be obtained.

MANDARIN
A Chinese fan of vivid colouring and decorated with faces in carved ivory. See also HUNDRED FACES.

MEDALLION
The medallion fan was contemporaneous with the CABRIOLET FAN (q.v.) and had a mount of finely-woven silk painted with a light

ground ornamented with three medallion subjects. The central medallion might be elliptical, rectangular or circular, the symmetry of the layout being maintained by a pair of smaller medallions, one to each side. The paintings were the work of highly-skilled minia- turists and displayed a detail quite as cleverly as on the more costly chicken-skin fans. See also the Glossary.

MINUET FAN

The term "minuet" is applied, with little foundation, to small brisé fans which appear to have been imported, and are (says Percival*) probably of Dutch origin. Small brisé fans of great beauty were made during the period of the Regency and William IV. Those to which the apellation "minuet" has been applied are of later origin and are usually decorated rather crudely with rustic scenes, floral designs or groups of *amorini*, sometimes pseudo-Watteau.

MODERN FANS

Fans are still manufactured today in the Orient, France and Spain. The better examples of this class of modern fans are made of sandal- wood, pierced by stamping, and have mounts of silk, satin or lace. Injection-moulded nylon and other plastics are also used. The fan today, though, is no longer a costume accessory and whereas in warmer climates it is used for its original purpose, the majority of modern fans are purely for novelty or decoration.

MOURNING FAN

There are several types of mourning fan, all intended for use during periods of family or public solemnity. These were sometimes un- coloured prints and etchings or engravings or pen-and-ink drawings. The subjects were sometimes of sadness, and at others classical or Biblical. They were in use in France at the time of the execution of Louis XVI and these contained portraits of the King and Queen, usually concealed in the general decoration or only visible when the fan was but partially opened. These Royalist fans, not unnaturally, aroused the fury of the Republicans. English examples were pub- lished at the time of the demise of George III and showed, in one design, the figure of Britannia placing a wreath at the foot of a pedestal carrying the bust of the late King. Another variety features

* *The Fan Book.*

a weeping girl and a pedestal carrying an urn, weeping willows behind parting to show a distant view of Windsor Castle. Other mourning fans are characterised by a lack or total absence of colour, black and grey overlaid with white toning the mount and dark-stained ivory sticks with simple embellishments in silver.

MYSTERY or PUZZLE

This type of fan was popular during the 18th century and is always of the brisé type. The sticks overlap by exactly half, this meaning that there are twice as many sticks in a mystery fan as there would be comparably-proportioned sticks in an ordinary brisé fan of the same size. The ribbon is so arranged that the fan opens equally well either way, i.e. from left to right, or from right to left. They are of particular interest since the fan carries not the usual two pictures (one on each side), but four. If the fan is opened left to right one pair of pictures is displayed, one to each side. If the fan now be opened from right to left, that part of each stick which was hidden by the overlap when opened the other way is now displayed to reveal two more pictures, the earlier two now being covered. The true mystery fan has four subjects of ordinary character, usually contrasting bright colours so producing an immediately detectable effect. Others, known as DOUBLE-ENTENTE (q.v.) concealed as alternative pictures subjects of a less innocent character.

NEAPOLITAN

There are two distinct classes of Neapolitan fans. The first has a figure as a central subject and this is usually taken from classical mythology. In the second type, the field is divided into panels, usually one superior and the other two inferior. The panels are decorated with views such as the Bay of Naples or Vesuvius in the central one with other Italian views such as the Colosseum in Rome in the others. There are large numbers of these fans and they date from about 1748 to 1800.

NECROMANTIC—See FORTUNE-TELLING

NORTH AMERICAN INDIAN

The fans of the North American Indians are usually formed of the feathers of the larger birds and amongst the Blackfoot nation, eagles' feathers were used as a standard of valour at the advent of the white man. The handle was of braided grasses, doeskin, deer hide or other readily-available material. Some fans were made of white duck quills by the Eastern Canadian Indians and one of these in the Doble collection has a birch bark handle ornamented by coloured quill and straw embroidery.

Fig. 48

The Pedal Zephyrion was a mid-Victorian invention intended to provide a cooling breeze whilst leaving both hands free. This was just one of the many largely impractical utility contrivances of the era.

OPERA-GLASS—See LORGNETTE

PALM

The natural fan provided by the leaves of the palm tree, particularly the curious natural folding leaves of the Ceylonese Talipot palm (see Chapter 12) has been used over the centuries in both domestic utilitarian and ceremonial duties.

PANORAMA

The panorama fan was a French invention dating from about 1830. It was always in the form of a rigid flat or screen-fan of more or less rectangular shape. In the centre was a rectangular window behind which was placed a travelling picture or panorama. This was rolled around ivory-handled spindles arranged vertically within the thickness of the fan at each side, the small, turned knobs protruding below the lower edge of the fan and at each side of the handle. Rotation of either knob would thus draw the picture back and forth behind the window. One is shown as Plate XXIV-7 in *Fan Leaves* published by The Fan Guild.

PARACHUTE—See BALLOON

PEACOCK FEATHER

The beauty of the peacock's feathers has always made them highly desirable as a material for fan construction and of all the feather fans made, these are the most sought after. Some folding fans of the last century were trimmed with these feathers but the real beauty is found in the total plumage of the fixed feather fan.

POMPEIAN

Most probably Neapolitan in origin, these fans have upon their leaves as principal decoration a copy of one of the frescoes from the excavations of the overwhelmed city of Pompeii. The composition usually occupies a rectangular central panel in the fan, the rest of the leaf being filled in with less important details. The colouring of these fans is governed by that of the original mural decoration and is thus rather heavy since the primary tones are black, red and rich buff, merging to orange with other colours. These fans date from the second half of the last century. (The major excavations were begun in 1863 following the discovery of a street some 113 years earlier. Pompeii, an ancient city of Campania, was buried by volcanic ashes from Vesuvius on the night of August 24th, AD 79).

PUNKAH

The punkah, from the Hindustani word *pankha*, is the name given to large swinging fans found originally in East India. These comprised cloth-covered frames hinged to hang vertically from the ceiling of a room and they were moved to and fro by cords usually controlled by servants. The punkah was kept in constant motion for two reasons— to cool the occupants of the room and to keep flies and other insects from alighting on foodstuffs. Punkahs were certainly in use in the early 18th century and around this time travellers took word of them to other parts of the world, particularly central America where they are sometimes found as part of the Colonial house. Although the true punkah is of cloth and often carpet-like in appearance, it has also been made in metal and wood.

PUZZLE—See MYSTERY

QUIZZING
Popular at the end of the 18th century and the beginning of the 19th was the quizzing fan, which had a large mount equipped with large peep-holes covered with transparent material so that when opened the fan showed a series of apparent perforations around its upper border. These would be concealed as part of the pattern. See also LORGNETTE.

REVERSIBLE—See MYSTERY: DOUBLE-ENTENTE

REVOLVING FAN or ROLL UP FAN
This is of Japanese origin and is known as the *Maki uchiwa*. It comprises a slender bamboo handle or guard. This is slotted for the major portion of its length and into this slot fits the circular face or mount of the fan. This consists of a large number of slender bamboo strips glued to a paper or silk backing in such a way that, like a roller shutter, the mount can be rolled up. It is cut into a circular shape and inserted into the slot in the handle, being secured in place by a central pivot. With the mount arranged so that the bamboo elements are at right-angles to the handle, it is a perfectly rigid fan. By rotating the mount through ninety degrees, it is then easily rolled round the stick and tied with thread.

RUBBER
A fan of hard black rubber which, when the handles were rotated, opened out into a $9\frac{1}{2}$ inch diameter circle, was patented by Henry B. Goodyear in May, 1858. The fan, which had nine leaves, was considered to be "a notable achievement" and one survives in the Doble collection.

RUSH

A form of primitive, grass fan popular in West Africa and found in the Hawaiian Islands, Samoa and similar locales. These are plaited into spear, spatula and kite shapes and sometimes used different coloured rushes.

SANDALWOOD

See reference in Chapter 8. A smooth, fine-grained wood which lends itself to fine carving and piercing without splitting. It has been widely used for many centuries for the manufacture of fans and is still in use today. The wood is aromatic and has a natural, fine colour.

SCENTED

Fans made of scented wood were introduced into the French court by Anne of Austria (wife of Louis XIII of France, born 1601; died 1666). The *peau de senteur* (fan of scented skin) was popular in France, Spain and Italy during the 18th century. Scented paper fans were also made, largely as an advertisement by perfume manufacturers (see under Rimmel in Chapter 12), during the last century both in France and England.

SCREEN FAN

Screen fans, rigid fans and hand-screens were introduced from China to Japan, according to Rhead* quoting unspecified native authorities, at the end of the 6th century AD. These have appeared in many shapes and forms, some as natural PALM (q.v.), circular, pear-shaped, heart-shaped and in other forms. The fan was either made of solid material or comprised a light frame covered with textile or other flexible substance. The earliest engraved fans were the hand screens used in Italy and elsewhere in the 17th century and the type received a renewed popularity in the 18th century.

SHAKER

The various Shaker communities in the United States produced a variety of fans during the last century, most of which appear to have been of feathers (those of the turkey and peacock being popular) with handles of woven quill, horn or wood. The turkey feather

* History of the Fan.

188

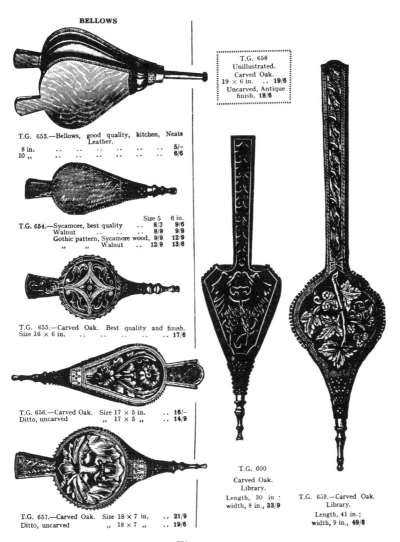

BELLOWS

T.G. 653.—Bellows, good quality, kitchen, Neats Leather.

8 in.	5/-
10 ,,	6/6

	Size 5	6 in.
T.G. 654.—Sycamore, best quality	8/3	9/6
Walnut	8/9	9/9
Gothic pattern, Sycamore wood,	9/9	12/9
,, ,, Walnut	12/9	13/6

T.G. 655.—Carved Oak. Best quality and finish.
Size 16 × 6 in. **17/6**

T.G. 656.—Carved Oak. Size 17 × 5 in. .. **16/-**
Ditto, uncarved ,, 17 × 5 ,, .. **14/9**

T.G. 657.—Carved Oak. Size 18 × 7 in. .. **21/9**
Ditto, uncarved ,, 18 × 7 ,, .. **19/6**

T.G. 658
Unillustrated.
Carved Oak.
19 × 6 in. .. **19/6**
Uncarved, Antique
finish, **18/6**

T.G. 600
Carved Oak.
Library.
Length, 30 in ;
width, 8 in., **33/9**

T.G. 659.—Carved Oak.
Library.
Length, 41 in.;
width, 9 in., **49/6**

Fig. 49

The Italian Egyptologist Rosellini, as well as discovering much about their use of the early fan, found that the Egyptians had found an alternative to the fire-fan at a very early date. In paintings which he found, Egyptians were shown in the act of blowing fires using bellows. Certainly the Romans used bellows and so this development of the fire-fan goes back almost 3,000 years. In 1920, London's Army & Navy Cooperative Society offered a choice range of modern bellows for sale.

fans are the most prolific and many resemble closely the feather fans of the American Indians.

SHOVEL or SCOOP
The name of this type of non-folding fan appears to owe its existence to the Fan Guild and aptly describes a fan of unusual shape which is used in a manner unlike the normal fan. The face of the fan is concave or scoop-shaped and the instrument is used by moving it in an arc towards and away from the face. The shape is achieved by a curved extension to the handle which is an integral part. This is bill-hook shaped but is generally so arranged that the point of the tip is in line with the handle, the back curving outwards. The framework of the fan extends from the shoulder of the handle to the tip and, when covered with leather or textile material, the result is this peculiar shape.

SPEAKING—See CONVERSATION

SWINGING—See PUNKAH

TEA FANS
The *Rikiu ogi* or tea fan first appeared in Japan in or around the period 1596–1601 and is used during the Tea Ceremonies. It is a narrow-opening, three stick fan covered with thick paper bearing designs drawn from the Impressionist school. Being reserved solely for handing round small cakes, its use in fanning is strictly taboo.

TELESCOPIC—See EXPANDING

THEATRICAL
These are an unusual variety and the earliest date from the first half of the 18th century. They are seldom well executed and the colours are generally rather dead and uninteresting. What is of interest though is that they show the styles of presentation used by players of the period characterised by the wearing of the ordinary dress of the day only occasionally modified to suit the supposed period of the action. As well as folding fans, the hand-screen also appeared in the theatrical form. Another variety, this time similar to the OPERA FAN (q.v.) was printed with the names of subscribers

together with the numbers of their boxes or seats at a particular theatre. These date from the second half of the 18th century and an early example, dated 1788, gives the plan of the King's Theatre; another the plan of the Opera House in 1797.

THOUSAND FACES—See HUNDRED FACES

TOPICAL

The topical fan was entirely a product of the 18th century. Rhead* states that it was the fan of the people, the poor relation of the more aristocratic painted fan. The engraved topical fan became the purveyor of history, presenting a running commentary on current affairs. Royal and distinguished personages, naval and military events, all were portrayed on the mounts of these relatively cheap fans.

TORTOISE SHELL—See references in Chapter 8

TRICK—See BROKEN

TROMPE-L'OEIL

Trompe-L'Oeil, from the French meaning still-life deception, is the name given to those fans whose mounts depict items of still life such as bowls of fruit, garlands of flowers, roses and suchlike, in particular when they are treated in a three-dimensional manner. Their period extended from the end of the 18th century through the 19th century and their style is both European and Asian. For this reason, any fan referred to as Trompe-L'Oeil must be qualified by further description.

TURTLE-SHELL

Turtle-shell has been used in the manufacture of small hand-screen fans, the two portions held together with metal plates and the whole fitted with a wooden or other type of handle.

VANNUS

Vannus (plural=*vanni*), feminine gender. The Latin name for a winnowing fan. See definitions at the head of the Introduction, page 25.

* *The History of the Fan.*

VENTILABRUM

Ventilabrum (plural=*ventilabri*), neuter. Derived from *ventus* meaning wind; *via ventilo* meaning to toss to and fro in the air or to fan. A winnowing fork. The modern equivalent would be something like a pitch-fork. The word subsequently used to describe ECCLESIASTICAL fans (q.v.).

Fig. 50

Man's first uses for the fan were as a dual-purpose utility object. He used it to cool his brow in the summer, and to blow his fire in the winter. *The Royal Magazine* for November, 1898, proved that the need still existed, and that it had been met with Victorian ingenuity.

1. White feather folding fan tipped with marabou. An extremely fine floral painting is executed on the feathers—a remarkable achievement considering the extreme delicacy needed to paint on this surface. Punched ivory sticks and well-carved guards. Chinese, *c*. 1820. 10 inches (26cm).

2. Painted vellum mount depicting a battle between Les Blondes et Les Brunes Putti, signed "Alexandre". Very finely pierced and carved mother of pearl sticks and guards, the guards bearing a ducal crown. French, *c*. 1850. 12½ inches (31cm).

3 and 4. Painted vellum mount showing Chinese figures with appliqué robes of iridescent mother of pearl and decorations made of pieces of real feather. The sticks and guards of tortoise shell ornamented with silver and gilt motifs. The reverse shows two figures in a garden scene. Oriental, c. 1780.

5. Mandarin fan, cloisonné enamelled silver sticks and guards, figures with ivory faces and brocade robes. Many of the painted figures are holding fans. Contained in black, glazed wooden case. Mid-19th century. 9 inches (23cm).

6. Finely finished sticks and guards of ivory are decorated with gilt and coloured lacquer. The mount is of paper with an assymetric painting showing a forest scene in the larger portion, and a ceremonial table in the smaller one. Chinese, probably early 19th century. 10½ inches (27cm).

7. Mandarin fan. Pressed ivory sticks and very finely carved guards. The mount is painted in vivid blues and reds with 100 figures with ivory faces on each side of the fan and many of the figures are dressed in robes of appliqué silk brocade. Chinese, mid-19th century. 11 inches (28cm).

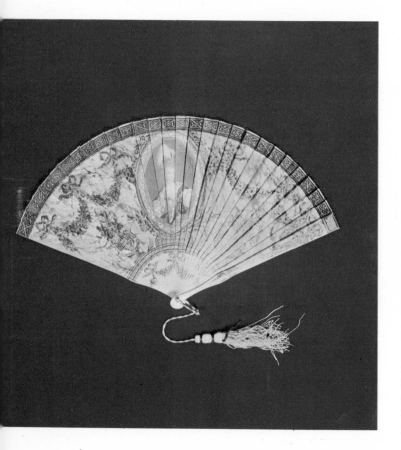

8. Small French ivory brisé fan rather crudely decorated with painted garlands of flowers. The centre medallion is a hand-coloured stipple engraving of Marie Antoinette. The fan may date from the last quarter of the 18th century but is more likely to be of Empire period or even later.

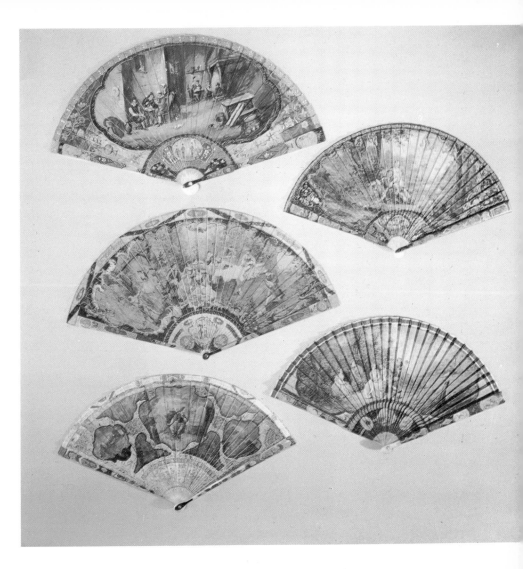

9. A group of Vernis Martin brisé fans, all *c.* 1740–50. Top left: A tavern scene with figures drinking and playing cards. There is a large fireplace around which a group is sitting chatting. The reverse shows a Tyrolean village scene. Chinese flowers are shown in the gorge reserves. 8½ inches (22cm). Top right: Rinaldo returning from battle with discarded armour on the ground as he is being comforted by Armida. Overhead is Cupid in a chariot. The reserve shows Chinese figures and floral decoration. On the reverse is a country mansion in a forest, the lower part showing a floral arrangement. 7½ inches (19cm). Centre: Painted after the style of Watteau with figures enjoying a fête champêtre, a maiden on a swing and figures dancing to a lute player. The reserve is in chinoiserie. The reverse painted with medallions of musical instruments and the centre showing a mountain village landscape. 8½ inches (22cm). Lower right: This fan displays more clearly defined, rounded shoulders and is painted with a rustic scene. Lower left: Unusual Chinese style of decoration, the centre cartouche showing a seated figure. The six other pictures, all in irregular-shaped cartouche, are in shades of the same colour or drab.

10. Orpheus with his lyre playing to the lambs, dogs and cows. Painted chicken-skin mount, ivory sticks decorated with musical instruments and guards of tortoise shell inlaid with mother of pearl, itself carved and inlaid. Italian, *c.* 1740. 11½ inches (29cm).

11. The reverse of the fan shown in *Plate 10.* Pan is seen with a nymph and Cupid with bow and quiver of arrows. Poseidon, God of the Ocean, reclines on the left.

12. Rinaldo returning home from battle (compare with brisé fan shown in *Plate 9* which has the same subject but with a different realisation). The sticks are pierced into an overall design. English, *c.* 1750. 11 inches (28cm).

13. Painted chicken-skin mount showing lovers seated beneath a tree surrounded by figures bearing garlands. In the distance a church on a hill, the whole with a decorative, floral border. The reverse is a pastoral scene. The sticks are pierced and decorated in a curious fashion and set with gilt and silver designs. The guards are well carved with tiny cameos. French, *c.* 1780. 10½ inches (27cm).

14. Mythological scene depicting Venus and Adonis. Ivory sticks embellished with fine miniature paintings of pastoral scenes and Chinese figures, the guards of mother of pearl inset with paintings. The reverse shows an abbey in ruin set in pastoral scene. The gorge of the sticks is divided into two sections: the upper one being worked overall into a delicate design and the lower one profiled in plain ivory. Flemish, *c.* 1740. 11½ inches (29cm). *15.* Right: detail from *Plate 14.*

16. Venus and Vulcan by his forge with the young Bacchus on the left. Finely-carved and pierced sticks with rounded shoulders worked overall into a design, the sticks likewise pierced and carved. Reverse: Chinese figures with centre one riding a chariot pulled by a doe. French, *c.* 1780. 10½ inches (26cm). *17.* Centre: detail from *Plate 16.* *18.* Below: reverse of the fan shown in *Plate 16.*

19. Very fine early gouache-painted chicken-skin fan, the sticks with square-cut shoulders, painted and inlaid with overall design, heightened by inserts of mica, the guards to match. The reverse shows a castle keep. French, *c.* 1780. 10½ inches (26cm). *20.* Below: enlarged detail from the fan shown in *Plate 19*.

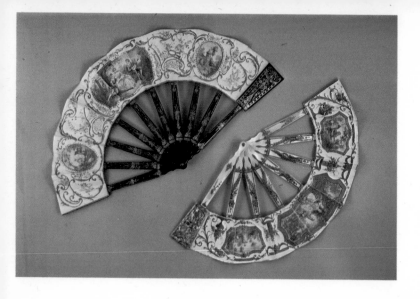

21. Two battoir fans. The first is painted on chicken-skin after Watteau, with sticks and guards of tortoise shell inlaid with gilt and silver piqué. French, *c.* 1840. 8½ inches (22cm). The second is also painted after Watteau, the sticks and guards with gilt decorative design on mother of pearl. 7½ inches (19cm).

22. Tortoise shell with over-laid silver sticks and guards, the design being arranged about unequal numbers of sticks. (ie 4, 2, 2, 1). The painting representing Venus and Adonis. Possibly German, *c.* 1820.

23. Lithographed mount with views in Madrid, the top panels depicting bull-fight scenes. The reverse showing angelic figures around a monument. Mother of pearl sticks and guards decorated overall with gilt. Spanish, *c.* 1850. Formerly in the possession of HRH Princess Royal. Enclosed in modern transparent plastic case. 9 inches (23cm).

24. Esther before King Ahasuerus. Chicken-skin mount painted in soft tones. Ivory sticks and guards, painted decoration, the fan housed in a transparent show case, *c.* 1700.

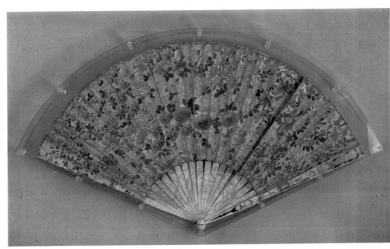

25. The reverse of the fan shown in *Plate 24*. Finely painted with a floral design overall. A curious feature is that the outline painting on the gorge corresponds with the painting on the other side.

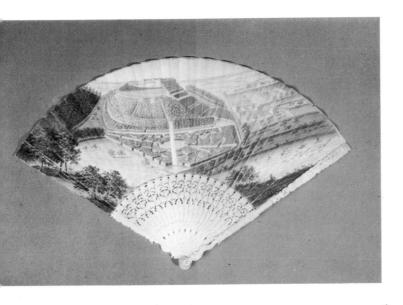

26. Printed mount showing a view of Belvoir Castle, Leicestershire, seat of the Duke of Rutland, before completion. The scene shows the south view of the garden layout below the east slope and the maze. A hunt is in progress in the right foreground, and, centre foreground, there stands an obelisk. The sticks and the guards are of carved ivory, the gorges being dolphin-shaped and the head carved like a shell. English, *c.* 1740. 11 inches (28cm).

27. Top Left, Ivory brisé fan depicting George Morland's *The Tea Garden* painted in 1790. The original (above) is in the Tate Gallery. English. *28.* Left, the reverse side of the fan shown in *Plate 27.* A full cover landscape.

29. Delilah depriving Samson of his strength by cutting off his hair with shears whilst the Philistines wait armed with a rope by which they will enslave him. Painted bone sticks with vignettes, the guards of ivory with mother of pearl overlay. French, probably late 18th century. 11 inches (28cm).

30. Painted chicken-skin mount portraying the Queen of Sheba with her train bearers approaching King Solomon seated. On the left is the tomb of Nestor, King of the Pylos and on the right are Roman gladiators. The reverse shows a shepherd boy with a distaff. The sticks are very finely carved and pierced into an overall design and the guards are likewise worked to extreme delicacy. English, *c.* 1760. 11½ inches (29cm).

31. Ivory brisé fan painted with central cartouche showing Constable's *Willi Lott's Cottage* flanked by two fine miniatures showing John and Mary Constable. English, *c.* 1830. *32.* Below, the reverse side of the fan shown in *Plate 31* showing the entire area given over to a copy of Constable's *Hay Wain.* The original of this is in the Tate Gallery. A print of the painting is shown below.

33. A pair of painted fan featuring the same centre subject on the painted mount the nobility feeding the poor who are seated around a table. The interesting feature is the style of decoration of the surrounds. Each appears complete and in keeping with the subject and yet each is different, so displaying the skills of the artists involved. The top fan has sticks and guards of pierced mother of pearl with silver and gilt decoration. The lower one has similar sticks encrusted with gold and the guards bearing convex oval mirrors surmounted by a ducal crown. The reverse of the upper fan shows a group of figures paying homage to Cupid: that of the lower one shows a group of figures in a riverside scene on either side of which are dancing couples. Probably French, mid-19th century.

34. Painted village scene with Chinese figures. A similar type of subject on the reverse. Pierced ivory sticks and guards. English, c. 1750. 10 inches (25cm).

35. Painted vellum mount showing the embarkation of troops and supplies to warships lying at anchor in the bay. Guards of mother of pearl, sticks of tortoise shell, both decorated with gilt inlay. Early 19th century.

36. The reverse of the fan shown in *Plate 35*. Three fans painted in the Chinese style, the one on the left showing a lady at her toilette, the central one a gentleman greeting a lady and her daughters, the one on the right showing a soldier escorting his bride and attendants.

37. Hand-coloured lithograph showing a garden scene with a gladiator presenting a boar's head to a seated maiden. The sticks and guards of finely-carved mother of pearl on thin pearl sheet, with gilt ornamentation. The reverse shows a group of maidens in conversation beside a well. Possibly German, *c.* 1840. 10½ inches (27cm).

38. Two feather fans with tortoise shell sticks. The top one is 12 inches long and is made of peacock feathers. The lower one has fine iridescent feathers in blue, green and gold. This one is 7 inches long and both are English, late Victorian.

39. Pair of fan-shaped bronze Chinese trays with gold inlay, also round cloisonné dish 12 inches diameter. Fan designs in coloured enamels. Oriental.

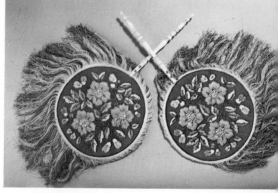

40. A pair of red velvet round fire screen fans embroidered in beadwork and pearls surrounded by a silk fringe, with turned ivory handle. Victorian. 8 inches (20cm).

VERNIS MARTIN—See reference in Chapter 8.

WALLPAPER—See DOMINOTIER

WAR

The Japanese iron war fan (see also GUN SEN) was used in the direction of troops. Two types are known. The first is the *uchiwa*, a flat rigid screen, and the other is the *ogi*, a folding fan. In both, the material of manufacture is iron and brass and the fan is of considerable weight. The front face of the fan is sometimes decorated in gold with a central red disc representing the sun. In use, it would serve as a visual signal and it is to be found in representations of battle scenes, the general on his war-horse in the heat of the battle brandishing in his right hand the fan as a symbol of both his authority and command. In close combat, the fan could be used both as a weapon and as a means of warding off close-combat attack. The folding fans usually had a mount of stiff paper.

WATER FANS

The *Mizu uchiwa* was made for use in the kitchen and dates from the 18th century. This Japanese fan is made of bamboo split into segments, covered with stout paper and then varnished or lightly lacquered. Some are found with painted decoration with figures and other subjects, the subsequent application of varnish being of a rich warm brown hue. The user of the fan would dip the fan into water and thus supposedly secure extra cooling during the process of fanning by evaporation.

WEDDING or BRIDAL FANS

During the 18th century, French brides always included a number of fans in their trousseaux for distribution among the lady guests as a memento of the occasion. On the occasion of a royal wedding, these fans would be extremely expensive and Percival* instances that those for the wedding of Maria Liczinska were made by Ticquet, fan-maker to the King, and the total of thirty-six fans came to 3,627 livres. When the Dauphin married his first wife, Marie-Therese Antoinette, daughter of Philip V, her thirty-six fans were valued at 3,855 livres. The Paris livre was worth about one shilling

* *The Fan Book.*

(1900 value) so some idea of the immense cost can be gathered. The Dauphin's second wife, Marie Josephe de Save, had thirty-five fans, one of which was described as "a fan of wood, mother-o'-pearl and ivory, decorated with carved gold work, and having a beautiful skin mount". This alone cost 456 livres. The wedding fan as described was normally one of a small batch of similar (but not necessarily identical) fans presented by the bride. The bridegroom would sometimes present his new wife with a very special and commensurately sumptuous fan and this was termed a bridal fan. The early wedding or bridal fans were of the brisé type and their decoration usually took the form of painted cartouche representing the bride being visited by attendants with floral offerings, dancing figures, musicians, and country life. Later, commemorative wedding fans were "published" by fan makers and these were usually cheap fans with printed, hand-coloured mounts. A marriage of the famed in nobility or state could mean good trade for the fan makers.

WIDOWHOOD
The subject of these fans usually takes the form of a woman in classical costume mourning over an altar, urn or tomb. The figure is executed in stipple or mezzotint and the landscape completed by hand.

WINNOWING FAN
See also VANNUS. This fan was held sacred by all the peoples of the ancient world. Its use was to winnow grain and took the form of plaited grass, the shovel fan, rigid fans of various types and the beater which last-mentioned also developed into the familiar carpet beater indispensible in homes in the pre-vacuum cleaner era.

WOODEN FANS
See also in Chapter 8. During the 18th and early 19th centuries wood was used extensively for fans, the fine, smooth grain and working characteristics of holly, satinwood, sandalwood and laburnum being most highly prized.

CHAPTER EIGHT

THE MANUFACTURE OF FANS

Within this section, we will take a look at the manufacture of fans as a trade and assess the status both of the fan-maker and of his industry. We will see how fans were made and enumerate the many materials which went into their fabrication. Finally we will look at the selling and distribution of fans and their prices.

As a specimen of utilitarian mechanism, the fan was intended simply as a means of agitating the air. This called for the provision of some form of continuous surface which could be presented to the air so that, when it was moved, it would cause the air also to move. But the fan had to be compact when not in use and ingenuity had already improved on Queen Theodelinda's primitive folding fan and devised the folding fan that we know today. So here then was a light frame which, either by the width of its component ribs (as in the brisé) or by the addition of a web or other and flexible substance (the mount), could be held in the hand and made to act in the desired manner. However, the elegance of fashion abhorred a plain and undecorated fan with as much vociferation as Nature abhors a vacuum. Consequently, although some fans were made which were quite plain (they are still made that way today), the costume fan of past times was required to be decorated to suit both dress and occasion. Later the fan transcended this elemental need to justify its presence as but a costume accessory and became a principal aspect of costume decoration. The fan maker therefore had to be not just a skilful mechanic with a sound working knowledge of the various materials at his disposal, but he had also to be a shrewd judge of convention, the whims of fashion and the insidious changes of taste.

The activities of the fan makers in Europe were governed by the early trade organisations and as early as 1673 during the reign of Louis XIV the master fan makers of Paris had a corporation of their own being the equivalent of our own City Guilds or Companies. Its patron was St Louis and it was governed by four jurors. To qualify for admittance as a master, the fan maker was required to have served a four-year apprenticeship and to have produced a test-piece to the satisfaction of the examiners. This rigorous procedure ensured the sustained high level of craftsmanship and the only exceptions to these admittance procedures concerned widows, sons and sons-in-law of master fan makers, as well as those marrying a deceased master's widow, who were allowed to obtain the facilities on easier terms.*

In Paris by the middle of the 18th century there were about 150 master fan makers and, the fashion of the fan being at its peak, the trade was lucrative and produced many rich and honoured manufacturers. An edict of August 11th, 1776, united the Fan Makers' Corporation with the musical instrument makers and the toy makers. Along with this new conglomerate—and its unlikely content must have created a goodly measure of protest and ill-feeling to begin with—went the fan painters, the decorators and varnishers and all the other smaller trades which together were necessary to produce a finished fan.

As one of the results of revocation of the Edict of Nantes on October 22nd, 1685, many Huguenots and among them many fan-makers, chose to seek their fortunes elsewhere and so fled from the Continent to London to escape religious persecution. Prior to this, when fans were introduced into England, they had for the most part been imported as related earlier. However, during the closing decades of the 17th century, there were but few London fan makers and their numbers were suddenly increased by this influx of fellow craftsmen from across the Channel. Since their trade was un-doubtedly an expanding and important one, it was decided to petition Queen Anne for a charter. So, on April 19th, 1709, the Worshipful Company of Fan Makers was granted its charter, the enrolment taking place in the Guildhall of London on October 5th, 1710. This was the last charter to be granted to any City Company. For the greater part of its history, the Worshipful Company of Fan

* See Chapter 4, p. 100.

Makers had no fixed habitation and held its meetings at various taverns in the City of London. In more recent times and up until the outbreak of World War II, it received hospitality from one or other of the old Livery Companies which possessed their own halls. In 1941, the Company met for the first time in the upper room of the reconstructed St Dionis' Hall, Lime Street, as its temporary headquarters, and dined in the Hall itself. Later, the Company was accorded certain rights for the use of the Parish Hall of St Botolph's Church, Bishopsgate. The Hall was an old parish schoolroom dating back to 1861 and situated in the gardens adjacent to St Botolph's Church. This old church, situated outside the walled city of ancient London, was one which only just escaped the Great Fire of 1666 and has served since 1952 as the meeting place for the Company which, classified as one of the smaller ones, has never been able to afford so sumptuous a headquarters as, say, the Cordwainers or the Goldsmiths. The function of the Fan Makers' Company was to protect the trading and manufacture of fans in this country so that the guild might control, watch and curtail the activities of the many Frenchmen and Italians who had arrived from overseas, these comprising both rightful masters of the trade and a number of speculators.

The Company's Charter survives bound up with a full-length portrait of Queen Anne dated 1714 and executed by one of the members by the name of Earle. The painting, completed in gouache, is of interest since it must have been the work of a fan painter and demonstrated some of the style of this period—a period from which actual fans have not survived in quantity. An examination of the Stamp Book of Admittances, which unfortunately goes back no earlier than 1747 and begins with the number 839, reveals the divisions of the trade. We have the fan maker, the stick maker, the ribbon weaver and the fan painter.

By a curious coincidence, the date 1747 also marks the date of another interesting reference to the fan maker. In that year, R. Campbell compiled his book *The London Tradesman* which was published in London by T. Gardner. Here, on page 211, he writes:

The Fan-Maker is an humble Servant of the Ladies, and makes Sticks for Fans of Box, Ivory, &c. and puts on the Mounts after they are finished by the Painter. The few that

197

Fig. 51

Two examples of carved guards from fans exhibited by Duvelleroy of London and Paris at the Great Exhibition in 1851. That on the left demonstrates the deeply-incised, three-dimensional carving while that on the right, in many respects equally ornate, shows a simpler style of carving. These styles, reminiscent in many ways of the Louis XIV period, show with what facility the manner of a previous era could be reproduced and thus many of the fans made during the Victorian era could hardly be classified as Victorian in style or execution.

198

are Masters, and keep open Shop, earn a pretty Livelihood; and the Journeymen, who are generally paid by the Dozen, may earn from Fifteen Shillings to a Guinea a Week.

Fan-Painting is an ingenious trifling Branch of the Painting Business. It requires no great Fancy, nor much Skill in Drawing or Painting to make a Workman; a Glare of Colours is more necessary than a polite Invention; Though now and then, if he is able to sketch out some Emblematical Figure, or some pretty quaint Whim, he has a Chance to please better than one who is not so adroit. The *Italian* Mounts are much more in Request than any thing of our own Manufacture, and large Prices are given for them. A great Part of our common Fan-Mounts are engraved and afterwards coloured, which is a great Discouragement to any Improvement at home in this fluttering Implement of the Ladies.

Harsh words against the painters of fans, and yet so many of the early fans, both oriental and European, display really exquisite artistry. Perhaps the jaundiced Mr Campbell was ignorant of the technical difficulties of painting on fans and had based his judgement on poor specimens as compared with, say, the finest Sevres miniatures.

The materials used in fan making are many and varied. Indeed, an inventory of substances appears to include just about every material known to contemporary workers and, from what we know of these artisans, this is indeed what we would expect to find. These men knew what effects they wished to create in their handiwork and their skills were equally developed in the use of wood, metals, glass, precious stones and even chemicals and pigments, for the fan maker preferred to mix both his own colours and his own varnishes.

Here follows a listing of the more common of these materials together with details as to how they are prepared, worked and used in the making or decorating of fans.

BAMBOO
One of the most useful materials is bamboo which, although woody in appearance, is in truth of the grass family. It grows in abundance in the Far East where it is used for house and furniture-building and

a wide range of articles, both utilitarian and decorative. The fan-makers of China and Japan sought out the thinner and more delicate growths of bamboo for the manufacture of their wares. The shoots or branches provide suitable materials which he cuts into the required lengths. The extremely fine, parallel grain makes it possible for these lengths to be split into even segments by the use of a sharp knife. These pieces form the ribs of the fan and best-quality fans now as a thousand years ago used the best bamboo which would be polished until the surface acquired a satin-smooth finish. The outer sticks—the Japanese call these the "parent" sticks—are made thicker than the inner—"children"—sticks. Bamboo lends itself to additional embellishment by means of inlay with various woods, ivory, mother of pearl, metals and so on. In its unadorned form, however, bamboo is extensively used in the manufacture of cheap fans and it has considerable strength and durability.

IVORY

Ivory is a hard substance which, although it has a far finer structure and great elasticity, is not unlike bone. It is essentially dentine, the substance from which teeth are naturally made. However, unlike human dentine which contains only about 25 per cent of organic matter, ivory comprises between 40 and 43 per cent of this constituent. It appears in its natural state as the tusks of the elephant, these tusks being the two upper incisor teeth which have developed into enormous proportions. The best ivory comes from near the equator and thus India and Africa have always enjoyed a valuable trade in ivory. The working of ivory is a craft at which the Chinese and Japanese excel. The relatively high strength and softness of the material allows it to be carved into delicate patterns with threads as fine as the best lace. Much of this extremely delicate knifework is done under warm water in a shallow bowl, the water acting as both a softener and lubricant, as well as trapping the shavings which can be converted into gelatine by prolonged boiling. Both China and Japan have produced exquisitely worked ivory fans and fan sticks and these have either been completed locally, or exported to Europe to be incorporated in fans with Parisian or London mounts. There have been many attempts at producing synthetic ivory but, not until the comparatively recent perfection of plastics has anything approaching the real thing been possible.*

WOOD

There are only a few woods which exhibit suitable characteristics
for the fan maker. It will at once be seen that a wood must be close-
grained, strong both with and across the grain, and yet capable of
taking carving, piercing, inlay and other decoration. The chief
kinds used are sandalwood, holly and laburnum. The first-men-
tioned has a pleasant odour and is extremely light both as regards
colour and weight. It can take piercing, and painting, but unless
used in thick sections, is prone to warping which means it is generally
unsuitable as a ground for inlay work. Holly is almost white in
colour but is rather brittle. It is sometimes used for guards and painted sticks. Laburnum, however, exhibits all the qualities for which
the fan maker looks. It is very tough, close-grained and is yellowish
in colour—an ideal base for subsequent staining and polishing. It
permits of fine piercing and inlay work. On the majority of fans,
even those with sticks of ivory, tortoise shell or mother of pearl, the
slips which secure the mount are usually of wood. The Japanese
use Japanese cedar (*cryptomeria Japonica*) which is easy to work and
has a natural fragrance but is very brittle, and a species of yew tree
called *charmaecyparis obtusa fam* and known locally as *hi-no-ki*. This
wood is soft and velvety in feel, light in weight, smooth-grained and
can be smoothed to a mirror-like surface. *Hi* wood, from which the
name of the *hi ogi* fan is derived, is also naturally immune to wood-
boring insects.

PAPER

Prior to the 19th century, all paper was made by hand. The paper
used for the etched and hand-coloured fans during the 18th century
is thin, tough and has a fairly smooth surface. It is doubtful if it

---

* Early in the present century, the Germans invented a synthetic ivory which
was used for making pianoforte keys, buttons, decorations, fans and, in fact,
almost everything which thin ivory had hitherto been used for. The imitation
ivory was processed from the ordinary potato. A good, sound "bog orange" was
washed in diluted sulphuric acid, then boiled in the same solution and then
slowly dried. Unlike real ivory, the synthetic potato-ivory discolours with time and
cannot be whitened up again. This is but one of a number of pseudo-ivory
substances which have been made over the years to combat the high cost and
shortage of the real thing.

was truly white to begin with; today it generally appears to have a creamy tint. It is a tribute to the care with which the paper was made and to the purity of the materials from which it was produced (boiled and ground-up rags) that it has in so many cases endured the years so well without becoming brittle. The first uses of paper in fan-making were in China and Japan.

TORTOISE SHELL

This beautifully-figured substance, which is similar in every practical way to horn, comes from the hawksbill turtle *Caretta imbricata*. The epidermic plates of the back or carapace number 13 and are arranged with five in the centre, from front to back, with four on each side. Rather like the slates on a roof, these overlap each other by about one-third of their total area and the largest plate may reach 8 inches by 13 inches with a weight of 9 ounces. The carapace has 24 marginal pieces called hoofs or claws which, together with those which form the belly, are of less beauty and size and hence less value. However, attractive this shell may be, its collection has always been a barbarous business, certainly in the past. The *Singapore Chronicle* published during 1824 an account of the procedure:

> When the tortoise was captured by the Eastern Islanders of Singapore, it was suspended over a fire kindled immediately after its capture until such time as the effect of the heat loosened the shell to such a degree that it was easily removeable. The animal, now stripped and defenceless, was then released to re-enter its native element. If caught again in the ensuing season, or at any subsequent season, the unhappy animal would be subjected to a second ordeal by fire rewarding its captors this time with very thin shell.*

Thus cruelly earned, tortoise shell was converted into many articles of beauty and adornment. The plates, flattened by heat and pressure and then split into thinner pieces, could be moulded by heat to form snuff-boxes, knife handles and picture-frames; pierced into combs and brooches; used for knife handles or used in the elaborate inlaying of cabinetwork known as Buhl furniture. For

* This story is also quoted in the *Mechanics Magazine* for 1825, and a further reference will be found in the *United Service Journal* for June, 1831.

202

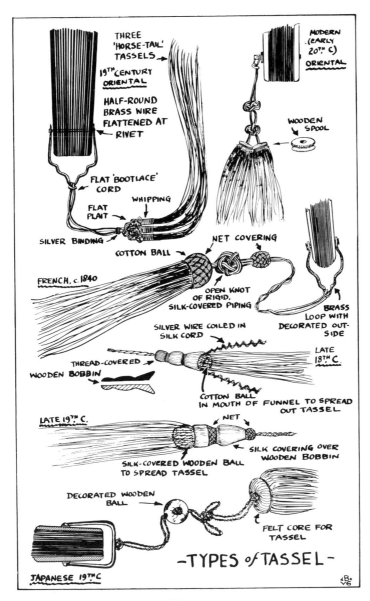

Fig. 52

Different types of tassels and how they are made and fitted. Most fans made before the end of the 18th century were not fitted with tassels. Subsequent repairers, though, quite often brought old fans up to ruling fashion by fitting tassels.

the fan-maker, it had the advantages of being light, strong, easily worked and very attractive. It was used in the making of both sticks and guards and sometimes as an inlay on and with other materials. Imitation tortoise shell was also used and this was manufactured from translucent horn which was stained. Generally this is easily recognised since, although the staining effectively goes right through the horn, the pattern looks far too clear-cut when compared with real tortoise shell.*

MOTHER OF PEARL

Among the most beautiful of all natural substances, mother of pearl has always been prized for its unsuspected colours and subtle hues which are reflected under changing conditions of light. The shells of a number of molluscuous animals display a brilliant pearly and irridescent lustre which is due to the peculiar manner in which the layers of calcareous matter of which they are composed have been successively formed. However, it is the shell of the bi-valve pearl-mussel *Meleagrina margaritifera* from which the majority of mother of pearl is produced. This mussel is a native of the tropics and is plentiful around the coasts of all tropical land. The shells vary in size and the largest reaches about 12 inches in length and weighs more than a pound. They vary in colour and thus it is possible to find a variety of textures and tones. In spite of its rather brittle nature, mother of pearl lends itself to carving and delicate fretting. A slightly less brittle variety called *dora* is preferred for carving and large quantities of this used to be brought up the Red Sea to Jerusalem where in the last century a thriving industry was formed to produce all manner of small articles in this material. Because of its layered formation, the shell can be softened in sulphuric acid (*aqua fortis*) and split into very thin layers. Alternatively, it can be ground down and polished to extreme thinness. The beautiful translucency of thin mother of pearl has long been recognised by fan makers who used it for guards, sticks, and for inlay in woods. Since the colours and textures often vary across a shell, the long

* A solution of gold in nitro-muriatic acid will give horn a red colour; a solution of silver in nitric acid will impart a black; and a solution of mercury in nitric acid a brown colour; so that by a judicious admixture of these three colours, with the natural yellow of the horn, a close resemblance to the tints of tortoise-shell may be produced. (*Penny Magazine*, August 4th, 1838, p. 300).

pieces of material which were used to form guards in particular are frequently found to have been formed of sections laminated together. The production of numbers of identical shapes such as fan sticks was carried out by sticking a number of pieces together to form a temporary laminate. After fretting, they were soaked in warm water to dissolve the glue.

VARNISH

Although not in itself a constructive substance, the enhancement of lacquer and painted fans was achieved with varnishes, in some cases many thin coats being applied to build up a brilliant transparency which survives even today. Brisé fans made before 1700 were varnished, the base substance being either ivory or wood. The varnish protected the surface—especially if it was delicately painted—as well as adding lustre. A general purpose varnish for fans was as follows: dissolve 2 ounces of gum-mastic, 8 ounces of gum sandaris, in a quart of alkohole (*sic*), and then add 4 ounces of Venis turpentine.* But the finest varnish of them all was the Vernis Martin.

There have been many claims to have discovered the secret of the several famed varnishes which have been introduced in the past by masters, whose work is characterised by that varnish, and the recipe for which has been taken with them to the grave. Similar in several respects to the beautifully clear, flexible Vernis Martin (literally Martin's varnish), was the Cremona varnish which characterised some of the prized violins which emanated from the masters of this Lombardic town. In 1904, George Fry, in his book *Italian Varnishes* laid claim to having discovered the secret of the process. His argument was that by the oxidation of ordinary resin and Venice turpentine (with or without the admixture of oil), varnishes might be produced that in colour, transparency and tenacity were identical with many varieties of Cremona varnish. The agent used in Fry's experiment was nitric acid and he presented a plausible case to endorse his claim.

Earlier, in 1887 to be precise, pianoforte-maker John Brinsmead claimed to have discovered the formula for the true Cremona varnish contained in a manuscript written by Antonio Parvardone in 1746.†

* *A Thousand Notable Things*, J. Gleave, Manchester, 1822.
† The subject of Cremona varnishes and the long-lost formulae was the centre

However, whatever the secret of the Cremona varnishes, nobody has yet been able to match successfully the full characteristics of "Martin's varnish" and thus this coating, which was applied not just to fans but other painted, decorated items, enjoys an enduring reputation with collectors. Not that its supremacy remains unchallenged, for other fan makers devised varnishes, both contemporarily and subsequently, which have been attempts to imitate the *vernis enseigne* with varying degrees of success.

LACQUER

Lacquerwork was devised in China and is a characteristic finish to many Chinese fans. The substance of lacquer, which is a form of resin, comes from the trunk of the *Rhus vernicifera* or lac-tree. As tapped, it consists of 70 per cent lac acid, 4 per cent gum arabic, 2 per cent albumen and 24 per cent of water and, although only slightly coloured, exposure to the air turns it black. A complex refining process is undertaken after which the lacquer is brushed on to the surface to be treated. A richness and pellucidity can be imparted to the lacquer by mixing with it finely-powdered gold whilst other additives include ground mother of pearl, cinnabar and gamboge, the last two being colouring materials. Japan derived the art of lacquering from China at about the beginning of the 6th century A D and subsequently carried it to a state of perfection far and away greater than that achieved by the Chinese. Lacquer was used as a ground for some fans whilst the later Japanese developments, which included three-dimensional decoration in lacquerwork, imparted some truly beautiful effects on Japanese fans.

ENAMEL

Enamelling has been practised in Western Asia since pre-Christian times and subsequently reached China about the 13th century. There are two kinds of enamelwork both of which are accomplished by the process known as incrustation. The first is *cloisonné* in which the pattern is raised on the surface of the metal by soldering on to it pieces of thin copper, silver or gold so as to form cells or *cloisons* to contain the coloured, fired and glazed pigment. This is also called

of an extended correspondence and a number of articles in *Musical Opinion* for the year 1887. Whilst the true Cremona is a tinted varnish, it bears a strong similarity regarding its other properties to Vernis Martin which is, of course, intrinsically clear.

Fig. 53

The mass-production of fans brought about the decline of the fan shops of former times. It also provided another item for the mail order stores. The Chicago-based firm of Sears, Roebuck & Company devoted almost a page of their giant 1902 catalogue to fans. Here is a montage of their stock. It may thus come as a nasty revelation for some collectors to find that their cherished fans are of no great antiquity and heralded not from some quaint old man working in a Dickensian olde shoppe at "ye Golden Fann", but from the sterile stockroom of America's biggest mail order business.

incrustation—cloisonné. The second is *champleve* in which the cells are punched or otherwise hollowed out of the metal itself so that the enamel remains flush with the surface. The Chinese produced some very fine filigree gold, silver or silver-gilt fans incorporating enamel decoration.

ADHESIVES

The glues and fixatives used by fan makers were many and various. Some were closely-guarded secrets which, as with so many similar demonstrations of the artisans' craft, died with their masters. Some have remained having been recorded in those curious, interesting and sometimes unintentionally amusing reference books compiled in the 18th and early 19th centuries. It is not to be implied that these fixatives should be used today when, even without recourse to synthetic resin adhesives, we have a wide variety of reliable, commercially-available glues from which to choose. However, here are a few of the cements used in times past. For fixing glass decorations on to wood, the common fixative was to use ordinary hot brown glue into which was stirred a quantity of finely-sifted wood ash. When the consistency of syrup was achieved, then the glue was ready for use whilst still hot. This glue was claimed also to be waterproof, but its proof against prolonged immersion is highly unlikely.

Fixing metallic objects on to ivory, tortoise shell or mother of pearl could be done in a number of ways. The most common relied upon the melting together of 16 parts of copal varnish, 6 parts drying oil, 3 parts Venice turpentine, 3 parts oil of turpentine and 5 parts liquefied animal glue. To this was then added 10 parts of powdered quicklime. Another mixture was to dissolve good glue in water and add half as much linseed oil and varnish and a quarter as much Venice turpentine to the amount of glue used. Yet another was to use 3 parts of copal varnish, 1 part linseed oil varnish, 1 part oil of turpentine and 1 part of glue.

Many materials lent themselves to fixing using egg cement. This remarkably strong fixative is prepared by diluting the white of an egg with an equal quantity of water and then beating this up with powdered quicklime into a thin paste. The cement then had to be used at once. Waterglass was also used, sometimes with the addition of casein cement in the proportions 6 parts of waterglass to 1 part of casein.

The pasting of fan-mounts required a thin, smooth, flexible glue which would not support mould. This was usually prepared from rice flour. Another formula was to use a mixture of equal parts of gum tragacanth and gum arabic which produced a thinner mucilage than either of these two fixatives alone. Tragacanth glues were made by mixing 1 dr. of powdered tragacanth in 6 dr. of glycerine and then adding water to make 10 ounces.

Horn being an amorphous substance was usually joined by heat and pressure but a glue which was sometimes used was made by dissolving 5 parts of mastic resin and 2 parts of turpentine in 6 parts of linseed oil. The resin required some time to dissolve and the mixture had to be kept in suspension by vigorous shaking. Ivory could be cemented by boiling isinglass in water until it became very thick. Enough oxide of zinc was then added to give the whole the consistency of molasses. Another recipe was to melt white wax and oil of turpentine together in an earthenware vessel over moderate heat so as to form a thick fluid mass. Colouring could be added if required.

Mica, used as an inlay, could be fixed by egg cement or by a gelatine cement made by soaking clean gelatine in water until it swelled. The water was then squeezed out between cloth. The gelatine was then gently melted in a hot-water bath and just enough proof spirit stirred in to make it fluid. A small quantity of gum ammoniac and gum mastic was then dissolved in rectified oil and then added while stirring. The mixture was then bottled and required to be re-heated before use.

There were three popular cements for tortoise-shell. The first consisted of 30 parts shellac, 10 parts mastic, 2 parts turpentine and 125 parts alcohol (methylated spirits). Another was 15 parts mastic, 45 parts shellac, 3 parts turpentine and 175 parts alcohol. The third formula was 5 parts mastic, 15 parts shellac, 1 part turpentine and 60 parts alcohol.

Unlike the fixatives available today, the majority of these glues were both slow-acting and slow-setting and required pressure and time in order to develop their strength. Of particular importance in the preparation of pieces to be glued was cleanliness and this is equally important today in repairing fans. This aspect, however, is covered in Chapter 9.

The processes involved in the manufacture of fans were lengthy

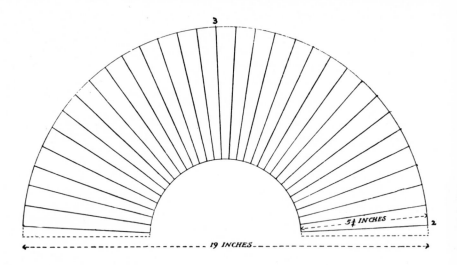

Fig. 54

The invention of the fan-leaf mould, drawn here, speeded up the production
of folding fans. The mould was formed of waxed card carefully creased and
folded. In use, the leaf was carefully positioned between the two thicknesses
of the mould and then creased when the mould was folded up concertina
fashion.

and delicate. Among these, that of pleating the mount was a tedious
operation calling for the utmost skill otherwise the fan would not
fold properly, nor would it open out flat. However, about the year
1760, a process was invented which ensured the accurate folding.
The inventor was named Petit and the manufacture of the special
pleating apparatus remained from thence-forward in the hands of
the Petit family in France.* After the leaf was painted and allowed
to dry, it was inserted in a mould comprising two pieces of thick,
strong paper or cardboard the surfaces of which were specially
prepared with a coating of an oily nature. The closing of the mount
in this mould automatically positioned the pleats and the brins or
sticks were then introduced between the folds and fixed by means of
glue (see Fig. 50). Duvelleroy, the famous fan maker who worked in
both Paris and London, commented:

* See Chapter 12 under DUCROT & PETIT. The mould is illustrated in
Fig. 54.

This operation of pleating, very simple at present, was formerly very complicated; it was necessary for the éventaillistes to exercise the most scrupulous exactitude; now the mould dispenses with this care.*

Charles Blanc, writing in *Art and Ornament in Dress*, enumerated that:

No less than fifteen or twenty persons are employed in the making of a fan, which passes through three series of operations: 1st, the work of the stick, in which are employed the cutter, the carver, the polisher, the gilder, the inlayer, the riveter, and sometimes the jewel setter who inserts the precious stones; 2nd, the leaf, which requires the designer, painter, or printer as the case may be; 3rd, the work altogether, employing the gluer, and in the case of spangled or embroidered fans, the embroiderer or sempstress, and the folder or pleater. After all this the last finished touches—the tassels, tufts, and marabouts† are added by the deft hand of a woman. When this formidable weapon of coquetry is completed, it is enclosed in a case like a well-tampered blade in its sheath.

Fan making in the Orient began, naturally enough, with the rigid type of fan. Charlotte M. Salwey recorded this description of the manufacture of the *uchiwa* or stiff fan:‡

About eighteen inches of bamboo is cut and prepared, of which about nine inches is split down to the node or joint, which prevents further splitting. As the grain runs perfectly straight, fifty or sixty segments are obtained by careful division of exactly the same thickness. In order to keep these in position, a diminutive bow of thick bamboo is inserted just below the joint, the segments are deftly arranged crossways, and a string having two strands is interlaced alternately between them and fastened securely; by this tension the whole framework is steadied. Though the handle is generally formed by the few

* *Rapports du Jury International, Exposition Universelle*, Paris, 1867, Vol. IV.
† Blanc meant *marabous* which are tufts of down from the wings or tail of the West African marabou bird and which were popular as trimmings for hats and fans.
‡ *Fans of Japan*, p. 28.

inches of bamboo left below the node, other substitutes are sometimes employed for the handles, which are left either plain or embellished; coloured and naturally curved bamboo, notched and carved in an open manner, is frequently resorted to for a change. When this is the case, a circular piece of thick paper or thin wood is doubled, so that the lower portion of the fan is dropped into a slot and fixed with a small brass nail or rivet; but the framework of this fan is always constructed on the plan previously entered upon.

In Japan, the fan makers worked in their own homes in the manner that true cottage-industry workers have laboured for centuries. They toiled hard for long hours with the utmost patience and were rewarded with only meagre pay. It did, though, cost little to live and the dedicated fan maker pursued his trade out of a love of the graceful lines of his handiwork.

The tools used by the workmen in making folding fans were extremely simple and were chiefly made of bamboo. Knives were set in bamboo handles and other tools included a roller for flattening down the folds in the paper and for fixing the papers together for the frames, and a bow-drill for making the hole into which the rivet was inserted. This rivet is called *Kana me* or "crab's eye" and it is made of wood, various metals or, occasionally, of paper string; this last substance being used exclusively for the fans of the Empress. The rivets of those fans which carried tassels were generally cylindrical and hollow, or else they were fitted with a ring at the rivet head, or a metal hanging handle. Except for the war-fan, which had an iron frame, the ordinary styles of fan were provided with frames of bamboo or ivory.

By the 18th century, vast numbers of Japanese fans were being produced for the cheaper markets and in order to produce sufficient quantities for export, the practice of division of labour was resorted to. Many people now carried on their employment in workshops, each being responsible for one part of the process and then handing his work on to another and so on through the different stages. There was still hardly anything in the way of machinery.

There are pattern designers, whose sketches fashion the work, houses which only furnish the bamboo frames, and others in which handles are lacquered and ornamented. Another group of persons undertakes the painting or printing of the paper, and so forth. Frames and decorated sheets for covering both sides are then given into the hands of other workmen, who are again divided in several groups, whose first work consists in folding the paper to correspond to the bamboo ribs.

A sheet of paper is pasted on one side of the frame, and a corresponding second painted sheet is fixed on the other side in the same manner, and when this is done the fan must be open and shut a good many times, and fixed here and there in imperfect places, so that the paper will lie easily in the folds, and spread without difficulty, as occasion demands, and as only a tough and pliant material will permit. This is the manner of proceeding with the *ogi* or folding fan.*

A similar sequence was used for the production of the sticks. The ivory, tortoise shell or bone was cut out roughly to shape by one worker who then handed his work on to another who, with the aid of scrapers, thinned the material down to the required thickness. This had to be done with great skill since the ivory is thickest at the rivet end, thinning off towards the shoulder so as to allow for the thickness of the leaf in order that, when closed, the fan would take on a parallel profile. A little extra thickness would be left if the stick had to be carved to show a design in relief. The stick then had the design marked out on it and was passed into the hands of the piercer who began his work by piercing small holes in the sticks using a fine drill. Through these holes he would then insert the thin blade of his piercing saw whose slender blade was set in a frame not unlike that of a fretsaw only with a much narrower bow. The superfluous ground could now be sawn out and discarded. Sometimes, particularly in the case of early and late fans, this completed the decoration. In the 18th century, the only ornamentation which fan sticks displayed was simple piercing. However, in the case of elaborately worked sticks, the carver now had his task to perform.

If the sticks were subsequently to be gilded or painted, this work was assigned to less skilful hands. For the best fans, from both

---

* *Industries of Japan*, by Johann Justis Rein, London, 1889.

oriental and western sources, the gilding was of a very high quality and put on in so many layers that it is spoken of as *encrusted*. Gold and silver leaf were both used; gold remains untarnished and bright, but today the silver has generally faded to a dull coppery or blackish shade.

Those fans made with sticks of mother of pearl usually had the delicately carved open work backed by an extremely thin skin of richly coloured pearl shell. The pearl being very brittle, this backing although itself fragile, added to the strength of the whole.

The use of fine vellum or chicken-skin (see Glossary) came back into fashion during the Restoration. In former times, it was imported from Italy where this extremely supple and endurable material was carefully prepared. However, over the years the art of preparation had been lost and the fan makers were forced either to find a substitute material or a substitute process for preparation. Finally, during the last century, a naturalist named Drevon was encouraged by the Parisian fan maker Désrochers, to devote his talents and efforts to finding a way of preparing vellum for fan mounts. Ultimately he succeeded and, in truth, succeeded with such accomplishment that the newly-processed material was even more flexible and translucent than in former times.

There is one detail which I think should be explained. The mount of a fan is frequently referred to as the leaf—indeed I have used both terms throughout this book and thereby implied their synonymity. In truth this is not altogether correct. The mount was always considered to comprise two pieces of paper or prepared vellum. These were each called a leaf, that forming the front of the fan usually being more richly embellished than that which formed the reverse. The two leaves, when glued together, formed the mount. The sticks of the fan were glued into pockets in the folds of the mount so that they were not visible beyond the shoulder. However, another form did exist and in many cases the mount was referred to as *à l'Anglais*. In this, there was only one leaf on to the back of which the sticks were simply glued. Naturally, the leaf was made of a thicker substance and, when viewed from the back, the sticks can be seen. Generally this denoted a cheaper, paper fan, but it was also an unavoidable characteristic of the fan with a textile mount.

One branch of the fan-maker's trade which may be thought too slight to warrant much attention is the tassel maker. However, an

examination of fan tassels will reveal that great skill and craftsmanship went into their making. It is unlikely that tassels were actually
made by the fan maker; they were most likely contracted from
specialists in this aspect of the embroidery trade.

Tassels were a late addition to the fan. Throughout the 18th
century, the fan was provided just with a rivet through the head
and only in the nineteenth century did it become stylish to use the
rivet to secure also the ends of an ornamental metal loop to which
could be attached a length of cord terminating in one or more
tassels. In spite of this, loops and tassels may be found on fans of an
earlier epoch since fans were often repaired and re-styled or brought
"up to fashion".

The purpose of the loop, cord and tassel was originally so that the
fan could be carried on the wrist, the hand being inserted between
the two lengths of cord. It was, though, to assume a purely decorative
function by the mid-19th century.

Sometimes the tassels were made of silk, but it was more usual to
use cotton or braided thread since this material tended to "fill out"
and look better. Its physical construction was, in many cases,
extremely interesting. The simple tassel would spring from a
tightly rolled spherical ball of cotton, but more enterprising styles
are to be found. Small, beautifully-turned wooden bobbins were
loop-sewn with thread to provide hard, flat tassel tops. On another
type, a lathe-turned wooden cone formed the centre of the tassel-
top, cotton being looped through its hollow centre and then bound
tightly to the sides. Finally, a pierced wooden ball, also loop-sewn,
would be drawn into the hollowed-out end of the cone to produce
an unusually attractive object rather like an ice-cream cornet.
Silver-wire whipping and sometimes silver-coiled wire-tinsel on
thread would add a brilliance, usually long since lost, to the
tassel.

Occasionally, as in Thornhill's patent fan incorporating a complete needlework set, the ball of the tassel would be of over-large
proportions and made of silk-covered wood in two distinct halves,
a small spherical space being left inside. This was to house (in the
Thornhill fan) a tiny seamstress's thimble. It may also have been
used to hold a miniature scent bottle.

Mourning fans were generally provided with black tassels but
costume fans for evening wear explored the whole spectrum of

colours. Those tassels made for oriental fans were rather different in that they were ornamented by small ivory or wooden balls which, in the case of fans in my collection, were decorated with painted butterflies.

Above the tassel, on some of my fans, an open knot was formed in stiff braided piping-cord. Some styles of tassels and their details of construction, are shown in the accompanying illustration, Fig. 52.

An intriguing insight into the manufacture of French fans is contained in Tallis's *History and Description of The Crystal Palace* (the Great Exhibition of 1851) which prefaces an account of the fans exhibited (quoted in Chapter 4) with the following description of the processes involved:

> Fan making has arrived at a high degree of perfection in France, and presents a remarkable instance of the sub-division of labour, as may be gleaned from the statement that about twenty different operations, performed by as many pairs of hands, are necessary to the production of a fan which sells for less than one halfpenny; and that these various processes are not all carried on in a single manufactory, but, on the contrary, form four distinct branches of trade, directed by masters employing the various artisans, who, for the most part, work at their own homes, and who are frequently assisted by their wives and children. A fan consists of the frame of solid material, called a "pied," which is composed of the inner ribs, or "brins," and the two outer ribs, or "panaches," and likewise of the flexible leaf, or "feuille." The frame is made of wood, bone, ivory, tortoise-shell, or mother-o'-pearl.
>
> The first operation is performed by sawing the material into the required form for the inner and outer ribs. These ribs then pass into the hands of another workman, who shapes them with a file, and they are then taken up successively by the polisher, the piercer, the sculptor, the gilder, and the workman who fixes on them the spangles and pins of gold, silver, and steel. The frame is now sent to the manufactory which furnishes the necessary drawings for the series of operations, where it is riveted, the rivet being frequently ornamented with a precious stone. The leaf, or feuille, is sometimes single, but more often double, and it is usually made of paper lined with silk or calico,

but also of parchment, lamb's skin, satin, and silk gauze. The richer kinds of feuilles are painted in water-colours on vellum, by artists known as *feuillistes*; and the highest and most expensive class by artists of celebrity, since Boucher and Watteau, Camille Roqueplan, Gavari, Clement Boulanger, and Dupré, have affixed their signatures to fans which they have decorated. The devices on the more ordinary descriptions of fans are printed from copperplates, and coloured by hand, and the most common sorts are ornamented by the process of chromo-lithography.

The feuille is folded in a mould of strong paper, and is then mounted on the frame and glued to the prolongations, or "*bouts*" of the inner ribs. The feuille of the best fans is after this painted on the edge with gold size, and gilt with leaf-gold; but the feuille of the common fans is printed in Dutch metal previous to its being cemented on the frame. The decorator now ornaments the frame with gold or coloured ornaments, and the fan lastly passes into the hands of the overlooker, who attaches the tassels, and selects the proper sized sheath, into which she places it. The frame, or "*pied*," is made in the parishes of Andeville, the Deluge, Boisière, Corbeil-Cerf, and St. Geneviève. In the district situated between Méru and Beauvais, in the department of the Oise, 2,000 workpeople, men, women and children, are employed in the fan-trade. The woods used are the beam-tree, the plum-tree, ebony, sandal, and the lime-tree. The dexterity and sureness of hand of the peasant workman are said to be quite wonderful. Considering his want of knowledge of the principles of drawing, his facility in engraving, sculpturing, and gilding, is certainly remarkable. The piercing is performed by means of minute saws, which the workman makes for himself with pieces of watch-spring. A remarkable piece of saw-piercing, in the shape of a mother-o'-pearl fan, was exhibited in the French Section, No. 149; it contained no less than 1,600 holes in the square inch. This *tour-de-force* was the production of one of these peasant artisans, named Désiré Henry.

The printing, the colouring, and the mounting of the feuille, and the final embellishment of the fan, are usually performed at Paris, under the direction of the fan-maker, called, *par excellence*, "Eventailliste," though he has really but little to do with the manufacture of the fan, and must be regarded rather as the collector into one focus, and arranger of the produce of others; yet his labours are not the less essential. The mounting of the feuille, its ornamentation with feathers, and final decoration, are the operations usually performed by a small number of work-people in his own establishment; besides which he furnishes the drawings to the peasant in the Oise; for the framework to suit the constant changes in fashion, he instructs his feuilliste as to the style of ornament; he groups together the frames and feuilles; and, finally, he overlooks the whole, to see that the workmanship has been well executed. Except the mountings of the feuille, and the final adorning of the fan, the other operations are usually performed by workmen at their own houses.

The number of fan-makers, or Eventaillistes, in Paris, in 1827, was 15, who employed 1,010 workpeople (344 men, 500 women, and 166 children), and sold about £40,420 worth of fans. According to the *Statistique sur l'Industrie à Paris*, drawn up by our colleagues, M. Natalis Rondot and M. Say, it appears that in 1847 there were 122 fan makers, comprising chamber-masters as mounters, feuillistes, painters, and colourers. The value of the fans made was £110,000. These masters employed 575 workpeople (262 men, 264 women, 29 youths, and 20 girls). The workmen, on the average, earn 3s. and the women 1s. 8d. per day. The men were, for the most part, copperplate engravers and printers, lithographic draughtsmen and printers, painters, colourers, and overlookers. Thus in twenty years it appears that the produce in fans had increased in value nearly threefold, whilst the number of workpeople had diminished to one-half. This change is to be attributed to the employment of machinery, especially of the fly-press in stamping out and embossing the ribs, and the extensive employment of chrome-lithography, an art not practised at the former period. By these means the French have been enabled greatly to increase their exports by the production of cheap fans, to compete with those made by the Chinese. P. Duvelleroy exhibited some small fans, the price of which was as low as 5d. per dozen.

So much for the materials of fan making, the method of manufacture and the state of the fan industry at the time of the Great Exhibition. To conclude this chapter, we are fortunate in having at our disposal a fine set of engravings from *Le Travail de l'Eventailliste*, part of the great encyclopaedia compiled by Diderot and published in 1765. These plates together with a translation of the original explanatory text, follow.

The four illustrations, reduced here from their original folio size, trace the different stages through which a fan passes from the time it entered the *atelier* (workshop) as a sheet of paper to its ultimate emergence as a finished fan.

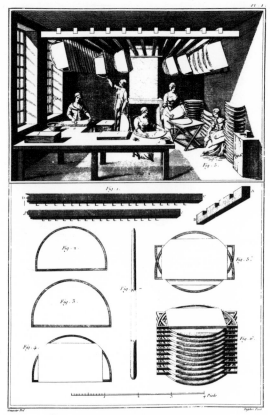

Eventailliste, *Colage et Preparation des Papiers*.

Fig. 55
PLATE I of *L'Eventailliste*

PLATE I.

The upper part represents the interior of a workshop where the fan papers are glued and prepared. This workshop is a large room with an open fireplace, in order to obtain the heat necessary for preparing the glue from shreds of hide. The ceiling has to be provided with numerous wooden beams at a height of about seven or eight feet. The lower parts of these beams are fitted with hooks in order that the hoops on which the glued papers are stretched may be suspended to dry.

Fig. 1. represents the girl who does the glueing by soaking a sponge (a) with glue from the earthenware glue pot (b) before her. The papers are then paired up and the two facing sides glued together. The plate shows a pile of glued papers (e), the earthenware pot for the glue (b), dry paper not yet treated (c), which is made into piles of a dozen or a gross, and a pile of glued paper (e).

220

Fig. 2. shows the raiser, who separates the pairs of glued sheets from each other and stretches them on hoops (f) to dry. She has at hand the pile of double sheets provided by the gluer (e), a double leaf stretched on a hoop (f), a receptacle containing water (g), and a sponge (h) to damp those parts of the paper which are to be attached to the hoop.

Fig. 3. The workwoman, called the stretcher, takes the hoops which are prepared by the raiser, and places them on the hooks.

Fig. 4. The cutter, when the papers are dry, takes the hoops one by one and removing the papers, piles them on the table; the empty hoops are placed on the floor.

Fig. 5. The rounder off, who cuts off the angles of the paper with scissors.

Fig. 6. A stone and mallet similar to those used by the bookbinders are also shown, these are used in gilding gilt fan papers.

Fig. 7. A drawing of the tool known as a *sonde* or probe. It is a kind of copper ruler rounded at both ends, and with very rounded edges. It is thirteen or fourteen inches long. In the illustration the centre part is not shown, as it would be too long to show in its entirety. The other objects can be identified from the account given above.

NOTES:

The double papers were glued together before the decorating or mounting was begun. If water-colour decorations had been done before the process of pairing up and stretching, which necessarily included the thorough damping of the leaf, the whole painting would have been ruined by the wet.

The glue was prepared on the premises because the workers believed in carrying out every detail of the work themselves. It was made by boiling down shreds of hide and skin until a gelatinous substance was obtained, which was similar to glue size but of sufficient consistency to stick firmly, yet not so hard that it could not be separated by the proper tool. This was a tool something like a paper knife (the *sonde* or probe) with edges carefully smoothed off that no roughness remained to catch in and tear the leaf.

The hoops or *rondes* on which the leaves were stretched were in reality, only half-circles, and the papers when stuck on to these were held as firm as the parchment of a drum, affording not only an excellent surface for the painter's brush, but also stiffening the paper so that when the time came for the folding of the leaf they took and held the marking of the folds most perfectly; bending but not breaking.

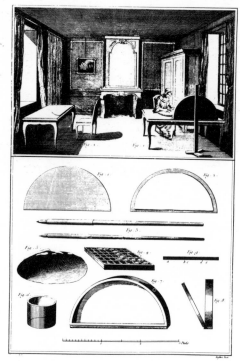

Eventailliste, Painture des Feuilles.

Fig. 56
PLATE II of *L'Eventailliste*

PLATE 2.

A workwoman seated at a table painting a prepared fan leaf on its *ronde*. Before her is the stretched paper and in front of her desk stands an easel for holding the drawing she is to copy at a convenient position in front of her eyes. The furniture of the room and the dress of the woman show that the position of the fan painter was superior to that of those who carried out the more mechanical details of stretching the leaves.

In the details below the main picture are seen (1) the surface of the leaf upon which the artist is to work, and (2) its reverse, showing the *ronde*. The other items shown form the utensils of the fan painter.

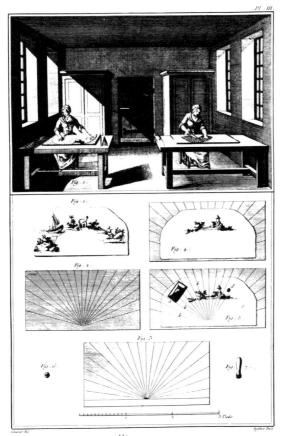

Eventailliste. Monture des Eventails.

Fig. 57

PLATE III of *L'Eventailliste*

PLATE 3.

Mounting fans—the uniting of the mount with the sticks. The engraving illustrates a room in which two girls are carrying out the operations of their trade.

Fig. 1. The workwoman who marks the creases in a leaf with a tool something like a burnisher, called a *jetton*.

Fig. 2. A woman working with a sonde or a probe opening the folds for the later insertion of the sticks.

Fig. 3. Large mould which gives a semi-circle. In both moulds the centre is indicated by a tiny copper plate, pierced with a hole, so that the exact centre shall be accurately preserved.

Fig. 4. Shows the method of finding the centre of a leaf, which is not always

223

in exactly the same place as that used by the painter and marked by him with the cardboard compasses shown on PLATE 2 as Fig. 8, because it is the task of the mounters to arrange matters so that heads of figures or other principal objects are not placed on a fold. To avoid this they move the leaf to and fro on the mount, so that the right side (which faces the wood) is arranged in such a way that the heads and other principal objects are neither in the grooves nor in the exact middle of the intermediate spaces. Once this position is found, the leaf is steadied by a piece of marble or other weighty substance as shown at (a) in Fig. 5.

Fig. 5. Here is illustrated the pleating of the leaf as shown in the part of the upper drawing which is marked Fig. 1. The leaf having been positioned as already described, the workwoman holds the leaf steady with her left hand and takes the smooth pressing tool known as the *jetton* in her right hand. This she draws along the grooves in the wooden mould, pressing the paper into these grooves and so creasing it in the form of rays.

Fig. 6. This little object is the *jetton* which is made of silver or copper and is about the size of a 24 sous piece. Sometimes the jetton is provided with a handle and in this form it is shown in Fig. 7.

To vary the number of sticks in a fan, or to modify the angle of the opened fan, different moulding boards must be used, but the principles of use are always the same.

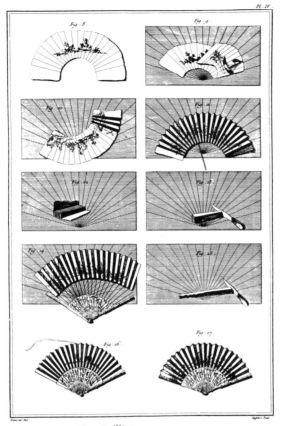

Eventailliste, Monture des Eventails.

Fig. 58

PLATE IV of *L'Eventailliste*

PLATE 4.

Fig. 8. The leaf fully scored with the rays for pleating. The unwanted part of the leaf—the gorge portion—has been cut off approximately with scissors.

Fig. 9. The pinching process in which the score marks are folded over where marked by the radiating grooves. The right side of the painting is maintained on the outside. Since the ordinary fan always opens from left to right (clockwise rotation of the guards), the painting which is to show must be arranged so that the folds coincide with the way the fan will open when completed.

Fig. 10. Now that the creases have been folded individually, the fan can be pleated properly as seen here. The process consists of dividing into two the spaces which were left between the folds already made (remember that in the mould only the "downwards" creases could be made: not until this stage can the "zags" be added to the "zigs" already folded).

Fig. 11. The most delicate of the processes is to separate the two pieces of paper which form the mount in order to make a passage for the slips of the sticks to pass. This passage must be made on every alternate fold and starting at the correct fold otherwise the mount will not fit on to the sticks. The tool used is the probe or *sonde* which is shown in Fig. 7 of PLATE I.

Fig. 12. The completely pleated and folded fan ready for cutting away any excess of paper on the first and last folds.

Fig. 13. The final trimmings to limits of the gorge portion of the mount.

Fig. 14. Here the slips of the sticks are carefully threaded into the openings produced by the probe at the stage shown in Fig. 11.

Fig. 15. Now looking much more like a fan, the upper end of the mount is trimmed back to the level of the ends of the guards.

Fig. 16. The outer edge of the mount is finished off by a narrow paper band, carefully folded and glued over the double edges of the mount.

Fig. 17. The finished fan. From here it may pass on to those who will attach tassels, feathers or other decorations to the completed article as it leaves the workshop of the fan maker.

CHAPTER NINE

CLEANING AND REPAIRING FANS

The order of the words which form the title of this chapter has been chosen for a particular reason. The processes of repairing, particularly those which call for the use of adhesives of one sort or another and including those repairs in which fresh substances are affixed to old, demand cleanliness of handling and cleanliness of the piece being worked upon. Again, not only does dirt affect the bond of a glued joint, but dirt encapsulated in a repair scheme will appear as discolouration if the fan is subsequently cleaned, so drawing attention to the repair.

However badly broken a fan is, the first operation should always be to clean it. The frailty of the pieces, the materials which together comprise the whole and the type of dirt to be removed must separately and severally govern the procedures of cleaning.

Let it be said at the start that far more damage can be done by careless or, as is more often the case, well-intended but ill-advised cleaning, than may be sustained in the normal lifetime of a fan. What we call dirt is usually an agglomeration of dust and fluff particles originally attracted to the surface, and now bound to it by moisture which, most commonly, was perspiration from the hands of those who used the fan and may have subsequently handled it. This dirt may not present an overtly distasteful appearance and, on a light-coloured background such as ivory, may appear as an acceptable patina. Indeed, on high-relief carving, the presence of this patina may well serve to throw into sharper relief the beauty of the workmanship. On a dark ground, however, the patina may not at first be apparent, although carved details and the inlay of metals or gilding may have dulled to the point of merging with the base colour.

I think it is not a bad idea to begin by listing the substances which should NOT under any circumstances be used for cleaning. Never use any chemical cleaner or solvent, patent or otherwise. There is no surer way of destroying original varnishing and decoration than some of the chemicals freely available today. By the same token, never use wire wool whether steel or brass, and do not use liquid polishes or metal cleaners. Also remember that bone, ivory and tortoise shell all absorb water and swell, so keep any use of moisture to a minimum.

Begin by setting up your work table under a strong light, clear everything superfluous off the table and pin, tape, or clip to its top a large piece of white shelf paper. Let this paper extend over and around the edge of the table where you will sit to work. For tools you will need a pair of sharp-pointed tweezers and either some manicurists' orange sticks or a supply of wooden (not plastic) cocktail sticks. For sundries you will need some of those useful things sold in chemists' stores for cleaning baby's ears—cottonwool buds. You will also need some cottonwool, some pieces of clean linen cloth and a jewellers' polishing leather. Now find a small metal tea-tray large enough to hold two saucers. Into one saucer put a few tea-spoonfuls of clean cold water. On the other saucer, put a slice of lemon. Why the tea-tray? In case you have a mishap and upset the water, the tray will contain it and avoid the risk of damage to the fan.

If you have an ivory fan with carved guards, keep the fan shut and clean both guards first using dry cloths and the polishing leather. To clean out the carving, use the cottonwool buds with just a spot of lemon juice on the end. Fine, delicate carving can be cleaned with a small pinch of cottonwool held in position with the tweezers and worked into the design gently using the cocktail sticks. Avoid using any sharp metal probe or scraper for cleaning as this will damage the ivory surface and, in addition, make it that much harder to clean properly. Don't ever use water to clean ivory. The most effective cleaner is a piece of linen moistened with just a drop of lemon juice. The rough cleaning can be followed by polishing with the leather. Any dirty spots can be polished with whiting. Always take care not to snag the cloth on the ivory and remember that any loose end of the cloth, hidden by your hand, can catch in and probably break off a part of the fan which you can't see.

Once the guards are cleaned, open the fan, one stick at a time, and gently clean each one with a small pad of cottonwool held between the thumb and forefinger and moistened with lemon juice. Do not rub too hard on painted ivory otherwise you may remove the varnish and the image.

There are on the market patent ivory cleaners, particularly those used for cleaning pianoforte keys and other ivory articles. These may be used on unpainted and unvarnished ivory but only sparingly. Take particular care on painted ivory—the painting may smudge or even lift right off.

The cleaning processes for a fan with a skin mount involve the careful and gentle treatment of the surface to remove loose dirt only. Any grimed-in material cannot easily be removed and I strongly recommend that any "deep cleaning" process must only be carried out by a skilled professional restorer. Ideally, of course, you should not attempt any cleaning of the mount at all. But sometimes a fan which has been stored closed in a dusty place will have accumulated dirt in the folds of the mount and this will look unsightly when the fan is displayed. Open the fan fully and holding it in one hand so that the mount only is on the table with the part from the shoulder to the head overhanging, rub the dirty portions with a ball of new bread (with the crust removed). If the mount is damaged in any way, do this job very carefully so as not to make matters worse. Do not use an india-rubber or any moisture at all.

Fans with lace or other fabric mounts are the most difficult to clean. You cannot apply any washing techniques for this would dissolve the animal glues securing the mount to the sticks and remove from the fabric any starch or size. Do your best to remove as much loose dirt as possible using a soft paint brush (an ordinary one-inch is just about right) after having shaken or blown off surface dirt first. With dark coloured or black materials, it is unlikely that any grimed-in dirt will show. However, light fabrics will show dirt and plain, undecorated areas (i.e. those free from spangles and painting) can be carefully sponged using a small pad of clean cottonwool and a little water. Try a small area first to see that the colour of the fabric is fast and that the mount may not be spoiled.

The most frequent stains found on fan leaves are those of iron-mould. These rust-coloured blemishes vary in size from tiny spots through to the foxed appearance of the pages of old books. They are the hardest of all stains to remove without damaging the surrounding area of the mount. Paper and chicken-skin should be treated very carefully since excessive moisture will spoil the mount. If the foxing covers any painted part of the mount, then the best you can do is to try to retouch the painting with water-colours. Plain areas of the mount may be gently dabbed with a fine artist's sable brush dipped in liquid detergent and water (a fifty–fifty mixture is suitable) followed by successive dabs with the brush dipped in clean water and instantly dabbed dry with a soft blotter. On dark-coloured fabrics, it is best to lightly sponge the area with damp cottonwool and then to camouflage the stain with ink or water-colours mixed to match and applied with the artist's brush. On fine, open-weave fabrics such as lace, extreme care must be taken not to disfigure the piercings of the material by using thick colour. The colour must be water-thin and several applications may be necessary, allowing each one to dry thoroughly before the next is applied. On white fabrics, you can use the merest touch of household bleach dissolved in four parts of water, again applied with a fine brush. Only treat the exact area of the stain, and as soon as it has faded, kill the bleaching action with a solution of liquid detergent and water applied with a cotton-wool pad.

Stains other than iron-mould on chicken-skin fan mounts are also demanding of particular care in treatment. Here you might try a very soft india-rubber which has been sharpened with a penknife to a point. Only work on the area of the blemish. Remember that a generally dirty fan mount, provided that it is intact, may be cleaned with a small block of new bread cut from the centre of a fresh loaf.

Generally speaking, if a stain shows resistance to your attempts to remove it, then leave it. Unskilled attempts at cleaning up a fan and clumsy efforts at concealing stains can spoil an otherwise good fan. If you have any doubts as to your ability or success in the cleaning operation, it is preferable to leave well alone.

Wooden guards are best cleaned by careful dry-polishing on soft linen. Where they are carved or inlaid with metals or enamels, this will usually serve to bring up the brightness. If not, and if all other efforts to clean are ineffectual, I have found patent cleaning wadding very useful if used sparingly. This is marketed under the trade-name Duraglit and is impregnated with a cleaning solution. A rub with this followed by soft cloth polishing will bring up polished wood, inlay and enamel like new.

Wooden sticks, usually of fine-pierced sandalwood, are hard to clean since the porous nature of their surfaces traps dirt. Whilst I personally prefer to leave these well alone, you may wish to try to clean away excessive dirt and if this is so, then a few drops of carbon tetrachloride on cottonwool may be used. This chemical, available as a cleaner under the trade-name Thawpit, is safe to use and is non-inflammable but if it is exposed to heat, or any person smokes near the fumes, these fumes transmute into phosgene which is a highly poisonous gas.

One form of fan that is just about impossible to clean is the fan which is made entirely of feathers or the feather-trimmed ordinary fan.

The all-feather fan will not respond to any normal cleansing treatment without ruining it. As any of my readers will know only too well if they have attempted to wash a hat feather, the barbs separate and the whole thing curls and frets, goes limp and assumes more the appearance of sheep's wool on barbed wire than a fine feather. No, the all-feather fan is best left as it is. The ordinary chicken-skin folding fan is occasionally found with peacock-feather frill. Each feather is mounted on the end of each stick in such a way that the natural curl of the feather forms an attractive adjunct to the appearance of the whole. Again, these feathers are best left un-cleaned or, at the very most, given just a gentle brush from bottom (quill) to top with a soft brush.

So much for basic cleaning. Now for the processes of restoration. Let me begin by saying that these processes are those which I have developed for my own use over the years. They are proven, practical processes which require the minimum of equipment and they are contrived so as not to impart further, secondary damage to the fan. By the same token, though, let me also say that these may not necessarily be the best processes (in consideration of speed, perman-ence or invisibility) and certainly not the only ones feasible. I offer this advice as a guide and if it serves as a starting point from which you can develop your own better processes, all well and good.

Before starting, do remember the important considerations which should be kept in mind by every restorer. Your work must be accurate, thorough and of the best possible standard. You owe it to posterity not to spoil your fans through thoughtless or careless work and above all you may suffer the personal grief of knowing that you have ruined a work of art which is no doubt considerably older than you and thus entitled to respect at least. If you do not feel capable of repairing your own fans then please do not try. Skip the rest of this chapter and find someone better qualified to impart new life to your broken fans.

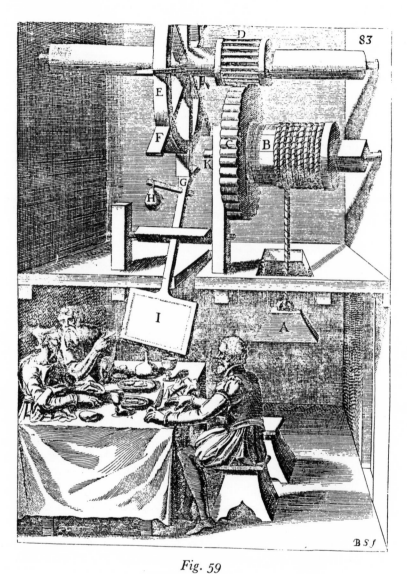

Fig. 59

Mechanical table fan, 17th century
Georg Andreas Böckler, "Theatrum Machinarum Novum", Nurnberg, 1973.

Fans, whether of wood or ivory, are prone to breakage at their weakest part—the rapid change of section at the shoulder where mount and gorge meet. Sometimes it is only the sticks which are broken, occasionally one or both of the guards. Finely-pierced ivory gorges are often so delicate that when they break, sizeable pieces of the material shatter and become lost with the result that there is a gap between the remaining portions.

The first step in repairing a damaged stick is to undo and remove the pin or rivet at the head, so allowing the sticks a measure of freedom. You will now be able to work on them without risk of damage to either the other sticks or the mount.

First, we will look at the case of the ivory stick which has a clean break and with no pieces missing. The repair method is straight-forward. Open the fan to reveal the broken stick or sticks and, using short strips of thick cardboard as cauls, clamp the fan in the wide open position using clothes pegs or paper clips. If the sticks are one-sixteenth of an inch thick or more, you can make an effective butt joint which will be quite strong enough for display purposes. A colourless acetate-based adhesive is suitable but a stronger bond can be achieved by using a cold-setting clear epoxy resin adhesive such as Araldite. At all times when glueing, use the absolute minimum of glue needed to make a satisfactory bond and remove any excess with a cocktail stick. Wiped-off glue smears the surface and, when hardened, will spoil the appearance of the repair. Also some adhesives of the Araldite type gradually yellow with age and can spoil the visual effect of an otherwise satisfactory repair.

To make a stronger repair such as is particularly necessary when repairing very thin pieces where the area of the glueline is minimal, the joint must be reinforced with a doubler or patch. This should be of stiff transparent material and celluloid has most of the right properties. However, celluloid does discolour with age and so water-clear rigid PVC is to be preferred. The reinforcing patch needs to extend to the full width of the repair and should overlap each side by at least three-eighths of an inch. The actual amount of overlap will depend on the break and the delicacy of the adjacent pieces. If you use transparent acetate sheet, an acetate-based adhesive can be used or Araldite. Both pieces of the stick should be arranged face down on a piece of glass and separated from it by a strip of polythene sheet which will act as a release agent. The pieces must be securely located using clips or small weights.

Sticks of mother of pearl which are broken can be repaired very neatly by glueing the pieces on to a doubler made of the same material. This can afterwards be polished and smoothed off so as to be almost invisible, even in the display of an open fan. A suitable surface for bonding can be achieved by dipping the new piece of 'pearl in dilute sulphuric acid for a few minutes, then washing thoroughly and drying before applying the glue.

Because of the need to position the pieces accurately and to enable them to lie flat and accessible, it may be necessary to separate the sticks by severing the tape (in the case of a brisé fan) or by slipping a thin piece of glass between the sticks.

Severely broken sticks, particularly those which are delicately pierced, may need different treatment. Where small pieces are completely missing, you may choose to try to make good the damage by setting the available pieces in a matrix of Araldite or similar resin which, when cured, you can then trim and pierce to resemble the missing original. Here you will have to work with files and a piercing saw but I must emphasize that major reconstruction of this kind does demand skill and patience and invariably calls for the complete removal of the piece to be repaired by dismantling the fan. The edges of the new piece can be polished with a thread of cotton rubbed with polishing rouge and passed to and fro through the piercings.

The fretting of delicate work should be done with a jeweller's piercing saw, obtainable from any good tool store. For cutting mother of pearl you will need the very finest blades made—the sort for cutting thin metal—to avoid chipping the edges of the brittle material. For ivory you still need a fine blade, though not quite as fine as that for mother of pearl—in fact if you use too fine a blade, the teeth will clog due to the heat generated in cutting causing the swarf to melt into the cutting edge. Delicate piercing, where it may not be possible to drill a small enough hole through which to thread the saw blade for the start of the cut, is best done with a jeweller's fine graver, NOT with a sharp blade. This is because the cutting edge of a graver is parallel in section whilst that of a blade is tapered and as the cut gets deeper, so a blade will cause the material to be pushed aside and possibly to break as a result.

Resin such as Araldite can be coloured to match in with the ivory by the use of a coloured filling mixed in with the adhesive whilst it is in the liquid form. This is called "flour" and is supplied by the resin manufacturers.

This type of repair is not really within the realms of the novice restorer and its application may seldom be justified.

An alternative to repairs of such magnitude is one which has been practised for a long time. This is the complete removal of the broken stick. The drawback of this type of repair is that it destroys the harmony of the fan and invariably means adjusting the mount to close up the void left by the missing stick. Whilst this may effectively be done on a plain fan with plain sticks, such fans are seldom worth repairing. It is the ornate fan with ornate sticks and delicately decorated mount where the problem arises. I can give no directive to the restorer on this point, other than to say that if the fan is of quality then there is no alternative but to make a copy of the damaged stick to the very best of your abilities.

Wooden sticks can be repaired using a polyvinyl acetate (PVA) woodworking adhesive such as Evostick Resin W and if the cross-sectional area of the joint is small, you can reinforce the back of the stick either with a narrow strip of nylon or terylene fabric glued on or by a narrow strip of wood veneer, cut so that the grain of the wood runs at right angles to the break in the stick. Use "bulldog" paper clips to apply setting pressure overnight, and thin the halves of the stick where the reinforcement is to be glued so that it does not produce a bulge.

These examples should only be taken as a guide to the repair of sticks since no two breaks will ever be the same and a technique which may suit one job may be unsuitable for another. Whereas it is said that doctors bury their mistakes, you will have to live with yours, so try to avoid them. Consider each repair in detail beforehand and decide the best approach. Some woods, being naturally oily, are difficult to glue. Horn and ivory are also difficult and flat surfaces need to be roughened slightly with the point of a sharp knife before a satisfactory bond may be made.

Of paramount importance is cleanliness—not just of your hands and tools but more important still the cleanliness of the pieces you want to unite. Even the almost imperceptible grease from your hands will affect the strength of a glued joint, so once you have prepared a joint, do not touch it, do not breathe on it; just cement it as quickly as possible. Handle pieces to be joined with tweezers

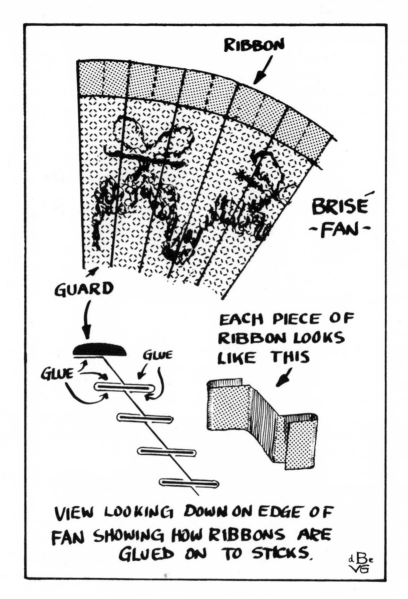

Fig. 60

How the blades of a brisé fan are joined by the tape. Note that the ribbon is cut into short pieces. It must be of very thin material and, for repairs, should be glued to the blades with a clear adhesive.

or in tissue paper (not paper handkerchiefs which do not prevent moisture from your fingers from reaching the piece you are holding). If the pieces have been glued before, then you must remove all traces of the old adhesive. When you come to glueing two pieces of a basically impervious substance such as mother of pearl or ivory, coat both surfaces evenly and thinly and then gently rub the two together before clamping. This excludes any air trapped between them which would naturally cause a weak joint.

Chicken-skin mounts on old fans may be damaged along the lines of the folds. The fold lines may fray either from abrasion during handling or whilst stored in the closed position. Unfortunately, any repair to the folds will reduce the flexibility of the edge and so any patching must stiffen the fold to the very minimum. Frayed folds which have not actually torn can be laid and consolidated by laying on a thin and narrow coat of acetate-based clear adhesive such as Durofix diluted to the consistency of water with acetone. This must be done carefully using a fine camel-hair brush. Alternatively, you can paint the frayed edge with thinned gum arabic or gum tragacanth.

Folds which have torn can be rejoined by glueing a quarter inch wide strip of rice paper or nylon fabric on to the back with the same acetate solution or gum. Although difficult to handle, a narrow strip of fine nylon stocking is very good for this job when a very blonde stocking fabric is used.

Grease spots on the mount should be removed with a small cottonwool swab dipped in benzine but if the surface is of skin, use the minimum of benzine since this may cause localised drying-up of the vellum which will show as a withered area.

The ribbon used on brisé fans which have the ribbon passing through slits in the blades is formed of a fine, closely-woven silk which is just wide enough to fill the width of the slits. If it is too narrow, it spoils the appearance whilst if it is too wide, it bunches up in the slot and interferes with the set of the fan when folded. In Vernis Martin style fans, the ribbon is fixed at the top of the sticks and is painted in keeping with the rest of the decoration. (See Fig. 60 for ribbon details.) Faded, frayed and discoloured ribbons are best replaced and if you cannot exactly match the colour of the original piece, you must experiment with dyes on the plain length of ribbon before fixing.

Victorian period fans usually had large tassels or ribbons attached to a metal loop which extended round the heads of the sticks from one guard to the other and secured with a rivet or pin. These were sometimes added to fans made earlier than the early 19th century as part of, possibly, an earlier repair. It is not advisable to wash these tassels, particularly if they are coloured, as the dyes may not be fast. Furthermore, the braided, plaited strands may unravel in the wash. It is best to leave these alone unless they are really bad when possibly the best thing is to try a suitable matching replacement.

Unless you have above-average skill, do not try to touch up or otherwise improve paintings, decorations or varnish on fans. Some modern materials react chemically with the old paints and varnishes with the result that the original is destroyed. To re-varnish a fan is sacrilege at the least; destructive at the worst; and foolhardy at all times.

CHAPTER TEN

POINTS FOR COLLECTORS

It should go without saying that fans are delicate, often extremely delicate, articles. Throughout the many years since first a fan was made, it will have succumbed inescapably to the inexorable forces of attrition. Its sticks will have become brittle and the leaf will have hardened and cracked. In the case of a silk or fabric mount, long exposure to the atmosphere will have set about turning the pliable threads into brittle strands devoid of almost all strength. Repeated use, careless handling and poor storage may also have taken its toll. For this reason, you should avoid treating an old fan as if it were a contemporary piece of everyday work. Repeated opening and closing, particularly careless closing, should be avoided since each time a fan is opened and closed, the folds in the mount become more marked and worn.

Of paramount importance is that a fan should not be fluttered or flicked. There is a temptation for those who handle fans without knowledge or forethought on the subject of fanology to wave them. On some people, indeed, this is almost a reflex action—give them a fan and they instantly wave it. Whilst modern cheap paper fans can be flicked in the manner customary to Spanish fan dancers, the very frailty of old fans makes such handling extremely risky. Sticks become dry and fragile with age and fan leaves deteriorate and become friable.

Avoid exposing a fan to direct or radiated heat as from an open fire or from sunlight since heat will frequently cause warping, particularly of ivory and thin wood. Even screen fans, whose original purpose was to protect the complexion from the heat of the fire, must be kept away from heat if they are to be preserved.

The question of sunlight has far greater importance from the aspect of storage and display. It is well known that both sunlight and skylight have a damaging effect on organic materials and varnishes. Although the ultra-violet component is the most damaging, it should not be forgotten that the visible radiation is also harmful. It is thus unwise to exhibit or store fans, either open or folded, in those parts of a room exposed to strong daylight. Wherever possible, a North-facing aspect should be selected.

Another point to watch concerns artificially-lit glass cabinets. Normal electric-light bulbs produce heat and, in the confines of a showcase, this heat can be appreciable. The cold light of fluorescent tubes is to be preferred, only here we are again faced with ultra-violet emission regardless of whether we use "white" or the so-called "daylight" tubes. Filters are available but an alternative solution is to use low-wattage tubes with metal reflectors to shield the fans from direct light, relying on reflection from, say, a white background or base to illuminate the piece.

If fans are of particular value or display a beautiful painted mount, then it is better to keep them wide open and mounted either in a showcase or a specially made fan-shaped glazed frame. This will prevent the wearing, cracking and probable eventual tearing of the mount at its folds. However, an important word of warning! Once a fan has been opened for exhibition in such a manner and left open for more than a few days, serious injury can be sustained by trying once more to close it. In fact a fan preserved in a fan case, unless of the "mountless" brisé type, may never again be folded without the mount splitting at the folds. This is particularly so with fans stored in unventilated cases or exposed to strong daylight.

From these initial remarks, it must be clear that a fan is not the easiest of ethnic ephemera to preserve. Indeed, chicken-skin fans require extra care if they are to be preserved adequately because, being formed of a once-living membrane, the substance is hyper-susceptible to heat and damp. Too hot an environment will cause the skin to harden and ultimately perish whilst damp produces mildew and stiffness when the skin is subsequently dried out. Warmth in excess can also harm ivory and cause the flaking-off of paint, gilding and varnish not to mention the deterioration of glues. In some early 18th-century fans, fish-glue was used in their manu-facture. This is very prone to deterioration, particularly in the confines of a show-case.

Temperature and humidity are thus extremely important and just as important is the relation between the two. Relative humidity should ideally be maintained at a constant in the region of fifty to sixty per cent. So long as the room temperature remains fairly constant and is not prone to extreme fluctuations, the actual temperature is not vital. However, you must remember that a variation in temperature affects the relative humidity. A low relative humidity, as I have indicated in the previous paragraph, means shrinkage, distortion and cracking together with a degree of brittleness in some materials. High relative humidity risks mould and attrition of the adhesives. A rise in temperature will lower the relative humidity. Air conditioning or, in climates prone to fluctuations, a humidifier are an enormous help. Again, the room in which fans are kept can incorporate features which will help smooth out potential harmful changes in relative humidity. Unpainted wood (i.e. natural wood) in showcases or drawers, curtains or backcloths of natural fibres and even thick paper or cardboard in the display case and the room can act as a natural moisture reservoir and retard a sudden loss of humidity.

One way to preserve fans, although not necessarily the ideal way of showing them off, is the fan cabinet. This is a chest of shallow drawers each divided up into narrow compartments large enough to accept a folded fan. This has the merits of allowing considerably more fans to be stored in a given space, is unquestionably cheaper than glazed individual fan cases and protects the collection from light and dust. Each drawer division can be lettered or numbered and related to a catalogue or card index system containing a description and history of each particular fan.

Where possible, each fan should be kept in its original case or, if that is no longer available, then valuable fans can be rolled in tissue paper or kept in a soft-fabric slip case.

If fans are to be preserved for posterity, it is incumbent upon you to take care to look after the fans in your collection.

I mentioned glazed fan cases. The original cases, which have been made for many years, have stout wooden frames and are sometimes of such massive proportions they have the same effect as thick horn-rimmed spectacles on a beautiful pair of eyes—they detract from the object of interest by overpowering the observer.

You can make a fan case (or have one made if you think your skills do not match the task) in several ways and probably the easiest way today is to use transparent acrylic plastics. The drawings offer some suggestions as to construction. The actual mounting of the

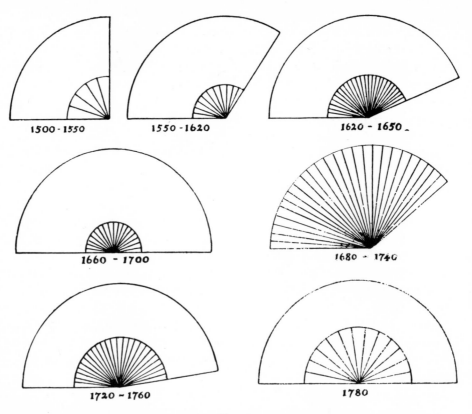

Fig. 61

The proportions of the folding fan throughout different periods. Whilst this can be taken as being a rough guide to the proportions of the fan at any given time, it must not be forgotten that there were exceptions to every example shown. Certainly during the 17th and 18th century, fans were produced which were not characteristic of the proportions ruling at the time.

fan in its case is naturally of great importance. If the fan is just placed in the case, then it can slip or partially refold. Delicate fans should never be pierced with a pin, although the pin is one of the easiest ways to mount your showpiece. To begin with, if you are to use pins, make certain that they are the plated, non-rusting variety and begin by arranging three or four pins to make a V of the right angle to hold the opened fan. The fan, supported on shaped acrylic blocks, is then rested in place between the pins and held there by a few more pins which can be placed through any existing opening in the fan such as the shoulder or beside the tops of the sticks. The task of holding the fan in the case is threefold: to restrain the fan from slipping to the bottom of the case; to prevent it from folding if the case is tipped; and to restrain the fan from moving at right-angles to the background.

Any form of adhesive tape, transparent or otherwise, should never be used, nor should metal clips of any sort at all. Even the plated steel pin is a little suspect and I personally prefer to attach my fans to their showcases using transparent acrylic rods. These can be cemented to the case, or attached with brass woodscrews through the back. The fan can be tied to these with fine nylon threads. Do not forget to make some ventilation holes in the back or bottom of the case. These can be fairly small (say a quarter-inch diameter) and if you think they look unsightly, you can cover them over with the lining fabric of the case—so long as it is not too thick. Failure to make these ventilation holes can accelerate the deterioration of the fan and in the very worst of changes in relative humidity, could cause condensation on the inside of the case, especially if the cases are entirely of plastics and not wood-backed.

So much for the mounting of fans and the storage of them in fan cabinets. I have already said that a fan should not be "fluttered". Another point to watch is that when a fan is opened, it should be opened carefully and slowly. This is particularly important with a chicken-skin fan although damage can also be done by the careless handling of a brisé fan since the vital ribbon may be perished. Delicate, fragile fans should be closed extremely carefully, gently closing each fold separately in the fingers. Avoid cupping a closed fan in the hand—the acid in the perspiration ever present even on a dry hand is harmful, and the closed fan displays on the edges the folds into which unsightly dirt is easily engrained.

FORMING A COLLECTION

The formation of a collection depends entirely on the tastes of the individual. Whilst there are those who are content to specialise in fans of a particular type, style or period, the majority of collectors tend towards a general collection to embrace all those fans which they may be lucky enough to find.

You may have the good fortune to own enough fans to form a

worthwhile general collection from which one or more thematic collections may naturally present themselves. Alternatively, you may set out from the beginning to compile a thematic collection. You may, for example, wish to concentrate on wedding fans, or historical fans. Again, a style collection may comprise nothing but brisé fans, or chicken-skin fans, or exclude folding fans altogether and dwell solely on screen fans.

In the final analysis, it is your collection and you should form it in the way which will give you the greatest satisfaction. People often ask "why do you collect?" There are so many answers to that question, many of them requiring some deep and very personal soul-searching. There are those who collect, maybe unwittingly, for the kudos which they may obtain by the ownership of a collection. There are others who collect because their friends are collectors of one sort or another, and they require the supposed social standing amongst their acquaintances which the reputation of being a collector may be considered to engender. This altruistic attitude may be enhanced to a varying degree by the investment value of fans.

It is always a dangerous thing to collect anything like fans purely for the potential monetary gain. True, some fans are very valuable; the majority are not. The real collector (or is this a jaundiced personal view?) is the person who enjoys ownership of a work of art because of the very personal effect it has upon his or her senses. Indeed, the very term "work of art" is not devoid of complexity, for what may to one person be simple, plain and lacking in merit may to another person represent beauty.

Far more talented people than I have tried to analyse the acquisitive urge in people and have plumbed the depths of Man's soul to fathom out what makes we collectors tick. Their conclusions are usually involved and leave the lay reader with a pervading sense of unease that his own cause is not being given justice. For this reason, I shall dismiss the reasons for collecting without further ado and just accept that people collect.

WHAT TO LOOK FOR WHEN BUYING
The collector, whether knowledgeable or neophyte, faces pitfalls in building up a collection. He or she (and incidentally some of the biggest fan collections of the past have been formed by men who

could hardly be dubbed feminists or fetishists!) will be confronted by vendors who, in the majority of cases, are notoriously ignorant about fans, and will have to use not inconsiderable acumen to make an accurate appraisal.

A word about faking. Whilst it can be argued that to produce a good counterfeit fan is surely to produce a fan of similar merit to an original, this misses the more esoteric considerations of age and originality. Counterfeit fans are quite on a par with forgeries in the art world and whilst such fakes may certainly be collectable (one only has to look at the sale of reproduction Rembrandts!) their true provenance must be recognised, even if for no other reason than to rationalise the selling price.

Cut vellum or découpé fans, for example, are very scarce indeed, mainly because the delicately pierced skin more often than not has long ago deteriorated. Percival infers that counterfeit specimens were produced in France during more recent times.* Again, a large number of fans was produced during the last century which featured 18th-century subjects on their mounts. Sometimes a fan leaf of a later date will have been affixed to a genuine early set of sticks no doubt following the deterioration of the original. A knowledge of 18th- and 19th-century styles of costume and hair thus becomes more than useful in weighing up the characteristics, apparent and otherwise, of a fan. Sometimes the 19th-century painter, working in the style of the 18th century, will show the coiffure as being white in colour whereas in reality 18th-century powdered wigs were grey in appearance.

A fan which has been repaired or restored will sometimes be found and here the collector must decide whether the amount of restoration and the quality of the restoration work detracts from the authenticity and appearance of the fan to the point where it is not worth acquiring. Repairs which have been carried out badly either by virtue of the choice of repair method or by slipshod workmanship will always look unsightly and you will have to assess whether it is going to be possible to undo the bad work and start afresh with a new repair scheme. Carelessly applied animal glues which have spread onto lace, for example, can be dissolved away with a little water and a lot of patience. Modern synthetic resins, on the other hand, are virtually impossible to remove from most

* *The Fan Book*, p. 188.

substances, particularly fabrics, without causing secondary damage. Occasionally, a painted fan will have been found to have been revarnished. If this has been properly done (it may have been done a hundred years ago or last week) this need not detract too much from the value or appearance of the fan. However, fan varnishing is not to be recommended either by the expert or the amateur restorer today and poorly applied varnish is virtually impossible to remove other than at great expense and by a picture-restorer.

The mount of a fan, whether painted or embroidered, is liable to damage due to its fragile nature. In past times, a fan so damaged would in preference to its being discarded, be repaired by having a painting of a later genre stuck on. During the 19th century, it was common for fan restorers to paste a second leaf on to the back of the sticks of an old fan being repaired. This served in some cases to support and thus reinforce the torn fragments of the old leaf and in others to form a ground for a new main or front leaf. This should be considered a legitimate attempt at repair rather than an underhand deception. It will, in most cases, serve to lower the value of the fan and again only an examination of the fan and its other characteristics will reveal the true period of a specimen which has been so treated.

As a general rule, the collector should not place too much faith in the opinion of the vendor but rather rely on his own knowledge and powers of observation. With a little practice, the collector can quickly determine the approximate period of the fan he is examining and should be able to judge whether it is original or restored and repaired. And although Queen Victoria (and Marie Antoinette) had many fans, the earnest assertion from the vendor that this particular one was one of her prized possessions, dubiously substantiated by a coloured lithograph of the personage involved, or by initials, should be taken *cum grano salis*. A knowledge of the various styles of European and Far East painting and decoration is of immense value since the art of each country possess various distinctive and unmistakable characteristics which can be detected in the art forms which that nation may produce.

French fans, not unnaturally, take prime place for their elegance, delicacy of workmanship and beauty of decoration. The exception to my earlier remarks on the identification of the country of origin is the fans of Spain. Large numbers of French fans were imported

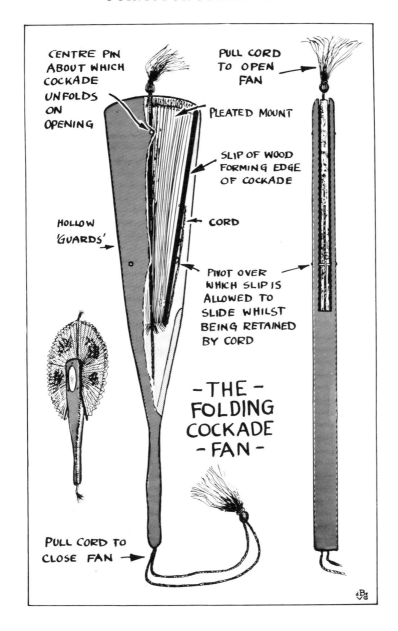

CENTRE PIN ABOUT WHICH COCKADE UNFOLDS ON OPENING

PULL CORD TO OPEN FAN

PLEATED MOUNT

SLIP OF WOOD FORMING EDGE OF COCKADE

HOLLOW 'GUARDS'

CORD

PIVOT OVER WHICH SLIP IS ALLOWED TO SLIDE WHILST BEING RETAINED BY CORD

- THE - FOLDING COCKADE - FAN -

PULL CORD TO CLOSE FAN

Fig. 62

The folding cockade fan and how it is opened and folded.

247

directly into Spain during the 18th century. This resulted in Spain having no early predilection towards styles of fan decoration with the outcome that later Spanish fans closely copied the styles of the French fans and it was not until comparatively recent times that more overtly Spanish styles have emerged.

Italian fans are identifiable by the excellence of the colour painting and the nobleness of the general design in the Renaissance style. They also are usually found with large mounts and comparatively short sticks. German fans are distinguished by somewhat heavy characteristics both as regards decoration and painting. Dutch and Swiss fans are of simple and rather formal design.

English fans are notable for their refinement of design and decoration frequently heightened by a classical style of treatment.

The earliest fans to bear coloured decoration were the hand-painted examples of the 17th and 18th centuries but by the second quarter of the 18th century, engraved and printed fan mounts were common; indeed the number of French printed fans of this period is prodigious. English fans sometimes bear the date and the name and address of their publishers in accordance with the provisions of the Act of 1735. The fact that some appear undated in spite of this law is probably due to the custom of printing this information on the lower edge of the mount, and this part would frequently be cut off in the manufacturing process of applying the leaf to the sticks (see Chapter 12).

These engravings were usually hand-coloured and should not be confused with the later coloured etchings. Coloured engravings printed from copper plates were perfected by Jacques Christophe le Blon (born 1670; died 1741) but the process was lengthy and costly and the fan leaf depicting a colour-engraved print is rare.

The majority of the late 18th and early 19th century printed fan leaves were decorated with etchings which were afterwards coloured by hand. These should not be confused with pen-and-ink drawings. The design was printed from an etched copper plate. Fans of this type are not of very great value from the artistic standpoint and there exists no comparison between these "mass-produced" decorations and the hand-painted fan mount. During the first half of the 19th century there was a veritable craze in Paris for fans decorated "in the old style" and etching gave way to lithographed outlines which were then hand-coloured, often with such a measure of skill that at first glance the printed outline may not be visible. However, close inspection with an eye glass may be needed to detect the light, faint printed outline over which the artist has painted. Elaborately carved sticks, although of workmanship which is coarse in comparison with the true early French fan, usually complete the attempt at deception and the unwitting buyer should be on the lookout for these fake Louis XV antique fans.

Around the same period there were simple fans which were lithographed and painted in figure groups in a very Watteauesque style. Percival relates that the drawing of these figures has a curiously "old-fashioned" flavour which is quite different to the style of the originals. It is rather puzzling why the designers at this date chose to evolve something of a similar sort out of their inner consciousness rather than just to copy the originals.

Similarly, many Spanish fans which almost always depict bull-fight scenes or scenes near the bull-ring appear considerably older than they really are. These, too, are lithographs subsequently hand-coloured and they are very seldom earlier than 1850 or so. Later still, fans of this type were printed by the chromo-lithographic process so even the artistic hand-finishing was superseded.

There is little straightforward in the identification of period or nationality of a fan and the collector has ever to be on his or her toes to avoid the many pitfalls. In the 18th century, for instance, fan sticks in lacquer and carved ivory were imported into Europe from China in large quantities. They were then assembled in Europe into fans with European mounts. Fans composed entirely of delicately carved ivory, horn or tortoise-shell and varnished all over were first made in Holland about 1734. These Dutch fans were imitations of Chinese lacquer work and are identified by the point that they are generally of small size and are painted with a garland or small wreath of flowers in which the predominant colours of the flowers are blues or pinks.

The beauty of the finely carved and pierced fans were copied by the French and so we can find Louis XV fans of carved ivory. These are of a larger size than those of Dutch origin and are stylistically French rather than copies of the Chinese origination. However, some are decorated in the Chinese manner whilst others have paintings after Watteau and Boucher. The considerably divergent styles seen here do, however, normally bear one character-

249

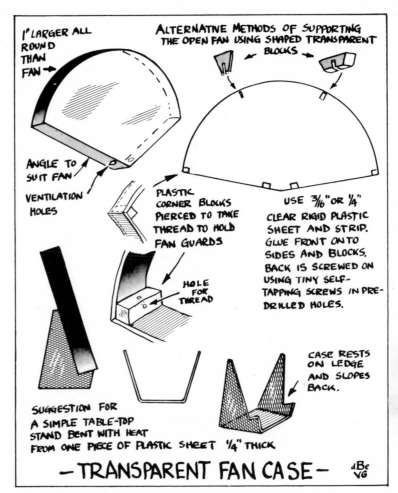

Fig. 63

How to make a display case for a fan. You can make cases out of wood with
a glass front or, as drawn here, you can make a fully-transparent case out of
clear acrylic plastic, so allowing both sides of the fan to be seen. How you
support the fan inside the case is dependent on the type of fan: for example,
a lace fan can have a loop of thread passed through the mount close to the
guards, whereas a paper or skin mount fan must be supported by a loop of
thread round the guard at the shoulder. Do not forget to make ventilation
holes in your case bottoms. The clear plastic stand can be used for resting
the case on a table or bureau. Alternatively you can cut keyhole slots in the
back of the case and hang it on the wall, or suspend it from a picture rail.
The fan must be supported at intervals around its mount so that it does not
flop around inside the case.

istic which is unmistakably French—the Vernis Martin which has a lustrous transparency and smoothness not found on Oriental work. Thus the collector must make a careful examination of the quality and texture of the painting and its varnish in determining both the age and nationality of a fan of this type.

Prior to the pierced ivory fan of the 18th century, Chinese fans of the 17th century sometimes have sticks and guards of silver or silver-gilt filigree work, ornamented with a plain design in translucent enamel. The same design appears on both sides.

The size of a fan is also a clue as to the period of its manufacture. As regards the European folding fan, it gradually increased in size during the reign of Louis XIV. Between then and the middle of the 18th century, the size was somewhat prone to fluctuation but then decreased to the proportions which became commonplace during the Directorate and Empire periods. At this time painting as a decoration for fans was almost entirely superseded by applied decorations in the form of sequins and spangles.

The proportions of the folded fan, as has the relative size of the fan, have varied considerably at different periods. During the latter half of the 16th century, the general proportions of the fan were approximately a quarter of a circle. The size of this segment of a circle gradually extended during the first half of the 17th century until towards the close of the reign of Louis XVI (1790) the fan had a deep mount opening to a semicircle. Between 1680 and 1740, the French fan had from fourteen to sixteen sticks. (See Fig. 61 page 242).

An even more direct comparison of the sizes of fans can be gauged from the consideration of the part which they played in fashion. The 18th-century fan, therefore, increased in size as skirts grew wider. As dresses reduced in size at the end of the century, so fans became smaller and smaller until fashions once again changed and the crinoline came in vogue in the 1860s. Fans once more became large and many mid-Victorian fans are of considerable proportions.

All that I believe I have done so far is to highlight the enormous difficulty in dating and identifying fans. Perhaps I have laid too much stress on the problem, great though it truly is, and so in mitigation I will set out a sort of "check list" of points to consider when you are looking at a fan.

251

1. SIZE   Consider the span of the open fan.

2. AREA   How far does it open? Bear in mind that the fan can generally be dated by its proportions. See Fig. 61 on p. 242.

3. MOUNT   Is it painted, hand-coloured lithograph, printed coloured lithograph, what sort of colours is it painted in—water-colour, gouache, oils, tempera, &c.

4. MANUFACTURE   Is it hand-made or machine-made? Look for punched decoration in guards and sticks rather than carved work. Watch for pressed designs rather than incised detail in wooden sticks.

5. DECOR   What style of decoration on sticks, guards, mount?

6. SUBJECT   What is the style and subject of the painting? Does it extend across the whole leaf? Is it contained in a bordered area such as a medallion or cartouche?

7. PERIOD   Baroque (1660–1735)
Rococo (1735–65)
Neo-Classical (1765–1800)
Regency (1810–20)
Empire (1804–14)
Minuet
Oriental Export (difficult to put a period to)
Victorian
Edwardian
Modern

8. NATIONALITY   Look for easily-identifiable signs such as subject, overall style of workmanship, historical events, places and people.

Remember that Louis XIV fans usually had between eighteen and twenty-one blades, the gorge featured a low shoulder and the painting was boldly executed in vivid colours. These fans opened to a half-circle. By Louis XV, the number of blades was from eighteen to twenty-two and they were usually narrower and therefore further apart. Somewhere around 1720, the shoulder was raised. The fans no longer opened out to a half-circle but were slightly less.

It is interesting to relate that the style which is usually known as Louis XVI was really in existence some years before he came to the throne and this once more highlights the difficulty in assigning a fixed date or even a period unless the fan happens to feature a datable event such as a royal wedding or birth or to commemorate a visit between sovereigns.

Folding fans made entirely of feathers were a 19th-century invention but the use of peacock and ostrich feathers as a decoration for an otherwise ordinary folding fan has been in vogue since the 17th century. The normal use of these would be as a decorative edging to the outer diameter of the mount, extending, to all practical intent and purpose, the area of the fan. Screen-shape fans made entirely of peacock or ostrich feathers have been made throughout the vogue-span of the fan and they are usually grouped in an ornamental handle with or without various other ornamentations of metals or minerals.

These somewhat condensed notes should act as a rough guide for the collector to be able to appraise with a fair measure of accuracy fans which he may be offered in his travels. I must stress again that there is so much very genuine ignorance amongst dealers who are unaccustomed to dealing in fans that you would be well advised to rely on your own practised judgement when buying rather than on the probably earnest but oft ill-advised provenance provided by the hopeful vendor. However, let me assure you of one point. It is a foregone conclusion that sooner or later you will fall victim to a bad buy. Everybody does this at some stage in their collecting and the three things to remember are first of all the very inevitability of this happening, secondly that if you are pleased with your buy (even if it is not what you thought it to be) you will retain a measure of that pleasure, and finally that this may highlight your own shortcomings in knowledge and spur you to ensure you do not fall victim again!

Of course, if all you want is quantity rather than quality, these words are superfluous. I recall once seeing an advertisement in a renowned newspaper for discerning people which stated, simply, "American desires library of about 6,000 books. Apply . . .". Lest I should offend any of my many American friends, let me add that there are some singularly cloth-headed Englishmen about as well!

CHAPTER ELEVEN

DECORATIVE ART AND THE FAN FORM

The semi-circle with radiating spokes from the centre which is the fundamental shape of the fan has certain properties which have been appreciated since primitive times. Every point on the circumference is at an equal distance from the centre, a basic geometrical fact which was applied to the design of the ancient stadium, the tactical positioning of warriors in battle and the arrangement of the concert orchestra. Architecturally, the semi-circle provided the earliest form of Man-made arch and a form which is still with us today. The arch above a door was frequently glazed with a semi-circular window—a fanlight. The word fanlight was used to describe these windows to distinguish them from the transom-light, naturally based on rectangular format.

Fan-shaped tracery in stone and cast iron was applied in architecture over many centuries and served not only to beautify but was also eminently practicable since it represented maximum strength for minimal material content.

Whilst these examples serve to illustrate the uses of the fan shape, the fan itself, or rather representations of it, have served widely over the years as a feature of decorative art. Tapestries, screens, carpets, even linoleums, were embellished with fans either as direct representations or as decorative shapes. Jewellery in the form of fan-shaped brooches has been produced since the middle of the last century and still today it is not uncommon to come across modern pieces representing the costume fan.

Table mats (place mats), menu holders, plates (both for practical table use and for decoration), firescreens and a host of other day-to-day objects have been produced over the years in the shape of fans. Some of these objects are shown in Plates 58, 59.

Although it is not unusual to see a woman on a bus or commuter train, or seated at the theatre, fanning herself with a newspaper or a programme, there must be few today who possess a fan and carry it

Fig. 64

Fan vaulting from Henry VII's Chapel at Westminster Abbey.

with them. The fan, though, is still considered to be a contemporary accessory of costume, and when Dorothy Wilding posed Her Majesty Queen Elizabeth II for her classic photograph, she portrayed her holding in her left hand a half-opened fan. If we interpret this accord-

255

ing to M. Develloroy's code, set out in Chapter 6, we find that Her Majesty is implying "Come and talk to me."

An impressive, titillating performance to watch is the Spanish Fan Dance where, as in many an opera and operetta, the skilful use of the fan plays an all-important part. More subtle, however, is the fan-dance of the Japanese which is the model of decorous behaviour. The Parisian fan-dancers imparted a far more overtly naughty connotation to the fan than may at any other time previous have been understood. It could, I have little doubt, be argued that this sort of performance was harmless enough since its messages were broadcast, so to speak, whilst the 18th-century lovers, secretly exchanging intimacies aided by the fan, at least intended to try to follow up what the language of the fan was alone allowed to imply.

There are many casual references to the fan and I believe that this short chapter is probably the best place in which to introduce several aspects of *fanology* which cannot conveniently be pigeon-holed elsewhere in this book. Although they are, from the historical aspect and also from the collector's point of view, somewhat in-consequential, I believe that it is as well to include them on the grounds that somebody, somewhere, might just want to know the meaning of certain phrases, or want to probe those sidetracks from the sturdy path of the costume fan.

A number of slang terms arose around the word "fan". During the last century, "fan" was widely used in certain quarters to refer to the waistcoat and John Camden Hotten asserted that the name emanated from Houndsditch. Matsell, on the other hand, wrote in 1859 that the expression was of American origin. A far more inter-esting and likely derivation is given by Barrère and Leland (*A Dictionary of Slang, Jargon & Cant*, London, 1897). Here we find that *fam* or *fem* is believed to be gipsy for hand, fem indicating five or the five fingers. However, the Romany word for five is *pange*. So fam meant, in gipsy language, to handle and came from the gipsy *fan* or *vangri*. But the word fan, as a verb, had two distinct meanings in more or less general useage. It meant to beat or to berate in one connotation, and in another it also meant to feel or to handle. Here it referred to the tactics of the petty thief* who would run his hands over a person in such a way as to determine if he had anything valuable in his pockets. The derivation here is clear to understand

* The *fogle-hunter* of Charles Dickens' *Oliver Twist*.

34. Chicken-skin mount painted with a scene showing St Luke descending from the clouds to cure a sick child. The sticks and guards of pierced ivory in paired decoration. The whole in a gilded fan case. French, *c.* 1750. 10 inches (26cm).
35. Painted vellum mount showing cartouche and medallions, the centre subject depicting two maidens being serenaded by a gallant. Carved and pierced mother of pearl sticks with thin iridescent pearl backing. The whole decorated with gilt. In an early bevelled-glass case. Probably French, mid-18th century. 11 inches (28cm).

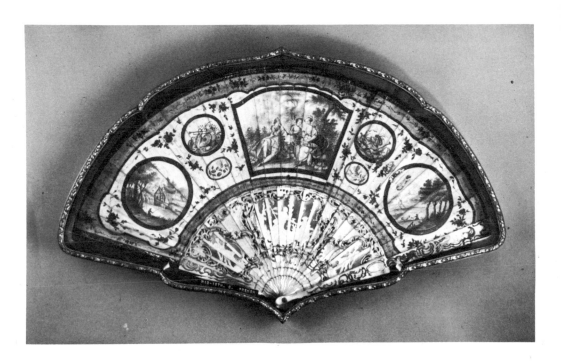

36. Chicken-skin mount painted with a large centre vignette showing a rural scene. Ivory sticks paired alternately from centre and ornamented with silver. Guards to match. In plain gilded fan case. French, *c.* 1760. 11 inches (28cm), and below 37. Two English printed fans. At the top is a calendar fan with flowers for the seasons and marked with events of Royalty, Church and University. The mount is dated 1794. Plain wood sticks. 11 inches (28cm). Below this is a fan printed with the instructions for five card games, this one dated 1792. Dark wood sticks and guards. 11 inches (28cm).

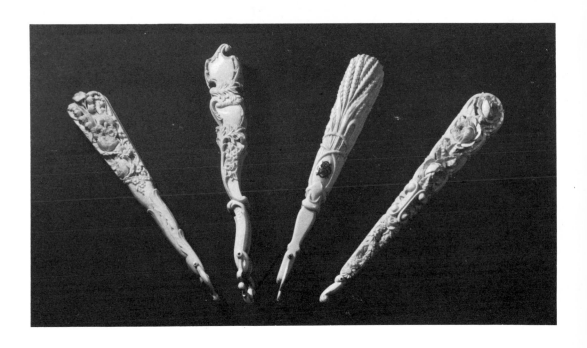

38. Four ivory brisé fans, each with plain ivory sticks, but with unusual and heavily carved ivory guards. English, *c.* 1830–40.

39. Lithographed mount showing four figures attacking Cupid who is protected by shields. The sticks of mother of pearl arranged in pagoda style with floral paintings, the circles at the shoulder no doubt serving also as peep-holes. English, *c.* 1830. 8½ inches (21cm).

40. Youghal lace mount with Tudor rose, thistles and shamrocks, plain mother of pearl sticks and guards. The whole enclosed in a black wood and gilt glazed case. Irish. Late 19th century. 9½ inches (24cm).

41. Flat Venetian point needle-made lace bridal fan denoting a marriage between members of two families bearing armorial insignia. A central figure in bridal gown with a surround of flowers and leaves, the family arms displayed at left and right. Sticks and guards of iridescent mother of pearl with gilt design. Late 19th century. 10¾ inches (27cm).

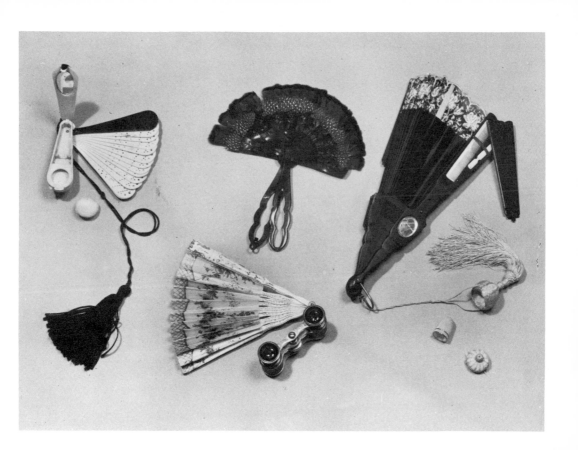

42. Four unusual Victorian fans with accessories. Top left: Punched ivory fan with a hollow handle which doubles as a toilet case. The lid opens to reveal a mirror and powder compact. Centre: Folding feather fan made to fit into a handbag, tortoise shell guards clip together in the open position to serve as handle. Top right: Black wood sticks and guards, lace net mount. Hollowed-out compartments in the thick guards are closed by swivelling panels and contain a comb and manicure implement, sewing requisites in the other guard including a tiny pair of scissors, with a thimble in the hollowed-out centre of the tassel bob. Patented by W. Thornhill *c.* 1895–1900. Below this is a fan with a painted mount and bone sticks and guards, attached by the rivet to opera glasses.

43. Folding cockade fan with a convex mirror in the handle. This fan operates in the same manner as that drawn in Fig. 62. Victorian.

44. Silk mount painted showing a couple in rural setting in the centre vignette. Floral decoration with spangles. The sticks gilt with silver on blonde tortoise shell with silver piqué. Mid-19th century. 9½ inches (24cm).

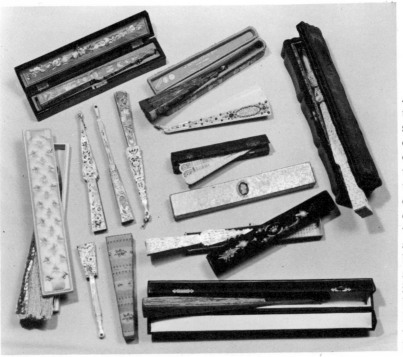

45. Group of fans in their original boxes showing the most common styles. That on the lower left is of wood covered in quilted silk taffeta; that on the upper right is of oriental lacquered wood. Bottom right is an early 20th-century box with double lid and to the left of it is a tapestry-covered box for a battoir fan. In the centre are various cardboard boxes.

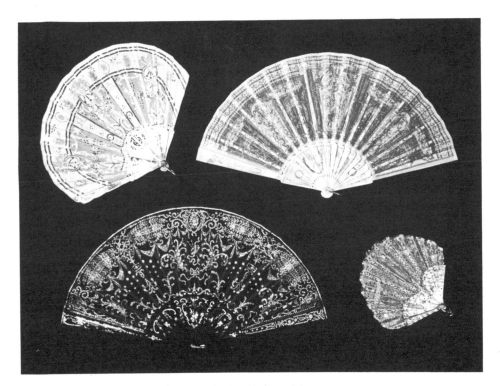

46. Fans with spangles. Top left: Shell-shaped spangled fan with silver-coloured mother of pearl sticks and guards decorated with piqué design. Silver-spangled mount of fine gauze. English, *c.* 1850. 8½ inches (22cm). Top right: Also English, this one dates from about 1900 and has sticks and guards decorated with silver and gilt quiver and laurel wreath designs. The mount is of fine gauze with gold spangles sewn with golden thread. The central panel shows musical instruments. 8½ inches (22cm). Bottom left: Tortoise shell sticks and guards with gilt ornamentation. The mount is of black gauze with fine gold spangles and thread pattern. French, Louis XVI. Bottom right: Small shell-shaped English fan with mother-o'pearl sticks and guards with clouté decoration. The gauze mount has silver and gilt spangles, *c.* 1930. 6 inches (15cm), and below 47. Advertising fan with a colour-printed paper leaf advertising a champagne. Plain wooden sticks. Modern.

48. The Lover's Quarrel. Black lace and gauze fan painted with figures in Kate Greenaway costume entwined by lovers' bows. The sticks of black wood decorated with gilt, the guards with carved and raised edelweiss flowers. English, mid-Victorian. 14 inches (35cm).

49. White ostrich feather folding fan with mother of pearl sticks and guards decorated with gilt and silver floral design and ladybirds. The ribbon is original. Its box shows it to have been made by Tiffany & Co. of New York and Paris, c. 1875. 12½ inches (31cm).

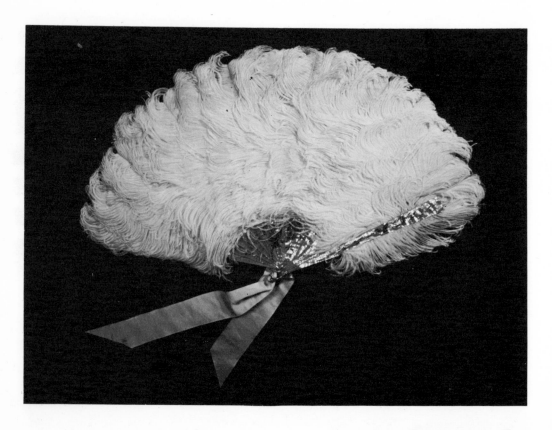

50. Jewellery in the shape of a fan. Earrings, clips, brooches and buttons all styled after the folding fan.

51. Bronze sculpture in the classical style by Pandiani, Milan. Size: 18 × 10½ inches (46 × 26cm). 19th century.

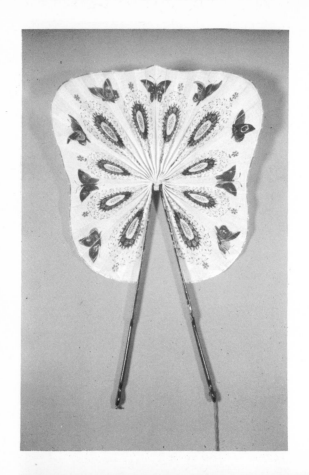

52. A modern scoop-shaped folding fan. This one was among the very last to be made by Duvelleroy in London and was given to the author by Mr P. Duvelleroy before he retired in 1965. London, 1965.

53. Silver tea service with fan-shaped tray 22 × 13 inches. Fan motif on tray, teapot, milk-jug and sugar basin. Hall-marked Birmingham, 1879.

54. Brass folding fire screen in filigree. 22 inches high.

55. Fan-shaped corner table and bronze fan-shaped wall clock with white enamel Roman numerals. French, *c.* 1870.

56. Coffee pot in Satsuma ware, lacquered tray with fan motif and fan-shaped lacquered trinket boxes.

57. Figure in gilded bronze 10½ inches high, standing on an ebony pedestal 2½ inches high. French.

58. Set of modern table mats printed with 18th-century fans.

59. Silver place menu holders. Victorian.

60. Modern Dresden china lady with a fan, a fan-shaped plate also in Dresden, and modern Dresden menu holders.

61. Decorated porcelain flower holder in the shape of folding and screen fans, and a hand-shaped half-open fan ashtray.

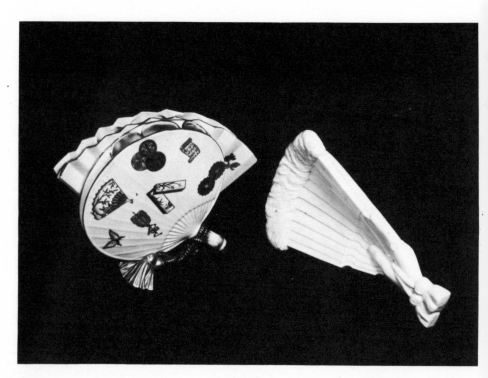

62. Minton china tea service, the saucers fan-shaped with painted butterflies on the handles of the cups, milk jug and teapot.

63. 18th-century Rudolstadt porcelain figure of a lady with a fan, a fan-shaped ashtray and a fan-shaped box with a hinged lid.

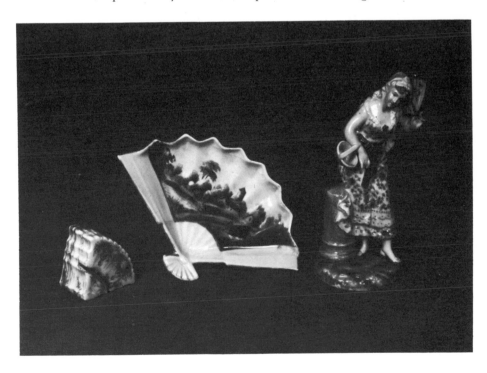

64. Chinese plate with fan motif, also Italian fan-shaped table lamp.

and it is easy to visualise the pick-pocket with his fingers fanned out quickly feeling the waistcoat of a potential victim. The connection between fan meaning a waistcoat, and to fan in this instance is circumstantial but would appear likely.

Queen Anne's Fan was the name given to what we generally know today as "cocking a snook". In the *Ingoldsby Legends* we read "He put his thumb unto his nose and spread his fingers out, to take a sight to make Queen Anne's Fan". A "sight"* was the name given to a gesture of derision and a "double sight" was made by joining the tip of the little finger of the hand already fanned in front of the nose to the thumb of the other hand, the fingers being similarly extended and emphasis being given by moving or wagging the fingers of both hands as if playing a piano.

The word "fan" remains very much with us today in another sense. We have sports fans, pop fans, fan clubs and so on. Here the word fan really does come from *vannus*, for the football fan is one who "fans up the spirits of his club", metaphorically blowing the flames.

Writing in *Fraser's Magazine* in May, 1879, H. A. Giles related the touching story of how the expression "autumn fan" used in China to refer to a deserted wife came into being. The tale, recounted in Woolliscroft-Rhead, is worth telling once more.

It seems that there was a favourite of the Emperor Ch'eng Ti of the Han dynasty, 32 BC, whose name was Pan and who for some time had been a confidante of His Majesty and the Queen of the Imperial Seraglio. Having persuaded herself that something more than an ordinary attachment of the hour existed between herself and the "Son of Heaven" and finding that her influence was on the wane, she was unable to conceal any longer her mortification, grief and despair. So she forwarded to the Emperor a circular screen-fan upon which were inscribed the following lines expressing the contrast between the summer of her reciprocated love, and the autumn of her desertion:

> O fair white silk, fresh from the weaver's loom,
> Clear as the frost, bright as the winter snow—

---

* This remains with us to this day in expressions such as to say to someone "You look a sight". However, "A sight for sore eyes" and expressions such as "That is a long sight better", whilst of equal antiquity, have other roots and derivations.

See, friendship fashions out of thee a fan:
Round as the round moon shines in heaven above;
At home, abroad, a close companion thou;
Stirring at every move the grateful gale,
And yet I fear, ah me! that autumn chills
Cooling the dying summer's torrid rage,
Will see thee laid neglected on the shelf,
All thought of bygone days, bygone like them.

Fig. 65

Exhibited at the Paris International Exhibition in 1878, this Queen Anne
style hanging clock was designed by Thomas Harris, F.R.I.B.A. and made
by Howell & James of Regent Street, London. The fan motif is evident in
the mantel, and the whole concept demonstrates the fondness of the
Victorians for objects of an earlier era in preference to a new creation.

And thus, from that time forward, the deserted wife in China has been known as an "autumn fan".

It probably goes without saying that the fan played an important part in music. Besides the fact that the ladies would deem any public function (including concerts and recitals) as an occasion for displaying their latest and finest fans, the fan was employed in numerous operas as a vital prop to the action.

One enterprising lady by the name of Madame Jeanne Dubost went so far as to devise a one-act ballet which she called *L'Eventail de Jeanne*, the Jeanne undoubtedly being herself. This was an interesting effort and quite as ephemeral as the fan. Madame chose not to write special music for her ballet, but to collect together a number of existing pieces by well-loved composers and weld them into a whole. Her ballet thus comprised music by Maurice Ravel, P.-O. Ferroud, Jacques Ibert, Roland-Manuek, Marcel Dellanoy, Albert Roussel, Darius Milhaud, Francis Poulenc, Georges Auric and Florent Schmitt. The first performance was on June 16th, 1927 and the orchestra appears to have comprised two pianos. The ballet was performed at least a second time (on March 4th, 1929), on this occasion before L'Academie Nationale de Musique complete with orchestra and professional choreography. The music was published by Heugel of Paris and it remains an interesting if rather trifling collection.

I have been unable to decide whether there is any incontrovertible connection between the fan and the musical fanfare which comprises a short passage (known in England in the past as a "flourish") for unison trumpets. Sir Charles Grove* states it to be a French term of unknown origin, possibly Moorish, possibly anomatopoeic. It could be said that the trumpets in a fanfare fan out, also that their sound fans out because in early times the trumpeters probably stood in a semi-circle, facing outwards, rather than in line abreast as is usual today. However, in organ-building, a fanfare of trumpets is the term used to describe a stop of beating reeds which produce a trumpet-like sound. These individual reed pipes are each fitted with a trumpet-like resonator and they are frequently arranged, unlike all the other pipes in an organ, horizontally projecting outwards in a fan shape from the front of the organ case. Traditionally

* *Dictionary of Music & Musicians*, 1st edition, 1889.

259

Fig. 66

Dating from about 450 BC, this funeral stele was made in Greece and
demonstrates the use of the fan motif as a crowning decoration. It now stands
in the National Museum at Naples.

a feature of the Spanish and Portuguese schools of organ-building
and only occasionally found on British and other Northern European organs, the other name for this arrangement is *en chamade*.

During this dress-making period it will "pay you" both in your appearance, your health and the fit of your gown if you try a pair of the Genuine Jackson Corset Waists.

If the proof of the pudding is in the eating, then the wearing of a pair of the Genuine Jackson Corset Waists is the proof of their excellence and usefulness in every avocation.

For Bicycle Riders they are simply perfection. They are an all-round necessity and companion. Your waist measure, stating whether you want white or drab, together with $1.25, will bring a pair to your house. Try at the Corset Dept. of your local store; they usually have them.

$1.25 a pair, postpaid. **JACKSON CORSET CO., Jackson, Mich.**

Fig. 67

The fan was used widely in advertising, usually with but passing connection with the goods being described. This notice appeared in *Munsey's Magazine* about 1895.

Whilst on this subject, the fan as a shape in organ building is quite frequently found. The great mechanical orchestrion organs which played music from pinned wooden barrels frequently had a fan-shaped row of reed-stop resonators arranged at the front of the instrument to enhance the appearance. The organ of this type which Messrs Imhof & Mukle of Vöhrenbach in Germany exhibited at the Industrial Exhibition in London of 1862 included just this feature and several organ builders, notably the Hull firm of Forster & Andrews, adopted a similar pipe arrangement for their "finger" organs. This firm exhibited an organ with two fan-shaped pipe arrays at the 1862 Exhibition and later built two concert organs in which the fan-shape played an important part of the appearance.*

The intrinsic strength of the fan shape with its radiating sticks from one fixed point is evident in Nature where we find that the shape of the shell (the bi-valvular mollusc species) has a similar functional design. Coincidentally, many 19th-century fans adopted the characteristic shell-shape being the greater part of an ellipse with the greater axis at the centre. A fan of this type is shown in Plate 46.

The fan also exists in another natural form and perhaps here I should add that this really is a folding fan. On the Island of Ceylon and the Malbar coast there grows a peculiar species of palm called the *corypha umbraculifera*, popularly known as the talipot tree. In many ways a remarkable tree, for it grows like a ship's mast to a height of a hundred feet or more before spreading its unusual foliage, its feather-light dark green leaves have all the characteristics of a brisé fan. When cut and dried, these leaves become a pale yellowish brown and can be opened and closed as if each slender fibre were hinged at the head. In Ceylon, which suffers both scorching heat and torrential rain, the natives have for centuries used Talipot fans to ward off the elements.†

One final variant of the fan is worth mentioning and this is one which is quite familiar to us today. The Scottish physician Dr Arnott in his *Report to the Poor Law Commissioners* in 1836, wrote:

> Not long ago the people working in cotton and other factories were observed generally soon to become pallid and sickly, and then scrofulous in various degrees, and many of them at last to sink into early graves; and this happened chiefly because they and their employers were ignorant of the fatal influence on their health of spending so much of their time in close apartments, of which the ventilation was either left to chance, or was even studiously prevented to preserve the warmth useful for the process of manufacturing. These work-people were crowded together, constantly breathing a polluted, noxious air, nearly

* The organs in the King's Hall, Hull (1913) and Queen's Hall, Hull (1907) as well as Holy Trinity Church (1900) and the Kinnaird Hall, Dundee (1865) had this feature. (*Vide: Forster & Andrews Organ Builders*, Laurence Elvin, 1968.)

† *Vide* article "The Talipot Tree of Ceylon", *Penny Magazine*, July 6th, 1833, pp. 257–58). See also Fig. 12 on p. 58.

as noxious to them as to the trouts of a mountain stream is the water of a stagnant pool. Recently, however, wheels or fanners for ventilating have been introduced into many of the factories, by which the air is drawn out or changed with any desired rapidity, while fresh air, artificially warmed, is admitted in its stead; and now, in places where these means have been adopted, the factory operatives, being further supplied with good food, and not over-worked, have become, as proved by late evidence, a most healthy portion of the working community.*

Dr Arnott went on to describe the elementary principles of air-conditioning and ventilation using a new variant of the fan. And so, in the 1830s, the rotating ventilation fan came into being, albeit driven by the factory steam-engine via the overhead shafting and belt-drive pulleys which represented the motive power of the "second Industrial Revolution". *Tempora mutantur, nos et mutamur in illis!*

* Dr Arnott's Report is given in the *Second Annual Report of the Poor Law Commissioners*, Appendix C.

CHAPTER TWELVE

AN INDEX OF FAN MAKERS, DESIGNERS AND PAINTERS

To the student of the fan and its development, three aspects become abundantly clear quite early on in his or her work with fans. To begin with there is the question of provenance. Apart from the difficulty in so many cases of even establishing beyond all doubt the basic country of origin of a commonplace fan, as shown in Chapter 8 the practice of fan painters signing their work was uncommon. The second problem is the identification of the scene depicted. The third difficulty is one which colours the preceding two—that of dating the fan by its mount.

If one were to attempt a complete listing of all fan makers one would be doomed to failure because there were so many and, because all did not mark their work, such a listing would be to all intents and purposes worthless.

Listing fan subjects also has its problems. The subject of a fan may be interpreted or positively identified as a scene from such-and-such an opera or classical happening, but if the novice collector is unable to recognise a description based on these terms as referring to a fan in his collection, then again our listing will have value only to the discerning and knowledgeable person of letters.

These, then, are the obstacles which stand in the way of the preparation of any listing which might help in identifying and dating a fan. One group of fans, though, automatically excludes itself from any of these limitations. This is that which includes the multitude of English printed fans which almost always had an identifiable subject and, where it had not been trimmed off in the process of mounting, the leaf always bore the printed date and the name of the publisher. A second group, only slightly less prominent than the printed fans, stands out. This includes those fans which portrayed historical events, fans of special, patented style or design and fans issued for special and readily-identifiable events.

What I have attempted to do is to list those fan makers whose

Fig. 68

The Youth's Companion. October 27th, 1898 contained this advertisement.

names most frequently appear on fan boxes, in advertisements or on common or interesting trade cards preserved in public, private or National collections. I have also included fan painters whose work is famous or identifiable. This listing also includes designers. Added to these names are those few who took out patents for special types of fan such as the mechanical or dual-purpose fans.

Fan subjects comprise such a vast field, both those forming the enormous repertoire of the classical, painted fan, and the popular and prolific printed fan. The early hand-painted fans were all, naturally enough, individually worked and although not unexpectedly the same scene was used on many fans, there were many such scenes, few of which were identifiable although many were taken from masters and skilfully adapted. In so many cases, then, identification of a fan mount may demand a thorough working knowledge of the works of Cruikshank, Angelica Kauffmann and other such artists. Here I have attempted to list the most common subjects which appear on fans, and this is intended to serve as a guide to the period of the fan.

England was the only country to make it law that printed fans should be dated and state the publisher. For this reason it is the English printed fan which is the only type of fan which may consistently be dated and attributed with certainty.

Because of the circumstances set out above, this list can never hope to be complete and, from the collector's standpoint, such a list is not needed. However, the present index is certainly the most complete so far assembled for the guidance of collectors. My sources of information, besides those fans in my own collection and in the collections of friends, associates and correspondents, include G. Woolliscroft Rhead and Lionel Cust's fine catalogue of the fans and fan-leaves in the Schreiber Collection which was published in 1893. The foundation of this listing builds on the first index which was compiled by MacIver Percival in 1920. His work also drew on *Le Livre de Collectioneurs* of Maze Sencier. With due acknowledgement to all these sources, I have embodied in one index all the relevant information which will assist in identifying and dating as many of the printed fans as possible. Coupled with this I have listed some positively ascribed fans that have come to light.

This Index is in two parts. The first comprises a list of engravers, artists, designers and publishers; and lists, where known, their published work either by title as printed on the fan, or by description of the subject. An attempt has been made to cross-reference this part so that designers and publishers of a fan—seldom the same person—can be found.

The second part of this Index lists the subjects alphabetically, again as printed or by description, and refers back to head-words in the first part. As an example, if you have a fan entitled *A Collection of Beaux*, consult the subject under Part Two of this Index, and look under "Collection" where you will find:

Collection of Beaux, A, *see* WILSON

If you now refer to Part One and look under the head-word WILSON, you will see that he was designer and engraver of this fan, but you will also see the title of the fan annotated "*see* READ". If you now find READ in this same part, you will discover that J. Read was the publisher of the fan.

Throughout this Index, reproductions of fan-makers' trade cards and signs have been introduced. These have come from four sources: my own collection, Paul Lacroix's *The XVIIIth Century* (1876), and the Heal Collection and the Banks Collection which are now both preserved in the British Museum.

PART ONE

AGAR
    Engraver: printed fans
    Oracle of Apollo, The
    Jupiter
    Tarquin and the Sibyl
    Widow, The
ALEXANDRE, M.   Paris
    Fans by this maker were exhibited at the Paris Exposition, 1867. One was painted on a silk leaf containing in one large cartouche a group entitled, "The four ages of Infancy, Youth, Manhood and Old Age". This was signed by F. Fossey
    Les Blondes and Les Brunettes
ALLEN FAN COMPANY   *see* HUNT, EDWIN SOPER
AMAURY, G.   62, rue la Boë Tie, Paris. Fan manufacturer
ANDRE, EUG
    Signature on Lithographed fan
    Three medallions of village life
AGRAND   rue Martin No. 357, Paris
    Publisher: Printed fans
    Five Senses and the Four Seasons—fan with nine medallions containing female figures representing the—
AREVALO, CANO DE
    Spanish fan painter to the Queen of Spain at the end of the 17th century.

ASHTON, SARAH 28, Little Britain, London.
    Sarah Ashton was admitted a member of the Worshipful Company of Fan Makers on February 1st, 1770.
    Publisher: Printed fans
    Duchess of York, 1792
    Botanical Fan, 1792
    Casino Fan, The, 1793 (Stipple engraving, hand-coloured)
    Conundrums, 1794
    Way of the World, The, 1796 (Stipple engraving)
    School for Scandal, 1796
    Shakespeare's Seven Ages, 1796
    World Grown Old and Crazy, The, n.d.
ASHTON, SARAH & CO.
    Publishers: printed fans
    Conundrums, 1797
ASHTON & CO.
    Publishers: printed fans
    Female Seven Ages, 1797
    Quiz Club, The, 1797
    Lady's Adviser, The, 1797
    Grotesque Subjects, 1797
ASHTON, S. & CO.
    Publishers: printed fans
    Dance Fan, A, 1798
ASHTON & HADWEN No. 28, Little Britain, London
    Publishers: printed fans
    Conundrums, 1800
    Union, The, 1801
    Peace Restored, 1801 (*see* WILSON)
    Divertissement pour tout Age, 1800
    United Sisters, The, 1801 (*see* WILSON)
BACH Madrid, Spain. Maker of quality fans who exhibited at the 1878 Paris International Exhibition.
BADINI, CHARLES FRANCIS
    Designer: Printed fans
    Fanology, 1797 (*see* WILLIAM COCK)
BALSTER, T. 7, Bedford Place, Rotherof
    Balster was admitted as member of the Worshipful Company of Fan Makers in December, 1777.

Publisher: Printed fans
George III, In Honour of, 1789
Queen's Royal Fan, 1821 (etching, hand-coloured)
Map of England, The
Vive le Roy, 1789 (George III and "Dieu et mon Droit")

BARLOW
Engraver
Royal Concert (after Cruikshank), 1781

BARTOLOZZI, FRANCESCO
Engraver: Printed fans
Theft of Cupid's Bow
Cupid & Psyche, 1779
Cupid & Arabesque, 1780

BAYLIE, ANN
Fan maker, Warehousewoman "At the Golden Fan and Sun at Chidley Court, near Carlton House, Pall Mall." Another trade card, in the Heal collection, reads: "Fan Maker & Warehouse Woman. From the late Nr. Marguss's India Warehouse, Bucklers Bury, Cheapside."

BEHRMANN & COLLMANN   London
Publishers: Printed fans
Aranjuez, March 19, 1808 (pub. November 1813) Aquatint-engraving, uncoloured.
Madrid, May 2, 1808 (pub. December 1813) Aquatint-engraving, uncoloured. (Two different versions showing different scenes. The second is a hand-coloured etching.)
Don Juan Palarea, 1813 (Aquatint-engraving, hand-coloured.)

BELLA, STEFANO DELLA
Engraver of Handscreen in the centre of which three couples are shown dancing a country dance (in Schreiber collection).

BELLETESTE, JEAN ANTOINE
Maker of ivory fan mounts, 1787–1832
Catalogue descriptif critique et Anecdotique des Objects (à Trianon) sous les Auspices de SM l'Imperatise (Eugenie), 1867. No. 70, "Un eventail scul(p)té a jour."

BELLEVILLE
"Belleville, Editeur, Imprimeur, Rue Portefoin No. 8" Inscription on uncoloured lithographed fan in Schreiber catalogue.

BELLI, FRA
"Invenit et Facit". The signature of a fan decorated on one side
with ten medallions representing Venus receiving from the
Tritons the tributes of the sea; on the other side five medallions
of subjects in the Pompeian style.

BELLINI LTD. "Artists in Fans, Mounters and Repairers",
189, Regent Street, London, W.1

BENIZY
Designer and Engraver: Printed fans
Charade Nouveau

BIRMAN, A. P.
Publisher and Designer: Printed fans
Marriage of Duke of York, 1791
George III, 1791 (*see* HINCKS)

BOITARD, LOUIS PIERRE
French engraver and designer in England
Pen drawings of cupids engaged in vintage in Schreiber collection,
signed "Boitard 196".

BOUCHER, FRANCESCO
Many fan leaves attributed to this French painter and engraver,
usually without justification. His period was 1703–70.

BROOKER, JAMES "Fan Maker at the Sun & Fan, the
corner of St. Paul's church yard near Cheapside. Makes, mounts
and sells all types of Fan." Fl. 1735.

BUNBURY, H. W.
Minuet at Bath, The (drawing reproduced on French Fan in
Schreiber collection).

BURNETT, MICHAEL
"Fan-maker at the Hand and Fan over against Friday Street in
Cheapside"
Advertised in *The Craftsman* 1732–3 as maker of "Lilliputian
fans" and others.

BURNEY, ESTHER "at the Golden Fan in Fenchurch
Street". 18th C. maker and repairer of fans
Designer: Printed fans, apparently published by AGAR (q.v.)
Oracle of Apollo, The
Jupiter
Tarquin and the Sibyl
Widow, The

CAHAIGNE
A finely-painted fan in gouache and dated 1766 is so signed.

CANU, JEAN DOMINIQUE ETEINNE
Engraver: Printed fans. Born Paris 1768
Horse Race, The
Lasso, The
Negro Labourers
El Mendigo

CARDON (presumably **PHILLIP**)
Engraver: Printed fans. Died in 1817
*George III with Nelson & Britannia (see **UWINS**)*

CAROY CO., SANCHEZ 5, Fernando VII, Barcelona, Spain. Fan manufacturer

CARRACEI, AUGOSTINO
Etched designs of hand-screens

CARRE, MDLE. ALIDA
18th-century Dutch fan painter

CHASSEREAU, FRANCIS
Admitted to the Worshipful Company of Fan Makers on November 3rd, 1758.
Designer: Printed fans
Pleasureboat, 1739
Garden Scene, 1741
Capture of Porto Bello, 1740
Shepherd & Shepherdess, 1741

In the Banks collection there is a trade card, probably *c.* 1750, bearing the name HONOUR CHASSEREAU "Fan-Maker & Stationer. At the Fan and Crown in Long Acre, London".

CHASSEREAU, FRANCIS (Snr.)

An early and important member of the Worshipful Company of Fan Makers who was admitted on December 4th, 1721, and was elected Member of the Court of Assize in 1729. See also CHASSEREAU, FRANCIS, his son.

CHAUDET, ANTOINE

French painter and sculptor, born 1763; died 1810
Designer: Printed fans
Napoleon Bonaparte (fan with medallions in honour of)

CHERRET, J.   18 R. Ste Marie Ternes, Paris.

Inscription and signature on a two-sided lithographed mount, partly printed in colours, and forming Rimmel's programme for a performance of Robertson's "Dreams" and Gilbert's "Robert the Devil", titled: *Programme of the Gaiety Theatre*

CHERRY, WILLIAM "Fann-Maker at the Mercury and Fann in Wardour Street near Soho Square . . . India Gold-Fanns of New Patterns Very Neat & Different from any yet Sold." Trade card, *c.* 1730, in Banks collection.

CHODOWIECKI, DANIEL NICHOLAS
Polish painter of miniatures and etcher, born 1726; died 1801
Designer and Engraver: Printed fans
Frederick William II
Apotheosis of Frederick II

CIPRIANI, GIOVANNI BATTISTA
Italian/English painter and etcher, born 1727; died 1785
Designer: Printed fans
Orpheus & Eurydice
Toilet of Venus

CLARK, S.
Designer: Printed fans
View of Greenwich, 1740

CLARK, ALFRED   33, New Bond Street, London
> Fan Maker, probably descendant from the fan-making family of Clarke, who made for the then Princess of Wales a fan which took from August 1900 to October 1901 to complete.

CLARKE, ROBERT   26, Strand, London
> A Robert Clarke was admitted member of the Worshipful Company of Fan Makers in 1756. His address is given as of "Mr. Clarke's in Bell Sauvage Yard, Ludgate Hill".
> Publisher: Printed fans
> *Fanology*, 1797 (Etching and stipple-engraving, uncoloured)
> *Love Scene*, 1795

CLARKE & CO.   "Fan Makers to their Royal Highness's the
> DUTCHESS & PRINCESS of GLOUCESTER at their Warehouse, No. 263 near Hungerford Street, Strand, London."
> Fl. 1780
> Publishers: Printed fans
> "Inventors of the much esteemed sliding Pocket Fan" (*Vide* trade card *c.* 1788)
> *Gipsy Fan* (at their Warehouse, The King's Arms, near Charing Cross, Strand, London.)
> *St James's Park*, 1741
> *King's Theatre*, 1788

CLARKE & SIMMONS
> Publishers: Printed fans
> *Eventail de Charades*, 1791

COCHIN, CHARLES NICHOLAS (the Elder)
> French engraver and writer, born 1688; died 1754

Engraver of Hand-screen showing the subject of the Triumphal Return of David with the head of Goliath.

COCK

Several men named Cock were members of the Worshipful Company of Fan Makers. ABRAHAM COCK was admitted January 5th, 1740. JOHN COCK of Wood Street was admitted December 5th, 1759. WILLIAM COCK was admitted November 5th, 1778. ABRAHAM COCK the younger was admitted March 19th, 1795. See also WEIGHT-MAN, THOMAS

COCK & CO.   36, Snow Hill, London
   Publisher: Printed fans
   Trial of Warren Hastings, 1788 (line engraving, uncoloured, central subject printed in brown)
   Heraldic Fan, 1792

COCK, J.
   Publisher: Printed fans
   Minuet, The, 1782
   Lieutenant-Colonel Tarleton, 1782

COCK, JOHN & CO. 21, Wood Street, London
   Publisher: Printed fans
   Medley of Puzzles, etc. 1791

COCK, JOHN, & CROWDER, J. P.   21, Wood St, Cheapside, London
   Publishers: Printed fans
   Drury Lane Theatre, 1794
   Allegorical Fan, The, 1794 (Etching, partly hand-coloured)
   Ten Country Dances & Five Cotillions, 1793

Almanack, 1796

English History, 1793 (*see* N E E L E)

History of France, 1793 (*see* N E E L E)

Oracle, The, 1800

Treaty of Amiens, 1801 (Illustrated in "Fan Leaves")

COCK, WILLIAM   42, Pall Mall, London "opposite Cumberland House". Fan-maker

Publisher: Printed fans

Original Fanology, The, 1791

New Opera Fan, 1797 (insc: "Publish'd . . . by permishion of the Manager of the Opera House, 42, Pall Mall")

Heraldic Fan, 1792 (insc: "Pub^d . . . by F. Martin . . . Ovenden sculpt . . . Sold by Wm Cock Fan Maker to the Duchess of York at No. 50 Pall Mall & 55 St. Pauls Church Yard") (Line-engraving, uncoloured)

COKER, B.   Fan Maker variously at 118 Fleet Street (in 1786) and 115 Fleet Street (1809) *vide* trade cards in the Banks collection. One reads: "Fans neatly repaired. Variety of S K R E E N S &c."

Publisher: Printed fans

Lord Howe's Victory, June 1st, 1794

COLIN

"Colin sc. Boulard, Rue St. Martin No. 112. Boulard No. 772. Depose." Inscription on fan in Schreiber catalogue.

COOPER, ROBERT
Engraver: Printed fans
Children with Dog
School for Scandal, The, 1796 (published by SARAH
ASHTON)

CORTONA, PIETRO DA BERRETTINI
Italian architect and painter, born 1596; died 1669. Said to have
painted a fan which was shown at the Exhibition of Fans
staged at Draper's Hall, 1878.

COUSTELLIER, FERNANDO DE, y COMP^{ia}
Spanish fan-maker. Several etchings, uncoloured, of floral designs
in Schreiber catalogue showing flowers with their names in
Latin and Spanish. Probably same as:

COUSTELLIER, FERNANDO y COMP^{ia} Fabrica di
Abanicos, Paris
Printed fans
El Telegrafo de Amor
Floral Fan

CROWN PERFUMERY CO., THE   177, New Bond Street,
London, also Paris and New York. Makers of perfumed paper
fans

DESAMEAUX, CHARLES
This name is found spelled in a number of ways including "De
Hames", "De Hantes" and "De Heaulme". The French
litterateur, A. Jal, mentions this master as being, in 1656,
"Marchand Edvantaillier et Ellumineur ordinaire de sa
Majeste." Percival attributes fl. 1680.

DESPARCS, F. CLAUDE LECTERE
"Fan Maker to His Majesty" *c.* 1680

DESROCHER, S.   Paris
19th-century fan maker who re-introduced vellum mounts.

DIEGO, CASA DE   Puerto Del Sol 12, Mesonoro, Romanos 4,
Madrid, Spain. Modern fan maker (1972)

DUCROT & PETIT   11, rue des Fontaines, Paris
Renowned fan makers. Petit was the inventor of the mould for
folding the fan mount. Exhibited at the Great Exhibition in
1851.

DUMOUCHEL, FRA   "at y^e Fann, & Crown, between
Charles Court, & York-House in the STRAND. Sells, all sorts

of Fans & Necklaces Wholesale & Retail, at Reasonable Rates."
Trade card, printed in French and English, in Banks collection
and dated 1803.

DUVELLEROY, PIERRE   Paris and London
  Famed Fan makers established in the early part of the 19th
    century at 17 Passage des Panoramas, Paris. Exhibited at the
    Great Exhibition in 1851. A London branch was opened in
    1849 at 167, Regent Street. The Royal Warrant was granted
    by Queen Victoria, Queen Alexandra, King George V and
    Queen Mary. The Regent Street premises were cleared when
    the rebuilding programme of 1924 began and a new building
    was leased at 121, New Bond Street where the business con-
    tinued until its final closure in 1965 as J. Duvelleroy. Duvel-
    leroy designed and made a great number of fans. Few were
    signed or marked in any way. One of his last, presented to the
    Author, is shown in Plate 52.
  Royal Fan, The (Queen Victoria, Prince Albert and their children).
    Published for the Great Exhibition of 1851 by JOHN TAL-
    LIS & CO.

278

J. DUVELLEROY,
BY APPOINTMENT
LONDON: 167, Regent Street, 167.
EVENTAILS ARTISTIQUES, MODERNES, ANTIQUES ET POUR MARIAGE.
FANS REPAIRED.

PARIS.   LONDON.

DYDE AND SCRIBE   Pall Mall, London
Publishers: Printed fans
Road to Ruin (etching, hand-coloured)
Charade Fan (*see* **SIMPKINS**)
ELIZABETH, PRINCESS
Designer: Printed fan
Rest by the Wayside, The
ELVEN, J. P.
Engraver: Printed fans
Medallions of Ships
EUREKA TRICK & NOVELTY CO.   P.O. Box 4614, 39,
Ann St. New York. U.S.A. Advertised as manufacturers of the
"Magic Trick Fan" in the 1880s. "Sent postpaid for 20c; two for
35c; $1.40 per doz."
FAUCON   "Evantails Artistiques", 61, Passage Panoramas,
Paris
FELIX, ALEXANDRE   40, rue St. Honoré, Paris
A renowned maker of quality fans whose wares were sold in
London by Graetzer & Hermann, 8, Huggin Lane, Wood St.,
Cheapside. Exhibited at the Great Exhibition.
FLEETWOOD, J.   48, Fetter Lane
Printed fans
Wheel of Fortune, The, (stipple engraving, hand-coloured)
FONTAINE
Designer: Printed fan
Napoleon Bonaparte (fan with three medallions in honour of)
FRANKS, H.
Engraver: Printed fans
Parliamentary Fan, 1741
FRENCH, J.   No. 17, Holborn Hill, London
Publisher: Printed fans
Church Fan, 1770 Later edition, 1776—etching, hand-coloured

GAMBLE, M.

Publisher: Printed (etched) fans

Orange Fan (Marriage of Princess Ann with William of Orange). 1733

Harlot's Progress (after Hogarth), 1732 and 1733

Henry VIII (after Hogarth), 1743

Church of England Fan, 1732–3

Excise Fan, An, 1733

Chinese Scene, 1738

Moses Striking the Rock, 1740

Damsel Mourning the loss of her Lover, 1739

Sailor's Wedding, The

Piping Shepherd, etc., 1739

Postorelle, 1738

Romeo & Juliet, 1742

Haymaking, 1744

Judgement of Paris, 1744

GANNE, J.

"Imp et Fabrique d'Eventails Rabiet. J. Ganné Succ^r, 63 Boul^d Ménilmontant, Paris. Degovrnay, Editeur, 28 rue Mazarine, Paris"

Inscription on lithographed fan depicting:

Souvenir de la Bastille (reverse side reads *Vive le Roy* 1789)

GERMO, LEONARDO

A fan painter who flourished in Rome around the beginning of the 18th century. The following fans bear his signature:

Venus and Adonis

Triumph of Mordecai

GIORDANO, LUCA

Fan painter

La Renommée des Dieux et des Déesses

GODEFROY

Engraver: Printed fans

Napoleon Bonaparte (fan with medallions in honour of)

GOODYEAR, HENRY B.

Patented a fan made of black, hard rubber on May 18th, 1858. Illustrated in *Fan Leaves*

GORDON "Ye Golden Fan and Crown in Tavistock Street, Covent Garden"

An original drawing for this fan-maker's trade card by William
Hogarth is recorded in Heal.* *The Craftsman* for February 6th,
1741, carried the following notice:
> "To be sold, at Gordon's Fan warehouse, The Crown and
> Fan in Tavistock Street, Covent Garden. All sorts of fans,
> Wholesale and Retail, very cheap. The Person leaving off
> trade."

The same publication, for February 12th, 1742, carried this
notice:
> "Gordon's Fan Warehouse, in Tavistock Street, Covent
> Garden. Mr. Gordon having left off trade, the Business,
> as usual, is carry'd on by his late journey-woman,
> MARY HITCHCOCK,
> At the same Place, where Ladies may be accommodated
> with all sorts of Fans, at the most reasonable Rates"

GOUPY, CHARLES "removed from Durham Yard to ye
corner of New Street, Covent Garden"
This information comes from a trade card in the Banks collection,
on which is also recorded that he was a fan maker. Goupy made
his name, however, as a fan painter. It is possible that he was
related to Joseph Goupy, the French/English artist who died
in 1763. Charles Goupy was a fashionable water-colour painter
who specialised in architectural subjects. A fan in the Schreiber
collection depicting three views in Rome is signed followed by
"1738 N.A.".

GRAETZER & HERMANN (*See* FELIX)

GUIDUCCI, ANGELO
Fan painter
Five Senses, The

GUILIELMUS, DOMINUS DE ERQUSTAN PINX,
1673
This signature appears on a fan painted with the following
subject:
Judgement of Midas

GUILLOT, JACQUES
"Fan Maker to the King" (Louis XIV) who flourished *c.* 1680

---

* *London Tradesmen's Cards of the XVIII Century*, Ambrose Heal, Batsford,
London, 1925.

HADWEN, J.
Admitted to the Worshipful Company of Fan Makers on November 5th, 1772.
Publisher: Printed fans
Allegory on the Triumph of Spain, upon which is inscribed in Spanish: Publicada segun la ley pr. I. Hadwen, cort de la Corona, Cheapside, London. See also ASHTON & HADWEN.

HAMILTON, T. No. 66, St. James's Street, London
Fancy goods maker who made and sold ostrich feather fans, *c.* 1830

HAMMOND
Designer and Engraver: Printed fans
Progress of Love, The (late 18th century)

HARDING, GEORGE
The *Boston News Letter* for August 8th–15th, 1704 contained the following announcement which was reproduced in *Fan Leaves*:

"FANS—George Harding lately from London, now at Mr. John Pitts, Confectioner in Cornhill, Boston, mounteth all sorts of fans as well as any done in old England. He likewise hath a large sortment of curious mounts which he will dispose of very reasonably, not purporting to stay long in these parts."

HARVEY 25, Boulevard des Capucinés, Paris

Fan manufacturer
HERAULT
Hand-screen in honour of the birth of the Dauphin, 1729, inscribed:
"Permit d'inprimer 23rd September 1729"
HERMET, F.   7 P^{ge} Dauphine, Paris
Name found on a lithographed fan showing the plan of:
International Exhibition, The, 1878
HINCKS, W.
Engraver: Printed fans
George III (*see* BIRMAN)
HITCHCOCK, MARY   (*see* GORDON)
HIXON, ROBERT   13, Bridges St., Covent Garden, London
Publisher: Printed fans
Bill of Fare for a Wedding Dinner, A (etching, uncoloured)
HÖRMAN, CHRISTOPH FRIEDRICH
Signed set of four Hand-screens representing ballet dancers
H.M., MRS   81, Haymarket, London
Publisher: Printed fans
Opera Fan, The (King's Theatre), 1788
HOLLIS, M.
Publisher: Printed fans
Casket Scene from "The Merchant of Venice", 1746
HOUGHTON, F.
An unusual fan, *c.* 1880 and depicting a youthful Shakespeare reading before Elizabeth I is illustrated in *Fan Leaves*. The signature is F. Houghton and the mount comprises vellum surrounded by a margin of Brussels needlepoint lace.
HUNT, EDWIN SOPER   Weymouth, Massachusetts, U.S.A.
In 1867, relates Esther Oldham in *Fan Leaves*, Hunt opened a fan factory to produce fans by machinery. Sticks of hornbeam were used and a carving machine costing $500 was designed and built. Hunt also perfected an imitation ivory. In 1876 his brother Fred Hunt and a Frank Allen took over the business. In 1885, the business was re-styled the Allen Fan Company in South Braintree. This enterprise finally closed about 1910.
HYLTON, RICHARD   "at the Golden Fan in Great George Street, Hanover Square"
Publisher: Printed fans

New Nassau Fan, The, 1733

IRELANDE   No. 28, Palais Royale, Paris
   Manufacturer and repairer of fans

I. S.
   Publisher: Printed fans
   Pensez à Vous, 1796

JATHALIE   169, Sloane Street, S.W. London
   Fan manufacturer

JENNER, J.   Strand, London
   Publisher: Printed fans
   Ruins of a Church
   Woman riding pillion behind a man who is talking to a priest

JONES, CHARLES   23, Ludgate Hill, London
   Publisher: Printed fans
   Perpetual Almanack, 1788

JOSSE L'AINE   Des quatres Saisons, a Paris. Rue Greneta. A
   trade card reproduced in Paul Lacroix's *The Eighteenth Century*
   reads: "Wholesale and retail manufacturer of fans of all sorts, at
   all prices to suit all tastes, for home and abroad. He undertakes
   all kinds of repairs, supplies the wood and the fancy designs for
   making them up, at a most moderate price." Part of Josse's trade
   card forms the title page to this present book.

JOUCY, JACQUES
   Fan maker to the King (Louis XIII), flourishing *c.* 1680

KAUFFMANN, ANGELICA
   Maria Anna Angelica Catherine Kauffmann was born at Coire
   in the Grisons in 1741 and took to painting at an early age.
   She came to London and was among those who petitioned the
   King for establishing the Royal Academy. She finally went to
   Rome in 1781 where she died in 1807. Her work was much
   admired during her lifetime but is best known today by the
   many engravings that were made from her designs by Barto-
   lozzi (q.v.) and others. Her style lost favour as the 19th century
   produced its own characteristic art forms.
   Designer: Printed fans
   Alexander Pope, Fan in honour of
   Theft of Cupid's Bow
   Shakespeare's Tomb, 1790

KEES, ERNEST   9, Boulevard des Capucinés, Paris

Manufacturer of fans

KEMP, BLANCH "at the White Bear & Star, opposite the India House, Leaden Hall Street." Trade card in the Heal collection. Fan maker, fl. *c.* 1740.

KERR, D.

Publisher: Printed fans

Fortune Telling by Cards, or the New Gipsy Fan. (Stipple engraving, hand-coloured)

KING, GYLES

Etching

Marriage of Princess Anne with the Prince of Orange, 1734

KLEINER, S.

Designer & Engraver: Printed fans

Vienna, 1756

Three Medallions painted on Silk

KYMLI

Painter to the Elector Palatine (Charles Theodore who inherited Bavaria in 1778)

Exhibited at Le Salon de la Correspondence in 1779 a fan featuring:

Toilet of Venus

LACHELIN, BENJAMIN 32, Avenue de l'Opera, Paris

Manufacturer and repairer of fans

LASINIO, CONTE CARLO

Designer: Printed fans

Made copy of F. Bartolozzi's fan leaf entitled: *Aurora*

LAURENT 2, rue Meyerbeer, Paris

Fan manufacturer

LAURIERE, J. St. James's Street, London

Publisher: Printed fans

Wellington (Portrait, head and bust; trophies of French flags and eagles seen both plain and coloured). No date but refers to Peninsula War and is probably 1813.

LE BRUN, CHARLES

French painter born 1619; died 1690. A fan painted by this master is recorded by Percival as having been sold in Spain about 1884. The subject was: *Phryne before her Judges*

LEGRAND, PIERRE

Fan Maker to the Duchess d'Orleans, *c.* 1663

LEROUX ET CIE   Fan's Manufact^r. 41, rue Notre Dame de Nazareth, Paris
Engraver & Publisher: Printed fans
Albert Smith's Ascent of Mont Blanc, 1851

LOUVION, J. B.
Engraver: Printed fans
Landscape, Shepherd, Shepherdess with Two Peasant Women

LA VEGA, FO.
Fan Painter. Two fans in Schreiber collection
Entry of Charles, King of the Two Sicilies, into Naples, 1734
Review at Gaeta, 1734

MARSAY, L. G. de   74, Faub-Poissonière, Paris
Lithographed fan showing sixteen humorous scenes representing dances from the time of Noah to "La Schotish (1850)" inscribed:
Histoire et Specimens De La Danse Pepuis Le Déluge Jusqu'à Nos Jours

MARTIN, F.
Publisher: Printed fans
Heraldic Fan, 1792 (*see* WILLIAM COCK)

MARTINI, P.
Engraver: Printed fans
Royal Family at the Exhibition of the Royal Academy, 1789

MAURER, W.
Publisher: Printed fans
Pyramid at Babylon, The

MONCORNET, BALTHASAR
Publisher: *See* COCHIN
Hand-screen with the subject of:
Triumphal Return of David with the Head of Goliath

NEELE, S. T.   352, Strand, London
Engraver: Printed fans
History of France, 1793 (*see* COCK & CROWDER)
History of England, 1793 (*see* COCK & CROWDER)

ONKRUIT, THÉODORE
A Fan painter who was flourishing *c.* 1660 at La Haye

OSBORNE, THOMAS   Gray's Inn, Holborn, London
Bookseller and Publisher who produced a souvenir fan to mark the occasion of his settling into his new house at Hampstead.

His fan, published on September 10th, 1754 (he died in 1767) was entitled:
Thomas Osborne's Duck Hunting, Mr, 1754

OVENDEN
Engraver: Printed fan
Heraldic Fan, 1792 (*see* WILLIAM COCK)

PARR, N.
Engraver: Printed fans
Ranelagh, 1751 (*see* SAYER)

PENBERTHY, FREDERICK "Fabrique d'Eventails", 390–392, Oxford Street, London

PERSIER
Designer: Printed fans
Napoleon Bonaparte (fan with medallions in honour of)

PETERS, REV. W.
Designer: Printed fan
New Church Fan Publish'd with the Approbation of the Lord Bishop of London. Stipple engraving, uncoloured, dated May 1st, 1796
Resurrection of a Pious Family or Glory to God in the Highest, 1796

PICHARD
"L'Almanach d'indication et d'adresse personnelle" (quotes Percival) refers to Pichard as: "Très connu pour la feuille d'Eventaille; il a chez lui d'excellents originaux"

PICKEARD, ROBERT "At the Swan and Golden Fan in Cheapside, near yᵉ Conduit, London". Trade card in the Schreiber collection.

PINCHBECK, JONATHAN The Fan & Crown in New Round Court, in the Strand
Publisher: Printed fans
Nassau Fan, The, 1733
Royal Repository
Grove at Bath, 1737
Bath Needles, 1757
Reason for the Motion, The (satire on Walpole), 1741
Humours at New Tunbridge Wells, 1734
Vauxhall, 1737
Dumb Oracle, The
Courtesy Fan, 1732
Old Man's Folly, The, 1734

Old Maid, The
Amours of an Old Bachelor, 1734
Bath Medley, The, c. 1757
POGGI, A. St Georges Row, Hyde Park, London
Publisher: Printed fans
Portraits of the Royal Family at the Royal Academy, 1789 (*see* MAR-
TINI, also RAMBERG)
Cameos, 1780
Children with Battledores, 1788
Power of Love, The, 1780
Cupid and Psyche, 1799
Children with Tops, 1788
Victory, 1782

PRESTON, J. "at his Music Warehouse No. 97 near Beaufort
Buildings, Strand"
Publisher: Printed fans
Royal Concert, 1781 (hand-coloured etching after Cruikshank)

PRESTON, T.
  Publisher: Printed fans
  King George III with words and music for four short songs, 1781
PYEFINCH, E.   "at the East India Warehouse, the Golden Fan,
  No. 30 Bucklersbury, near Cheapside, London." Importer of
  Japanese and Chinese fans. fl. *c.* 1730

RABIET aîné
  "Fab^que d'eventails Rabiet aîné Boul^t Ménilmontant 63" (Paris)
    is the inscription on a hand-coloured lithographed fan showing
    five humorous scenes representing comic incidents on the
    Seine steamboats with inscriptions, entitled:
  Omnibus-Gondoles
  See also GANNE, J.
RABIET, E.
  "Fabrique d'Eventails E. Rabiet 63 Boulevard Ménilmontant,
    Paris" is inscribed on a lithographed fan depicting:
  Hippodrome de Paris
RAMBERG, P.
  Designer: Printed fans
  Royal Family at the Exhibition of the Royal Academy, 1789
READ, J.   133, Pall Mall, London
  Publisher: Printed fans
  Prince and Princess of Wales, 1795
  Female Seven Ages, 1797

Progress of Love (undated)
Good Swain, The, 1790
Good-for-Nothing Swain, The, 1795
Altar of Love, The
Ladies' Bill of Fare, The
Selection of Beaux, The
RENAU, M. LE CHEVALIER
Designer: Etched fan
Gibraltar

John Roberts
at the Queen's Head *in*
Holborn; near Hatton Garden; LONDON.
Sells all Sorts of Fine China Ware;
The Finest Hyson and Congou Teas,
Fine Double Flint Drinking Glasses, &c
and India Fans.

RIMMEL, EUGENE "Importer of Parisian and Viennese Fans." 76, King's Road, Brighton; 96, Strand, 128, Regent Street and 24, Cornhill, London, and 17, Boulevard des Italians, Paris. Maker of Rimmel's New Perfumed Fans: "*The Surprise Bouquet* sweetly scented and expanding into an elegant Screen Fan, from 3/6d." In addition to this folding circular fan, Rimmel, who was Perfumer by Appointment to HRH the Princess of Wales, sold "American Fans" of white holly wood (1/6d, 2/6d and 3/6d), "The Floral Viennese Fan" (which cost from 3/6d) and the "Rich Parisian Fan, ornamented with real lace or choice paintings" from one to ten guineas. For some years

until about 1868, Rimmel had an arrangement with the neigh-
bouring Lyceum Theatre whereby the theatre programmes were
scented, presumably in return for the advertising space—the
whole back cover—which Rimmel took. Several of these scented
programmes, alas! now devoid of their one-time olfactive
properties, survive in the Guildhall Library in London.

ROBERTS, JOHN   "at the Queen's Head in Holborn, near
  Hatton Garden, London." Sold imported Indian fans and
  oriental goods (*Vide* trade card in the Banks collection), fl. *c.* 1780

ROMANELLI
  Signature recorded by Percival on a fan with the subject: *Rape of
  the Sabines, The*

SANDERS   "Fan Maker, No. 59 Cornhill." Trade card in the
  Banks collection dated *c.* 1787.

SANSOM, MARY   "at ye Golden Fan next door to the Nagg's
  Head Tavern." Trade card, *c.* 1780 in the Banks collection.

SAYER, ROBERT
  Publisher: Printed fans
  Ranelagh, 1751 (*see* PARR)

SETCHEL, J. F.   23, King Street, Covent Garden, London
  Publisher: Printed fans
  Bartholomew Fair

SILBERBERG, B.   Königl, Honlieferant, Hamburg, Germany.
  Manufacturer and repairer of fans

SIMPKINS   Clements Inn, London
  Engraver: Printed fans
  Road to Ruin
  Charade Fan (see DYDE & SCRIBE)
  Royal Emblems
  Vive le Roy, 1789 *(see* BALSTER, T.)

SLEEPE   Three fan makers bearing this name are known to have worked in London during the mid-18th century. RICHARD who operated *c.* 1753 in the parish of St. Michael-le-Querne. MARTHA was in business "next door to the Black Swan, the North Side of St Paul's Church Yard." Her period would appear to be around 1750 and it is possible that she was either the mother or the sister of the most illustrious of the Sleepe family, ESTHER who was born on May 19th, 1723 and later was in business as a fan maker "At the Golden Fan and Seven Stars, opposite the Old Jewry in the Poultry." This same sign was used by MARTHA and the possibility is that the addresses, with the vagueness practised at the time, were the same. ESTHER was to become the wife, in 1749, of Dr Charles Burney, the famed musicologist who was three years her senior. It is unlikely that ESTHER gave up fan making upon her marriage since Burney was still on the threshold of his career. Since he was elected organist at St. Dionis-Backchurch, Fenchurch Street in the year of his marriage, Burney and his wife probably took rooms in that area. Burney contracted consumption and so, in 1751, moved to Lynn-Regis in Norfolk (now King's Lynn). In 1760, fully recovered, he returned to London and on September 28th the following year, his wife Esther died in Poland Street, thirty-eight years old.

SLOPER, C.   Lambeth Road, London
  Publisher: Printed fans
  Ferdinand VII (line-engraving, examples both coloured and uncoloured)

SPEREN, G.
  Publisher: Printed fans
  Pump Room, Bath, 1737
  Orange Grove, Bath, 1757

SPRINGSGUTH JUNIOR
  Engraver: Printed fan
  Music

SPRINGSGUTH, S.
Engraver: Printed fan
Duke of Wellington
STOKES, SCOTT, and CROSKEY 18, Friday Street,
London
Publishers: Printed fans
Surrender of Valenciennes, 1793. (Etching, painted in blue ink, the
reverse hand-coloured)
New Caricature Dance Fan for 1794, 1794
New Puzzle Fan, 1794
Dance Fan, 1794 (etching, uncoloured) *see* ASHTON, S. & CO.
STOTHARD, THOMAS
English book illustrator born 1755; died 1834, and painter. One
of his designs, *Three children with a dove and cage*, was reproduced
on a French fan in the Schreiber collection.
Designer: Printed fans
Lieutenant-Colonel Tarleton, 1782 (*see* WELLS)
Young Girl and Doves
STRANGE, SIR ROBERT
Engraver: Printed fans
Prince Charles Edward Stuart & allegorical figures
Cameron of Lochiel as Mars & Flora MacDonald as Bellona, 1745

STUNT "Fan Maker. Wholesale Retail & for Exportation. No.
191 Strand. Opposite St Clement's Church Yard, London. The
Old Established Shop, late Sudlow." The latest recorded date
for an issue from Sudlow's Fan Warehouse (q.v.) is 1795. The
trade card quoted above (from the Banks collection) is dated *c.*
1798.

SUDLOW'S FAN WAREHOUSE 191, Strand (*see* also STUNT)
Publishers: Printed fans
Royal Wedding, 1795
Prince & Princess of Wales, The, (stipple engraving, hand-coloured)

TALLIS & CO., JOHN London & New York
Publisher: Printed fans
The Royal Fan (Queen Victoria, Prince Albert and their children). Engraved for the Great Exhibition of 1851 by P. DUVEL-LEROY, Paris

THIELCKE, H.
Engraver: Printed fans
Rest by the Wayside, The

THORNHILL, W. & CO. London
Manufacturers of the "dressing-case fan" *c.* 1895–1900 which was said to have been invented by Dame Madge Kendal.

TIFFANY & CO. Union Square, New York; Avenue de l'Opera 56, Paris. Fans sold and repaired. Probably not makers

TIQUET FACIT
Signature on a fan listed in the Sale Catalogue of the Walker Collection (1882) which depicted:
Personages of the Court of the Regency playing Blind Man's Buff

UWINS, THOMAS
Designer: Printed fans
Neptune and Britannia with George III (*see* CARDON)

VAUGHAN, EDWARD Fan maker, at the Golden Fan near the Chapel in Russel Court, Drury Lane
Printed fan
Necroman Trick Fan, The, 1734

VIGINET, V. & CO. 48, Rue de Luxembourg, Boulevard des Capucinés, Paris. Fan makers

VOIRIOT, LES
The Voiriot family were fan painters of some standing. Flourished about 1639; his son CLAUDE followed on and finally his (Claude's) son NICHOLAS flourished *c.* 1679

WARD, A. "Successor to the late Mrs Vanhorn. No. 9 the lower End of King Street, Westminster, near the Abby. Deals in all Sorts of fine India & Ivory Fans as usual." *Vide* trade card in Banks collection dated *c.* 1784.

WATTEAU, JEAN ANTOINE

This French painter, whose style has so often been copied, was
born in 1684 and died in 1721. It is not known for certain if he
ever painted a fan or mount, but he has frequently had such
work attributed to him, frequently on slender grounds. The
majority of Watteauesque fans, if not all, are stylistic works by
clever artists. Percival lists two fans allegedly sold for high
prices and said to be by Watteau. Their subjects were:
A Fête at Versailles
Une Fête a Cythère

WEBB, THOMAS & SONS   Melbourne, Australia. Probably
fan importers only

WEIGHTMAN, THOMAS   No. 255, St Paul's Church Yard
Publisher: Printed fans
Portrait of Duchess of York surrounded by dance music, 1791 (also
mentions "L. Cocks from Snow Hill")

WELLS, LEWIS   Warwick Street, Golden Square
Publisher & Engraver: Printed fans
Gretna Green, A Trip to, or *The Real Way to Get Married*
Views of Margate, 1798, (aquatint engraving painted on green
paper with the address 26, Leadenhall Street)
also Engraver of:
Lieutenant-Colonel Tarleton

WERNDLY, WILLIAM "at the Golden Fan in Leicester Square." Several trade cards survive in the Banks collection. On one he describes himself as "Fan Painter" and on another, to exactly the same design, the words read "Fan Maker". Probably fl. 1760–80

WILSON, GEORGE 108, St Martin's Lane, London
Designer & Engraver & Publisher: Printed fans
Ladies' Bill of Fare, The (*see* READ)
Selection of Beaux, A., 1795 (*see* READ)
Collection of Beaux, A., 1795
Good Swain, The, 1795 (*see* READ)
Good-for-Nothing Swain, The (*see* READ)
Union, The, 1801
Peace, The, 1801 (hand coloured stipple engraving, *see* ASHTON & HADWEN)
Advisor & Moralist, 1797
Lady's Physician, The
Quiz Club, The, 1797
Seven Ages, The
Female Seven Ages, The (*see* READ)
United Sisters, The (*see* ASHTON & HADWEN)
The Ladies' Bill of Fare was published in two versions: that issued on February 14th, 1795, bears the inscription: "Publish'd as the Act direct (*sic*) by G. Wilson." A very similar design, quoted by Percival, bears the inscription: "Geo. Wilson del[t]. London, Published Feb[v]. 20, 1795, by J. Read, 133, Pall Mall".

WILSON, JOHN Cary Street
  John Wilson was admitted a member of the Worshipful Company
    of Fan Makers on December 7th 1757. He may have been the
    father of GEORGE WILSON (q.v.)
XAVERY, FRANCIS
  This name and the date 1763 has been seen on a fine painted fan
    depicting:
    An Affianced Pair led by Hymen to the Altar of Love

PART TWO

Abduction of Helen of Troy (French, subject found on Louis XV
    brisé fans)
Achilles and Deidamia (French, late 18th century)
Advisor and Moralist, see WILSON
Albert Smith's Ascent of Mont Blanc, see LEROUX ET CIE
Alexander Pope's Bust crowned by the Graces (English, stipple and
    line engraving, several versions from Kauffmann original design,
    mid-18th century)
Alexander Pope, Fan in honour of, see KAUFFMANN
Allegorical Fan, The, see COCK & CROWDER
Allegory on the Triumph of Spain, upon which is inscribed in
    Spanish Publicada segun la ley pr. I. Hadwen, cort de la Corona,
    Cheapside, London, see ASHTON & HADWEN
Almanack, 1796, see COCK & CROWDER
Altar of Love, The, see READ
Amours of an Old Bachelor, see PINCHBECK
An Affianced Pair led by Hymen to the Altar of Love, see XAVERY
Ancient Marriage, An (French, late 18th century)
Apollo and the Muses (Italian, late 18th century, after Guilio
    Romano)
Apotheosis of Frederick II, see CHODOWIECKI
Aranjuez, March 19th, 1808, see BEHRMANN
Assembly of the Notables, The (French, both hand-painted and
    printed versions, 1787)
Aurora of Guido (numerous portrayals, Italian and French, mid-
    18th century)

George III and Queen Charlotte (small landscape on reverse, Etching, hand-coloured)
George III, In honour of, see BALSTER
Gibraltar, see RENAU
Gipsy Fan, see CLARKE & CO
Glory to God in the Highest, see PETERS, Rev. W.
Gods on Mount Olympus (German, *c.* 1770)
Good-for-Nothing Swain, The, see READ, also WILSON
Good Swain, The, see READ
Good Swain, The, see READ, also WILSON
Gretna Green, see WELLS
Grotesque Subjects, see ASHTON & CO
Grove at Bath, see PINCHBECK
Harlot's Progress (after Hogarth), see GAMBLE
Haymaking, see GAMBLE
Henry VIII (after Hogarth), see GAMBLE
Heraldic Fan, see COCK & CO, also OVENDEN
Heraldry Fan, see MARTIN
Hercules and Omphale (Italian, *c.* 1780)
Hippodrome de Paris, see RABIET
Histoire et Specimens De La Danse Pepuis Le Deluge Jusqu'a Nos Jours, see MARSAY
History of England, see NEELE
History of France, see COCK & CROWDER, also NEELE
Horse Race, The, see CANU
Humours at New Tunbridge Wells, see PINCHBECK
International Exhibition, The, see HERMET
Jephtha's Daughter (French, late Louis XIV)
Judgement of Midas, see GUILIELMUS
Judgement of Paris, The (French, late Louis XIV)
Judgement of Paris, see GAMBLE
Jupiter, see BURNEY, also AGAR
King George III, see PRESTON, J.
King's Theatre, see CLARKE & CO
La Renommee des Dieux et des Deesses, see GIORDANO
Lache qui t'abandonne (French, stipple engraving, Louis XVI and Marie Antoinette. Post Revolution)
Ladies' Bill of Fare, The, see READ, also WILSON
Lady's Adviser, The, see ASHTON & CO

Neptune and Britannia with George III, see UWINS

New Caricature Dance Fan for 1794, see STOKES, SCOTT & CROSKEY

New Church Fan Publish'd with the Approbation of the Lord Bishop of London, see PETERS, REV. W.

New Game of Piquet now in Play among different Nations in Europe, A. (English etching, hand-coloured, alluding to the intrigues of European diplomacy concerning the affairs of Poland, probably 1807 after Treaty of Tilset)

New Nassau Fan, The, see HYLTON

New Opera Fan, see COCK, WILLIAM

New Puzzle Fan, see STOKES, SCOTT and CROSKEY

New Union Charade Fan, The (Stipple engraving and etching, hand-coloured, inscribed "Published by the Proprietor and sold at No. 42, Pall Mall, First of April, 1801")

Offering to Hymen, The (French, Louis XVI)

Old Maid, The, see PINCHBECK

Old Man's Folly, The, see PINCHBECK

Olympus (French, late Louis XIV)

Omnibus-Gondoles, see RABIET aîné

Opera Fan, The (King's Theatre), see H.M., MRS

Oracle of Apollo, The, see AGAR, also BURNEY

Oracle, The, see COCK and CROWDER

Orange Grove, Bath, see SPEREN

Original Fanology, The, see COCK, WILLIAM

Orpheus & Eurydice, see CIRPIANI

Il Paese del Matrimonio (Italian printed, mid-18th century)

Parliamentary Fan, see FRANKS

Pastorelle, see GAMBLE

Peace, The, see WILSON

Peace Restored, see ASHTON & HADWEN

Pensez a Vous, see I.S.

Perpetual Almanack, see JONES

Phryne before her Judges, see LE BRUN

Piping Shepherd, etc., see GAMBLE

Pleasureboat, see CHASSEREAU

Portrait of Duchess of York surrounded by dance music, see WEIGHTMAN

Portraits of the Royal Family at the Royal Academy, see POGGI

Shepherd and Shepherdess, see CHASSEREAU
Souvenir de la Bastille (reverse side reads *Vive le Roy* 1789), see GANNE
Storming of Jerusalem & Healing of Godfrey de Bouillon's Wound (Italian, late 17th century)
Surrender of Valenciennes, see STOKES, SCOTT and CROSKEY
Tarquin and the Sibyl, see AGAR and BURNEY
Telemarque and the Nymphs (French, Louis XV)
Telemarque on the Isle of Calypso (French, Louis XV)
Ten Country Dances and Five Cotillions, see COCK & CROWDER
Testament de Louis XVI (French, stipple engraving, Louis XVI portrait with son & daughter. Post Revolution)
Theft of Cupid's Bow, see BARTOLOZZI, also KAUFFMANN
Thomas Osborne's Duck Hunting, see OSBORNE
Three Children with a dove and cage, see STOTHARD
Three medallions of village life, see ANDRE
Three medallions painted on Silk, see KLEINER
Toilet of Venus, see CIPRIANI
Treaty of Amiens, see COCK, J., & CROWDER, J. P.
Trial of Warren Hastings, see COCK & CO
Triumph of Mordecai, see GERMO
Triumphal Return of David with the Head of Goliath, see MONCORNET
Une Fête a Cythère, see WATTEAU
Une Folie Chasse L'Autre (French, mid-18th century)
Union, The, see ASHTON & HADWEN, also WILSON
Vauxhall, see PINCHBECK
Veduto Generale della Solfettura pre de la Citte d'Pozzuoli (Italian, 1760–70)
Venus and Adonis, see GERMO
Venus & Adonis (Italian, early 18th century)
Venus & Vulcan (French, late Louis XIV)
Victory, see POGGI
Vienna, see KLEINER
View of Greenwich, see CLARKE
Views of Margate, see WELLS

Visit, The (French, Louis XVI)
Vive le Roy, see SIMPKINS, also BALSTER
Way of the World, The, see ASHTON, SARAH
Wheel of Fortune, The, see FLEETWOOD
Widow, The, see AGAR, also BURNEY
Woman riding pillion behind a man who is talking to a priest, see
  JENNER
World Grown Old and Crazy, The, n.d., see ASHTON, SARAH
Young Girl and Doves, see STOTHARD

APPENDIX A

Edict of Nantes, April 13,
1598, revoked by Louis XIV
October 22, 1685

Year	France Monarch	France Period	England Monarch	England Period
1600	Henry IV (1589–1610)	Henry IV	Elizabeth (1558–1603)	Elizabethan
	Louis XIII (1610–43)		James I (1603–25)	
	(1612–19 Marie de Medicis was Regent)	Medicis Regency	Charles I (1625–49)	
1650	Louis XIV (1643–1715)		Charles II (1660–85)	Commonwealth (1649–59)
			James II (1685–8)	
		Louis XIV	William III (1689–1702)	William & Mary
1700	Louis XV (1715–74)		Anne (1702–14)	Queen Anne
	(1715–23 Philippe Duke of Orleans was Regent)	Louis XV	George I (1714–27)	
	Marquise de Pompadour, King's mistress.		George II (1727–60)	Georgian
1750	Died 1764. Succeeded by Madame du Barry		George III (1760–1820)	

306

Louis XVI   Louis XVI
  (1774–89)   French
Marie   Revolution
  Antoinette   (1789–92)
  became Queen

              First Republic
                (1792–9)

1800

              The Consulate
                (1799–1804)
              The Empire   Regency
                (1804–14)   (1810-20)

Louis XVIII   George IV
  (1814–15;   (1820–30)
  1815–24)   William IV
                          (1830–7)
Charles X   Victoria
  (1824–30)   (1837–1901)

1850 Louis Philippe
      (1830–48)   Second Republic
              (1848–52)   Victorian

      Napoleon III
      (1852–70)   Napoleon III
              (1852–70)

1880   Third Republic
              (1870–9)

                            Edward VII
                            (1901–10)   Edwardian

APPENDIX B

FAN BOXES

When fans were manufactured, they were placed in boxes for storage both prior to sale and for the subsequent safe keeping of the fan in the lady's dressing room. Some of these boxes were extremely attractive and beautifully made and a few words about this aspect of fanology may not be out of place.

It is not easy to trace the history of so apparently simple an artefact but it is probable that the first fan boxes were made in China and are of comparatively recent origin.

There is reason to suppose that the fan box is peculiar to the fan in the West since in Japan and China it was customary for the fan to hang from the waist in a sheath or to be secreted in the folds of the dress. These sheaths were of shagreen or embroidered fabric, sometimes embellished with designs formed in gold or silver thread. Several in my collection bear certain common characteristics: the sheath is made of two stiffened pieces of material, edged with a diaper-patterned blue band and Peking stitch, the end of the sheath being formed of a circle of soft leather or satin brocade.

Yet another form of fan protection was provided by the tassel cord in the length of which would be formed a loop of such diameter and at such a distance from the attachment point of the tassel cord to the rivet that the loop could be slid up the closed fan to keep it shut.

The need for fan boxes may have been Western, and the first fan boxes may well have been made in the Orient as an adjunct to the fans exported to Europe. The brightly-coloured fans which were made for sale in the West around the beginning of the 19th century were usually supplied in lacquer boxes made of wood and decorated in the standard manner for such pieces. Sometimes this decoration would extend to the familiar gesso, so popular in the second half of the last century. These lacquered fan boxes attained the peak of their popularity around the time of the Great Exhibition in 1851 in London and were frequently to be valued, by a later generation, in excess of the fan which they formerly contained. For this reason, these boxes sometimes turn up in junk shops (those happy hunting grounds of relic which fad has seen fit to rechristen as "antique shops") *sans* fans and offered as trinket boxes. Their former purpose is usually evident from their long and slender shape although be warned that some similarly-shaped boxes were made in composition and *papier maché*—and supplied with a Japanese lacquer, Chinese lacquer or relief gesso decoration which were intended for jewellery and dressing-table knick-knacks. These were similar in many ways to the painted and lacquered *papier maché* pen boxes and pen cases of Persian origin.

As for the design and development of the fan box as a special purpose-built case intended purely for a fan, this may safely be said to have been the province of the French where Parisian fan makers took the extra trouble to make their wares more attractive. Indeed, so expensive were some of these fans (some cost the equivalent of £1,000 today) that it would have been impossible to consider their contemporary preservation and storage without some form of suitable case. Although provided by the fan maker, he was not responsible for their manufacture. This was the province of craftsmen whose speciality was this branch of trade. Called *gagniers*, these men made cases for *etuis* and other fancy and valuable goods. In the hands of these masters, the fan box became a thing of beauty in its own right and a suitable object to grace the boudoir *table de toilette* of the noble and the élite. Finely-finished shagreen leather cases lined with satin, velvet and silk gimp were turned out for the fan-makers' wares. Boxes with quilted exteriors made of silk, velvet and embroidery were frequently made with shaped interiors which formed a support for the closed fan and protected it against damage from movement inside its sheath. These were made from around the early 18th century onwards. Strange as it may seem but during the closing years of the great era of the fan, the fan-box displayed art and skills almost superior to those of the fan which it contained. Although more often French than English in origin, these boxes could be said to span the Victorian era.

Whereas most boxes were rectangular, a few were made which were the shape of the closed fan, wider at one end than at the other. I have one in my collection which is made of ebony and shaped like the profile of the closed fan, one guard of which swivels on a rivet to reveal the space contained within. This is a late box, with appliqué mother of pearl over the lid and down the sides.

As the epoch of the fan waned, so the relatively short era of the fan box also underwent change—a change for the cheaper. The delicate fan box was now made of cardboard covered with decorative paper. These boxes were still well made, being double thickness and fully lipped to make a nicely-closing case, the the hinge was of paper-covered linen. The fan maker usually placed his name inside the lid or on the bottom.

For the collector, a fan in its *original* box (and here I do mean the box made for the fan and not one which has been found to be an approximate fit) has a greater value than one without a box. Naturally, this statement can only be taken to refer to fans of the middle to late 18th century for which boxes were made. These were most frequently ivory fans, sometimes with *incrustation-cloisonné* guards, and usually with lace mounts.

Most of the fan-boxes which have survived, and here I am referring to the ones covered with various fabrics, have faded and on some the stitches have become fragile through exposure to sunlight and air. My advice to collectors is not to attempt to clean, dye, re-cover or otherwise restore these boxes. They are so easy to spoil and a faded, even a torn box in its original condition is better than a bright, newly-covered one which has been divested of its historical value and the patina of generations.

APPENDIX C

Throughout the history of the fan, it has taken its place along with other examples of fine and delicate craftsmanship and beauty as a fitting gift to present to royalty. It is significant that the ancient fans played so vital a part in the affairs of dynastic pomp and ceremony. The first fan which appears to represent the folding fan belonged to a Queen—the Lombardic Theodelinda. So it has been down through the centuries. To list a Royal fan is to list Royalty *in toto*. Here, though, is an abbreviated list of some of the more important Royal fans which have a place in the history of the British Isles.

MARY STUART   Born on December 7th, 1542, she became Queen of the Scots only seven days later when her father, James V, died in his thirtieth year. She was just sixteen years of age when she married the French dauphin (Francis II). Two years later she was a widow. She married her cousin, Henry Stuart in 1565 but was imprisoned in 1567. After nearly twenty years in captivity, she was beheaded. In the 45 years of her unhappy life, she endured a turbulent existence from which, not surprisingly, very little has survived in the way of personal property. Among the few such relics preserved in the National Museum of Antiquities in Scotland is her fan. This is described by Seton*

Its mount is of silk and silver tissue; it is of brocaded floral design of conventional character, disposed in two bands, one red and the other green, with the design in silver thread; below, other bands in red, blue and yellow, are so graded in colour that the general appearance of the mount has a rainbow effect. The fan mount opens from a central handle of tortoise-shell, in which pivot the "panaches" or guards; this enables the fan, when closed, to pass to the bottom of the handle and, supported at the sides by the "panaches" to become enclosed, as it were,

* *The Penicuik Jewels of Mary, Queen of Scots*, Walter Seton, London, 1903.

311

in a tortoise-shell case. The handle terminates below in an ivory knob, the lower portion of which is missing. The width of the fan, extended, is $10\frac{3}{16}$ ins. From the centre of the pivot to the top of the ivory knob it measures $2\frac{3}{16}$ ins.

This type of fan would be classed as a semi-cockade type folding and partly telescoping into the hollow handle. Manufacture of this style continued through to the last century. The Earl of Leicester's present to her is described as being of white feathers, the gold handle, thickly jewelled, bearing a lion rampant with a muzzled white bear beneath his foot. On New Year's Day, 1579, she received a gift of "two fannes of straw wrought with silke of sundry colours".

ELIZABETH I Born in 1533, Elizabeth, daughter of Anne Boleyn, came to the throne of England on November 17th, 1558. Her long reign saw the face of England change dramatically. It saw the re-establishment of the Church of England and the completion of the translation of the Bible. She died in 1603 to be succeeded by the son of Mary, Queen of Scots, James I of England. Elizabeth acquired a large number of fans, no fewer than 27 being recorded in the inventory of her personal possessions at her death. One of these was a gift from Sir Francis Drake whilst another was richly jewelled and said to have been valued at the time at no less than £400. It is on record that Elizabeth regarded a fan as a suitable gift for a queen,* and she has subsequently been referred to as the "Patroness of Fans".

MARY Catherine of Aragon's daughter Mary came to the throne of England at the age of 38 in 1554—and died just four years later. One of the New Year's gifts which she is recorded as having received in 1556 was: ". . . seven fannes to kepe the heate of the fyre, of strawe, the one of white silke".†

ANNE OF DENMARK Anne was born in 1574 and was eight years younger than James, future King James I of England, when they married in 1590. She became James's queen on his accession to the throne in 1590. Although James's reign was a turbulent one (he was the Protestant son of Mary, Queen of Scots, and his reign saw the

* *History of the Fan* by G. Woolliscroft Rhead, p. 102.
† *ibid*.

Gunpowder Plot, the death of William Shakespeare and the start of the Thirty Years War), his Queen apparently did little to leave her mark in history. She died in 1619, six years before her husband. An engraving exists (reproduced in *Chats on Costume**) which was made by the Flemish/English engraver, Renold Elstracke (fl. 1590–1630). This illustration shows the King and the Queen, who is holding a feather fan in her left hand. Inscribed at the bottom right-hand corner is the legend "Are to be sold at the White Horse in Pope's Head Abbey, by John Sunbury and George Humble." The particular significance of Queen Anne is that it was during her reign that, on April 19th, 1709, the Worshipful Company of Fan Makers was granted its Charter.

CHARLOTTE SOPHIA   The daughter of the Duke of Mecklenburg-Strelitz, Charlotte Sophia was born in 1744. The year after he came to the throne of England in 1760, 22-year-old George III of England sought the hand of this beautiful girl of whom it is said that the beauty of her arms combined with her dainty hands served to accentuate the appearance of a beautiful fan.† Queen Charlotte died in 1810, ten years before the King. A painting exists by Thomas Gainsborough (born 1727; died 1788) which is preserved in St James's Palace, London.

VICTORIA   When her uncle, William IV, died in 1837, Alexandrina Victoria, only daughter of Edward, Duke of Kent, succeeded to the throne and so began an era of progress and development on a scale hitherto unknown in England. The eighteen-year-old Queen, styled Queen of the United Kingdom and Empress of India, married her cousin, Prince Albert of Saxe-Coburg and Gotha in 1840, who assumed the title of Prince Consort. The Queen had many fans, among them the so-called Royal Fan made for her in Paris by F. Duvelleroy and printed and published by Tallis. This was exhibited at the Great Exhibition of 1851, and is reproduced here as Fig. 41. On the occasion of her Diamond Jubilee in 1897, she was presented with a fan by the Worshipful Company of Fan Makers.

---

* *Chats on Costume* by G. Woolliscroft Rhead, London, 1906.

† This statement may be apocryphal: it appears in *Fan Leaves* published by the Fan Guild of Boston, U.S.A.

ALEXANDRA   The death of Victoria brought her son, Albert Edward, to the throne in 1901 as Edward VII. Born in 1841, he married Alexandra Louise Julia, Princess of Denmark, who was three years his junior, in 1863. At the coronation ceremony in 1902, she was presented with a fan by the Worshipful Company of Fan Makers. Their reign was short-lived, the King dying in 1910. Queen Alexandra outlived him by fifteen years.

MARY   George V came to the English throne in 1910 and at his coronation in 1911, Queen Mary was presented with a fan by the Worshipful Company of Fan Makers.

Other Royal occasions marked by the presentation of a fan include:

THE PRINCESS MARY—on the occasion of her wedding in 1922.
QUEEN ELIZABETH (of George VI)—at her coronation in 1937.
PRINCESS ELIZABETH (daughter of George VI)—at her wedding in 1947.
DUCHESS OF GLOUCESTER—on the occasion of her receiving Freedom of the Company in 1948.
QUEEN ELIZABETH II—on the occasion of her coronation 1953.
PRINCESS MARGARET—on the occasion of her wedding in 1960.
PRINCESS ALEXANDRA—at her wedding in 1963.
PRINCESS RICHARD OF GLOUCESTER—1972.

Fans also formed valued gifts throughout the turbulent times of the French monarchies and other European royal families. It would be uncharitable not to include reference to the fans which were also presented to the wives of American Presidents, although these particular fans, certainly in later years, were more in the realms of being private gifts than State presentations. An account of some of these fans is contained in *Fan Leaves* published by the Fan Guild, Boston, Massachusetts in the United States.

If Queen Elizabeth I gained for herself the reputation today of having slept in what must appear to be almost every house more than a hundred years old (and the raised eyebrows are almost as legion!) then Royal presentation fans are almost as numerous. True there were very many owned by court ladies and the lesser royalty.

BIBLIOGRAPHY

Listed below are some of the more important works of reference regarding the fan and fanology. Also listed are some modern writings which are considered worthy of mention.

Art Journal: *Catalogue of the 1851 Exhibition*, page 313.

Art Journal, 1875, page 103.

Baró, Carlos M. and Escoda, Juan: *Éventails Anciens*, Payot Lausanne, 1957.*

Blondel, Spire: *Histoire des Eventails chez tous les Peuples at à toutes les Epoques*. Librairie Renouard, Paris, 1875.

Bouchot, Henri: *L'Histoire par les Éventails Populaires*. (Two articles contributed to *Les Lettres et Les Arts*.) Paris, January & July, 1883.

Bush, George: *Der Fächer*, Düsseldorf, 1904.

Catalini, Carla: *Waaiers*. Van Dishoeck, Bussom, Holland, 1966.

Collins, Bernard Ross: *A Short Account of the Worshipful Company of Fan-Makers*, Favel Press, London, 1950.

Crystal Palace, Tallis's History & Description of the, Volume 1, pp. 214–19. London, 1851.

Cust, Lionel: *Catalogue of the Collection of Fans & Fan Leaves presented to the Trustees of the British Museum by the Lady Charlotte Schreiber*. Longmans, London, 1893.

Encyclopaedia Britannica (article on Fans). Volume IX, Ninth edition, A. & C. Black, Edinburgh, 1879.

Erler, M.: *Der Moderne Fächer* (article in *Kunstgewerbe-blatt*, September, 1904.

Fan Leaves. The Fan Guild, Boston, Massachusetts, U.S.A., 1961. (Limited to 100 copies.) [A copy is to be found in the Library of the Victoria & Albert Museum.]

Fans of All Countries, A series of twenty photographs of Spanish, French, German, Italian and English fans. Arundel Society, London, 1871.

Flory, M. A.: *A Book About Fans* (with chapter on fan-collecting by Mary Cadwalader Jones). Macmillan & Co., New York, 1895.

* This volume, published as part of the Orbis Pictus series, was also published under the title *Alte Facher* and comprises pictures of a fan collection from Barcelona.

Giles, H. A.: *Chinese Fans*, article in *Fraser's Magazine*, London, May, 1879.

Great Exhibition, The: Official Catalogue of, London, 1851.

Heath, Richard: *Politics in Dress* (article contributed to *The Woman's World*), London, June, 1880.

Hughes, Therle: *A Flutter of Fans* (article in Discovering Antiques, Pt. 28, London, 1971).

Joly, Henri: *Legend in Japanese Art*.

Knox, Thomas W.: *The Boy Travellers in Central Europe*. Harper & Bros., New York, 1893.

Leisure Hour, The: London, 1882 (article on fans), pp. 417–21.

Magazine of Art: Greek Myths in Greek Art (articles), Vol. VI, pp. 57 & 466, London, 1883.

Marcel, Gabriel: *En Eventail Historique du dix-huitième Siècle*. Paris, 1901.

Mongot, Vincento Almela: *Los Abanicos* (Fans of Valencia), Spain.

National Encyclopaedia, The: (article on Fans). Volume V, Mackenzie, London, *c*. 1880.

National Cyclopaedia, The: (article on Fans). Volume VI, Chas. Knight, London, 1849.

Oldham, Esther, various articles in American magazines, 1948–72.

Parr, Louisa: *The Fan* (article contributed to *Harper's Magazine*, London, August, 1889, pp. 399–409.

Percival, MacIver: *The Fan Book*. Fisher Unwin, London, 1920.

Petit, Edouard: *Etudes, Souvenirs et Consideérations sur la fabrication de l'éventail*. Versailles, 1859.

Rhead, George Woolliscroft: *History of the Fan*. Kegan Paul, Trench, Trübner & Co., London, 1910 (limited to 450 copies).

Robinson, F. Mabel: *Fans* (article contributed to *The Woman's World*). London, January 1889.

Rondot, Natalis: *Rapport sur les Objets de Parure, de Fantaisie et de Goût, fait à la Commission Française du Jury Internationale de l'Exposition Universelle de Londres*. Imprimerie Impériale, Paris, 1854.

Salwey, Charlotte Maria (née Birch): *Fans of Japan*. Kegan, Paul, Trench, Trübner & Co., London, 1894.

Schreiber, Lady Charlotte: *Fans & Fan Leaves—English*. John Murray, London, 1888.

Schreiber, Lady Charlotte: *Fans & Fan Leaves—Foreign*. John Murray, London, 1890.

Standage, H. C.: *Cements, Pastes, Glues & Gums*. London, Crosby Lockwood & Son, 1920.

Standen, Edith A.: *Instruments for Agitating the Air* (article in *The Metropolitan Museum of Art Bulletin*), Vol. XXIII, No. 7, March, 1965. New York.

Thornton, Peter: *Fans* (article in Antiques International, Rainbird, London, 1966).

Uzanne, Octave: *The Fan*. Illustrated by Paul Avril. Nimmo & Bain, London, 1884 (English translation from French original).

Woman's World: article on fans, London, January 1889, pp. 115–20.

Worshipful Company of Fan Makers: *Report of Committee, &c. Competitive Exhibition of Fans, held at Draper's Hall*, London, July 1878.

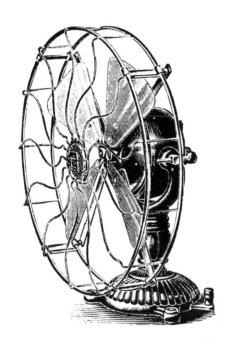

INDEX

Because certain sections of this book are self-indexing, *i.e.* the index of fan-makers, designers and painters, and the index of fan-leaf subjects, names and titles contained in these sections are not re-indexed in the following. However, where names which are mentioned in these parts are also referred to in the remaining body of the text, they will be found in the index. For information on a particular fan-maker, for instance, the name should first be sought in Chapter 12, and then this index checked for any textual references.

Plate numbers in roman type refer to black-and-white illustrations assembled in two gatherings: Plates 1 to 33 being between pages 128 and 129, and Plates 34 to 64 being found between pages 256 and 257.

Plate numbers shown in *italic* type refer to coloured illustrations which are to be found between pages 192 and 193.